THE HEART *of* COMPASSION

Books by Dilgo Khyentse

The Heart of Compassion:
The Thirty-seven Verses on the Practice of a Bodhisattva

The Heart Treasure of the Enlightened Ones:
The Practice of View, Meditation, and Action

The Hundred Verses of Advice:
Tibetan Buddhist Teachings on What Matters Most

The Wish-Fulfilling Jewel: The Practice of Guru Yoga
According to the Longchen Nyingthig Tradition

The Heart of Compassion

The Thirty-seven Verses on the Practice of a Bodhisattva

A Commentary by

DILGO KHYENTSE

Translated from the Tibetan by the
Padmakara Translation Group

SHAMBHALA · *Boston & London* · 2007

SHAMBHALA PUBLICATIONS, INC.
Horticultural Hall
300 Massachusetts Avenue
Boston, Massachusetts 02115
www.shambhala.com

© 2007 by Shechen Publications
www.shechen.org

9 8 7 6 5 4 3 2

Printed in the United States of America

♾ This edition is printed on acid-free paper that meets
the American National Standards Institute Z39.48 Standard.
Distributed in the United States by Random House, Inc.,
and in Canada by Random House of Canada Ltd

Designed by Lora Zorian

LIBRARY OF CONGRESS CATALOGING-IN-PUBLICATION DATA
Rab-gsal-zla-ba, Dis-mgo Mkhyen-brtse, 1910–
The heart of compassion: The Thirty-seven verses on
the practice of a Bodhisattva / Dilgo Khyentse; translated
from the Tibetan by the Padmakara Translation Group.
p.   cm.
"Oral and written teachings were translated from the Tibetan"
—Introd. Includes bibliographical references and index.
ISBN 978-1-59030-457-0 (alk. paper)
1. Rgyal-sras Thogs-med Bzan-po-dpal, 1295–1369.
Rgyal-sras lag len so dun ma. 2. Enlightenment (Buddhism)—
Requisites. 3. Spiritual life—Buddhism. I. Rgyal-sras Thogs-med
Bzan-po-dpal, 1295–1369. Rgyal-sras lag len so dun ma. English.
II. Padmakara Translation Group. III. Title.
BQ4399.R463R33 2007
294.3'420423—dc22
2006102332

Contents

Translator's Introduction   1

About Gyalse Ngulchu Thogme   9

THE ROOT TEXT   27

TEXTUAL OUTLINE   39

THE COMMENTARY   43

Appendix 1: Supplementary Commentaries
   on the Spiritual Teacher   205

Appendix 2: Supplementary Commentary
   on Desire   211

Appendix 3: Supplementary Commentaries
   on Transcendent Concentration   215

Appendix 4: Supplementary Commentaries
   on Transcendent Wisdom   223

Appendix 5: Mind-Training Prayer   227

Notes   235

Bibliography   253

Index   261

Translator's Introduction

In 1984, Kyabje Dilgo Khyentse Rinpoche gave what is probably his most extensive recorded teaching on the practice of the Mahayana path, at Tashi Pelbar Ling, his residence in the Dordogne, in southwest France.

The teaching was based on one of the most revered texts of Tibetan Buddhism, *The Thirty-seven Verses on the Practice of a Bodhisattva,* composed in the fourteenth century by Gyalse Ngulchu Thogme. This concise, profound poem in thirty-seven *shloka*s became widely known throughout the Tibetan world and, over the centuries, has been of immense benefit to countless practitioners. Easy to memorize, it is considered to be a distillation of another seminal Mahayana work, Shantideva's great masterpiece *The Way of the Bodhisattva* (*Bodhicharyavatara*), and has been the subject of many teachings and commentaries by the great masters of all traditions of Tibetan Buddhism.

Khyentse Rinpoche's explanations draw on the unparalleled depth of his wisdom and experience, and are oriented above all to those wishing to put these instructions into practice in everyday life. With great mastery, he shows how all the different facets and levels of the Buddhist teaching, when properly understood and applied, form a seamless, integrated whole.

While preparing the English version of these teachings, the

translator was able to request further explanations from Khyentse Rinpoche, which have been included in the footnotes. Khyentse Rinpoche also instructed the translator to include a number of additional quotes taken from the vast commentary on the *Seven-Point Mind Training* written by his root teacher, Shechen Gyaltsap Rinpoche, and from a few other texts. Substantial excerpts of an inspiring biography of Ngulchu Thogme, by his disciple Palden Yeshe, have also been included as a prelude to the actual text and commentary. Concerned that it might be wrong to translate only selected excerpts rather than the whole text, the translator sought advice from Kyabje Dilgo Khyentse, who kindly said that there would be nothing wrong in presenting the essential points of Gyalse Thogme's life in this way, and that, just as a piece broken off a big lump of molasses is as sweet and delicious as the whole thing, these excerpts would be no less valuable in kindling the reader's faith.

The oral and written teachings were translated from the Tibetan by Matthieu Ricard. Final editing was by John Canti. Both belong to the Padmakara Translation Group. Many other people made major contributions and gave valuable advice at various stages in the long gestation of this book, and we are most grateful to all of them, especially John Newnham, Terry Clifford, Vivian Kurz, and Camille Hykes.

This version of the root verses is based on a number of different translations, including one by the Padmakara Translation Group, one by Constance Wilkinson, and one by Matthieu Ricard. Where alternative interpretations presented themselves, the commentary written by Minyak Kunzang Sönam (also known as Chökyi Trakpa), a learned disciple of Patrul Rinpoche, was followed.

Work on the final stages of this book was made possible by the generosity of the Tsadra Foundation.

More than twenty years after they were first spoken by Khyentse Rinpoche, we are delighted to be able to offer these treasurelike instructions to all practitioners.

ABOUT DILGO KHYENTSE RINPOCHE (1910–91)

Dilgo Khyentse Rinpoche was one of the last of the generation of great lamas who completed their education and training in Tibet. He was one of the principal lamas of the ancient Nyingmapa tradition, an outstanding upholder of the practice lineage who spent twenty-two years of his life meditating in retreat, accomplishing the fruits of the many teachings he had received.

He composed numerous poems, meditation texts, and commentaries, and was a *tertön,* a discoverer of "treasures" containing the profound instructions hidden by Padmasambhava. Not only was he one of the leading masters of the pith instructions of Dzogchen, the Great Perfection, he was also the holder of hundreds of lineages, which he sought, received, and taught throughout his life. In his generation he was the exemplary exponent of the *Rimé* (nonsectarian) movement, renowned for his ability to transmit the teachings of each Buddhist lineage according to its own tradition. Indeed, there are few contemporary lamas who have not received teachings from him, and a great many, including His Holiness the Dalai Lama himself, who venerate him as one of their principal teachers.

Scholar, sage, and poet, teacher of teachers, Rinpoche never ceased to inspire all who encountered him through his monumental presence, his simplicity, dignity, and humor.

Khyentse Rinpoche was born in Denkhok Valley, in eastern Tibet, to a family descended from the royal lineage of the ninth-century king, Trisong Detsen. His father was a minister to the king of Derge. When still in his mother's womb, he was recognized as an extraordinary incarnation by the illustrious Mipham Rinpoche, who later named the infant Tashi Paljor and bestowed a special blessing and Mañjushri empowerment upon him.

Even as a little boy, Rinpoche manifested a strong desire to devote himself entirely to religious life. But his father had other ideas. His two elder sons had already left home to pursue monastic careers; one had been recognized as an incarnate lama and the

3

other wanted to become a doctor. Rinpoche's father hoped that his youngest son would follow in his own footsteps, and he could not accept that he might also be a *tulku,* or incarnate lama, as had been indicated by several learned masters.

At the age of ten, the boy was taken ill with severe burns; he was bedridden for nearly a year. Knowledgeable lamas advised that unless he was allowed to embrace spiritual life, he would not live long. Yielding to everyone's entreaties, his father agreed that the child could follow his own wishes and aspirations in order to fulfill his destiny.

At the age of eleven, Rinpoche entered Shechen Monastery in Kham, eastern Tibet, one of the six principal monasteries of the Nyingmapa school. There, his root guru, Shechen Gyaltsap, enthroned him as an incarnation of the wisdom mind of the first Khyentse Rinpoche, Jamyang Khyentse Wangpo (1820–92), the peerless lama who—along with the first Jamgön Kongtrul—set in motion a Buddhist renaissance throughout Tibet. All contemporary Tibetan masters draw inspiration and blessings from the Rimé movement.

Khyen-tse means "wisdom and love." The Khyentse tulkus are incarnations of several key figures in the development of Tibetan Buddhism. These include King Trisong Detsen and Vimalamitra, who, along with Guru Rinpoche, brought tantric Buddhism to Tibet in the ninth century; the great Gampopa, disciple of Milarepa and founder of the Kagyu tradition; and Jigme Lingpa, who, in the eighteenth century, discovered the *Longchen Nyingthig,* the *Heart Essence of the Vast Expanse.*

At Shechen, Rinpoche spent much of his time studying and meditating with his root guru in a hermitage above the monastery. It was during this time that Shechen Gyaltsap gave him all the essential empowerments and instructions of the Nyingma tradition. Rinpoche also studied with many other great masters, including the renowned disciple of Patrul Rinpoche, Dzogchen Khenpo Shenga, who imparted to him his own major work, the *Thirteen Great Commentaries*. In all, he received extensive teachings and transmissions from more than fifty teachers.

Before Shechen Gyaltsap died, Khyentse Rinpoche promised his beloved master that he would unstintingly teach whoever asked him for Dharma. Then, from the ages of fifteen to twenty-eight, he spent most of his time meditating in silent retreat, living in isolated hermitages and caves, or sometimes simply under the shelter of overhanging rocks, in the mountainous countryside near his birthplace in Denkhok Valley.

Dilgo Khyentse Rinpoche later spent many years with Dzongsar Khyentse, Chökyi Lodrö (1896–1959), who was also an incarnation of the first Khyentse. After receiving from Chökyi Lodrö the many empowerments of the Rinchen Terdzö, the collection of "revealed treasures" (*terma*), Rinpoche told him he wished to spend the rest of his life in solitary meditation. But Khyentse Chökyi Lodrö's answer was, "The time has come for you to teach and transmit to others the countless precious teachings you have received." From then on, Rinpoche worked constantly for the benefit of beings with the tireless energy that is the hallmark of the Khyentse lineage.

After leaving Tibet, Khyentse Rinpoche spent much of his time traveling all over the Himalayas, India, Southeast Asia, and the West, transmitting and explaining the teachings to his many disciples. He was often accompanied by his wife, Sangyum Lhamo, and his grandson and spiritual heir, Rabjam Rinpoche.

Wherever he was, he would rise well before dawn to pray and meditate for several hours before embarking on a ceaseless series of activities until late into the night. He accomplished a tremendous daily workload with total serenity and apparent effortlessness. Whatever he was doing—and he was often giving his attention to several different tasks at the same time—seemed to make no difference to the flow of his view, meditation, and action. Both his teachings and his lifestyle combined into a harmonious whole all the different levels of the path. He made extensive offerings, and during his life offered a total of a million butter lamps. Wherever he went, he also supported many practitioners and people in need, in such a discreet way that very few people were aware of the extent of his charity.

Rinpoche held that building stupas and monasteries in sacred places helps to avert conflict, disease, and famine, promotes world peace, and furthers Buddhist values and practice. He was an indefatigable builder and restorer of stupas, monasteries, and temples in Bhutan, Tibet, India, and Nepal. In Bhutan, following predictions he had received for the peace of the country, he built several temples dedicated to Guru Padmasambhava, as well as a number of large stupas, gradually becoming one of the most respected teachers of all the Bhutanese people from the royal family down. Rinpoche made three extended visits to Tibet in the 1980s, where he inaugurated the rebuilding of the original Shechen Monastery, destroyed during the Cultural Revolution; and he contributed in one way or another to the restoration of over two hundred temples and monasteries in Tibet, especially the monasteries of Samye, Mindroling, and Shechen. In India, too, he built a new stupa at Bodhgaya, the site of Shakyamuni Buddha's enlightenment beneath the bodhi tree, and initiated plans to construct stupas in each of the seven other great pilgrimage places sacred to Lord Buddha in northern India.

In Nepal, he transplanted the rich Shechen tradition to a new home—a magnificent monastery in front of the great stupa of Bodhnath. This became his principal seat, and it currently houses a large community of monks, led by their abbot, Rabjam Rinpoche. It was Khyentse Rinpoche's particular wish that this should be a place where the Buddhist teachings are continued in all their original purity, just as they were previously studied and practiced in Tibet, and he invested enormous care in the education of the promising young lamas capable of continuing the tradition.

After the systematic destruction of books and libraries in

Tibet, many works existed in only one or two copies. Rinpoche was involved for many years in publishing as much of Tibet's extraordinary heritage of Buddhist teaching as possible, a total of three hundred volumes, including the five treasures of Jamyang Kongtrul. Until the end of his life, Rinpoche was still seeking lineages he had not received, and transmitting to others those that he had. During his life, among countless other teachings, he twice transmitted the 108 volumes of the Kangyur and five times the 111 volumes of the Rinchen Terdzö.

He first visited the West in 1975, and thereafter made a number of visits, including three North American tours, and taught in many different countries, particularly at his European seat, Shechen Tennyi Dargyeling in Dordogne, France, where people from all over the world were able to receive extensive teaching from him, and where several groups of students undertook the traditional three-year retreat program under his guidance.

Through his extensive enlightened activity, Khyentse Rinpoche unsparingly devoted his entire life to the preservation and dissemination of the Buddha's teaching. What brought him the greatest satisfaction was to see people actually putting the teachings into practice and their lives being transformed by the blossoming of bodhichitta and compassion.

Even in the last years of his life, Khyentse Rinpoche's extraordinary energy and vigor were little affected by his advancing age. However, he began to show the first signs of ill health in early 1991 while teaching in Bodhgaya. Completing his program there nevertheless, he traveled to Dharamsala, where, without apparent difficulty, he spent a month transmitting a set of important Nyingmapa empowerments and transmissions to His Holiness the Dalai Lama, which the latter had been requesting for many years.

Back in Nepal, as spring advanced, it became obvious that his health was steadily deteriorating. He passed much of the time in silent prayer and meditation, setting aside only a few hours of the day to meet those who needed to see him. He decided to travel to Bhutan, to spend three and one-half months in retreat opposite the "Tiger's Nest," Paro Taktsang, one of the most sacred places blessed by Padmasambhava.

Completing his own retreat, Rinpoche visited several of his disciples who were also in retreat and spoke to them of the ultimate Guru, beyond birth and death, beyond any physical manifestation. Shortly afterward, he was again showing signs of illness. On September 27, 1991, at nightfall, he asked his attendants to help him sit in an upright position. In the early hours of the morning, his breath ceased and his mind dissolved in the absolute expanse.

About Gyalse Ngulchu Thogme (1295—1369)

The great sage Gyalse Ngulchu Thogme was born in Phuljung, a few miles to the southwest of Sakya Monastery, in Tsang, central Tibet. His father, Konchog Pal, "Glory of the Three Jewels," and his mother, Chagza Bumdron, had pure minds and great faith in the Dharma. His mother had felt great joy, and her compassion had deepened, throughout the time he was within her womb. He was given the name Konchog Sangpo, "Excellence of the Three Jewels."

As soon as Gyalse Thogme learned to speak, it became evident how full of compassion he was. One day, as he sat on his mother's lap, he saw a leaf whirled up into the air by the wind. He began to cry intensely.

"Why are you crying?" asked his mother.

He pointed a finger at the disappearing leaf and said, "An animal has been carried away into the sky!"

On another occasion, after he had begun to walk, he went outside but returned only a few minutes later, naked—to the great surprise of his mother.

"What have you done with your clothes?" she asked.

"There was someone out there who was feeling cold," he replied.

She stepped outside to see who it was, and saw that her son had put his clothing over a frost-covered bush. Stones had carefully been placed on the corners to keep the coat from flying off.

When he played games with his friends, Gyalse Thogme never minded losing. Indeed, he felt sad if others lost rather than he. Scouting for dry wood with the other children, he would feel glad when they found some, even when he himself came away empty-handed. But if he found wood and the others did not, he would either help them in their search or give them his own wood, for fear that their parents might scold them. As a game he used to make little stupas, or make believe that he was receiving teachings, or giving a teaching himself.

A few pages of a holy book in his hands would instantly turn any sorrow into happiness. But when people allowed their clothes to brush over the holy scriptures, or when they showed any other form of disrespect toward them, he would feel sad.

In short, like all great beings, Gyalse Thogme suffered more than others when they themselves suffered, and he felt happier than others when they were happy.

He was three years old when his mother died, and lost his father when he was five. His grandmother raised him until he was nine, and then she, too, died. From then on, until he was fourteen, he was cared for by his maternal uncle, Rinchen Tashi, "Auspicious Gem," who taught him to read and write. Gyalse Thogme was always grateful to the uncle who had set him on the spiritual path.

One day, he said to his uncle, "From now on, give up attachment to this life and simply practice the Dharma. I'll provide you with food and drink by going to beg for alms. This will be my way of repaying your kindness."

He kept his word, and that is how they lived from that time onward.

At the age of fourteen, having realized that the joys of samsara are like a dreadful burning pit of red-hot embers, he took the vows of a novice monk and received the name Sangpo Pal, "Splendor of Excellence."

The proper activities of a monk comprise study, reflection, and meditation, and accordingly, from the age of fifteen onward, he received teachings from numerous spiritual teachers of all schools.[1] Never flagging in his studies, he soon became exceedingly learned. He not only memorized most of the texts he studied—sometimes upon hearing them only once—and penetrated their meaning without difficulty, but was also able to answer questions in public on the most subtle points of doctrine. His teachers declared him to be a second Asanga (Asanga—Thogme in Tibetan—was a great Indian *pandita* famous for his universal knowledge),[2] and from then on he became known as Thogme Sangpo, "Excellent Asanga." He was only nineteen. His learning in the sutras and tantras grew, and through meditation he developed authentic experience of the meaning of the teachings. His sincerity, motivation, and endeavor were such that during a month in retreat he made more progress in his spiritual realization than others might achieve in three years.

At the age of twenty-nine, he took the full monastic vows at the Monastery of É. He observed the discipline of a monk in an exemplary way until the end of his life, never neglecting even the minutest of vows. Aware of the negativity associated with animal furs and skins, he carefully avoided wearing clothes of such materials. He began to give regular teachings on fundamental Mahayana texts such as *The Way of the Bodhisattva*[3] and *The Transcendent Perfection of Wisdom*,[4] and composed numerous commentaries that clearly explain the profound meaning of these teachings.[5] Gyalse Thogme was truly like the sun, radiating rays of compassion and wisdom toward all beings.

> Shining from the great sun of his wisdom and love,
> Warm rays of teaching, debate, and composition
> Dispelled the darkness of ignorance
> And made the lotus garden of the Buddha's
>   teachings bloom.

In the course of his studies and teaching, he encountered a period of great material hardship. Various people proposed that he learn how to give initiations and perform rituals in order to earn money without much effort. His response to such no doubt well-intentioned but misguided suggestions was to compose *The Thirty-seven Verses on the Practice of a Bodhisattva,* which sums up the whole bodhisattva path.

When Gyalse Thogme was thirty-two, he accepted the position of abbot at the Monastery of Tara, and remained there until he was forty-one. But when the Monastery of É insistently invited him to be its abbot, he declined, saying that someone better should be sought. He recommended the famous Khenpo Wanglo, who was duly appointed. Everyone was satisfied.

Throughout his life, countless beings were drawn to Gyalse Thogme by his kindness, his gentle speech, his flawless behavior—always in accord with what he taught—and his skillful way of teaching in a manner appropriate to each individual's nature and capacity.

> Greet them with the flag of generosity,
> Appeal to them with gentle speech,
> Inspire their confidence by acting with consistency,
> Attune yourself to them and give them perfect
> advice.

His generosity was indeed limitless. As it says in *The Ornament of the Mahayana Sutras,* "There is nothing a bodhisattva will not give: his wealth, his body—everything."

That was just how Gyalse Thogme, from his early youth, used to give away everything without restraint, giving whatever he had to friends and to the poor, regardless of his own poverty. To those who affectionately tried to stop him, saying that if he gave so much, he would have nothing left to live on, he would reply, "I won't die of starvation. And even if I do, I don't mind!"

Once, when a student came to see him, the only thing Gyalse Thogme had to give him was a precious stupa. Just afterward, one of his disciples, who could not bear to see his master part with such a sacred object, went to the student, bought the stupa from him, and offered it back to his master. But Gyalse Thogme gave it away to another person, and the same thing happened again several times. From his youth he had totally severed all ties of desire and attachment. He was a wonderfully good person.

During a period of acute food shortages in Ngulchu, someone offered him some barley flour. Soon, Gyalse Thogme was giving away a full plate of it to any beggar who came by. Beggars came repeatedly until he hardly had anything left to eat himself.

One beggar saw this and scolded the others, saying, "Don't you see he has no more than a cupful of flour left? Isn't it unfair to keep on begging from him like that?"

One day, Gyalse Thogme gave a beggar a fine woolen undergarment from central Tibet. And when the same man returned the following year, he gave him a new woolen cloak. The beggar was delighted, but Thogme, thinking that he could have given him something even better and that it was wrong not to do so, handed him his own long woolen cloak. However, the beggar stayed rooted to the spot, not daring to take it.

When someone told Gyalse Thogme that to be excessively generous to others and allow them to take whatever he had might not be truly beneficial to them, he replied, without any pretense, "I am truly happy that others use my possessions as much as they like." And he added, "The Dharma Lord Jamsar said, 'Since I do not have the slightest feeling that I am the owner of my belongings, someone who takes them all away can hardly be a thief.' The great Kashmiri Pandita Shakya Shri,[6] Lord Götsangpa,[7] and many other sages took the vow never to own anything. Compared with their generosity, my own is like the tiptoeing of a fox compared with a tiger's leap. Yet, since I try to emulate them, I feel that when people use my things and take them away, not only are they untarnished by the fault of theft, but their well-being is truly increased."

The many beggars who used to live nearby said he always

spoke gently to them; they never heard a single word of scolding from him. Gyalse Thogme himself sometimes said that he was never able to say harsh words to anyone. As he always attuned his words to the nature of others, there came a time when whatever he said was a spiritual instruction.

When trouble broke out in Sakya, Jamyang Dönyö Gyaltsen and his brother[8] had to flee farther east into central Tibet.

Lama Rinyewa confided to Gyalse Thogme, "When all these annoying things happen, I somehow manage to control my mind by applying the right antidotes. But what a lot of thoughts of attachment and anger I have! Does that happen to you?"

"All the joys and sufferings of this world are just projections of our minds and the result of our past karma," Thogme replied. "As I have a little understanding that in relative truth everything is like an illusion, and that in absolute truth everything is utterly beyond conceptual fabrications, I don't experience attachment and hatred at all."

Gyalse Thogme retired to the hermitage of Ngulchu at the age of forty-two. He remained there until he was sixty-five, dedicating himself entirely to spiritual practice, and showing in body, speech, and mind every aspect of perfection. Until the end of his life he seldom lay down, but instead stayed sitting upright, cross-legged, day and night. Yet his health was not affected and his face always looked young and radiant.

His inner realization was revealed on many occasions in miraculous deeds and in feats of clairvoyance. Once, when he and a few companions were on their way to meet the master Sönam Trakpa,[9] they came to a dry, desertlike place called Shangda.

"Let's eat here," he suggested.

His companions objected. "There's no water," they said.

But Thogme replied, "Go and collect some dry wood. I'll take care of the water."

When they returned, they found that Thogme had made a

depression in the sand. It was full of water. After their meal, the water was still there, but not long afterward there remained no trace.

On another occasion, when he was giving an empowerment of Amitayus, the Buddha of Longevity, his face looked to some of those present as dazzling white as a snow peak. During the call for blessings, his face turned an orange-red, and during the expulsion of hindrances,[10] it turned dark red and wrathful, and his hair stood on end.

Another time, some especially devoted disciples saw him as Eleven-Faced Avalokiteshvara,[11] the Buddha of Compassion.

Once, when an army from central Tibet was approaching Ngulchu, Gyalse Thogme told all the inhabitants to run away. But they wouldn't listen. Since the northerners had won last time, they said, and nothing had happened, surely there was no need to worry this time.

Thogme was insistent. "This time you must escape!" he said.

But they still did not move. The northerners lost, and when the army from central Tibet invaded Ngulchu, everyone panicked and flocked around Thogme. Just as the five *rakshasa*s were unable to harm anyone in the kingdom of King Strength of Love,[12] so too, when the ruthless soldiers appeared brandishing their bloodstained swords and spears, they only had to see the face of the Dharma Lord for their hatred to subside, and they became filled with faith. Prostrating before him, they asked him for protection cords. They wanted to receive his blessing, but dared not approach.

"We are evil people," they said. "We may defile you."

"I can put up with that," Gyalse Thogme replied, and he gave them his blessing.

Some of them could not withhold their tears, and weeping with regret from the depth of their hearts, offered him their confession. Everyone gained strong faith in his foreknowledge and in the power of his blessing.

He could effortlessly take upon himself the sickness of others, as happened on several occasions—when Butön Rinpoche and Khenchen Changtse,[13] in particular, fell ill. Gyalse Thogme had countless visions of deities, such as Avalokiteshvara, Tara, and many other buddhas and bodhisattvas, and heard the Dharma from them. It is also said that he received teaching from the Khasarpani image[14] at Nesar, and from the image of the Eleven-Faced Avalokiteshvara at Chagö Shong, which spoke to him as though it were a living person.

He spent his days and nights allowing compassion to permeate his whole being. Sometimes, he seemed to have fainted, but he was actually having visions of buddhafields, making offerings to the buddhas, and benefiting countless beings.

Fully mature spiritually, he could bring others to maturation without effort. People had only to meet him once to conceive faith, renunciation, love, and compassion, and to develop the mind of enlightenment—the wish to bring all beings to buddhahood. For those who stayed near him for a long time, the effect was even more profound and far-reaching.

Above all, he had such love for beings that he never minded undergoing any physical hardship, or even risking his life, if that could be even a small service to others.

Once, when Gyalse Thogme was sixteen, someone who had been giving him some material help asked him to leave for Sakya on an important task and to return the next day. Halfway to Sakya, in a desert plain, the young Thogme came upon a bitch who was starving to death. She was on the verge of eating her own pups. He felt great pity for her, and wondering what he could do to help, decided to carry them all back to É, his monastery; he would then have to travel all night to make up for the time lost. He set off, carrying the dogs on his back. It was very hard. Finally, however, he arrived back at É and finished taking care of them. Before setting off again, he thought he had better have a sip of water. It was then that he came upon the man who had sent him on his errand.

Astonished at seeing him there, the man asked, "Hey, didn't you go?" When Thogme explained what had happened, the man cursed him, and said, "There's such important business at stake, and here you are with your great compassion!"

Thogme had been rebuked so sternly that he did not dare take his sip of water. He set off again at once, walked all night, and accomplished his task in Sakya early in the morning. Returning immediately, he arrived back at É just before sunset.

Seeing this, the man who had sent him was amazed. He begged Thogme to forgive him for the scolding he had given him. He added, "What you did is wondrous indeed!"

Another time, when he was about twenty, all the monks of É were leaving for Chöbar, when Thogme saw a crippled woman weeping by the main door of the monastery. He asked her what was wrong. She explained that she was crying because the monks were leaving. As she would be left behind, there would be no one left to give her alms. Thogme told her not to despair. He would return to fetch her, he promised.

He carried his belongings up to Chöbar and rested for a short while before leaving again with a rope. His friends called him from afar, asking where he was going. Thogme said that he was going back to get the crippled woman, but they did not believe him.

When he got back to É, however, he found that he could not carry both the woman and her things. So first he carried her clothes and mat a certain distance, and then came back to carry the woman. In this way, carrying in turn the woman and her belongings, he eventually reached Chöbar. His friends were astonished. They had thought at first that he'd just gone to collect firewood, they said, but what he had done was something truly marvelous.

When Gyalse Thogme was about thirty, a sick beggar used to stay outside near his door. His body was completely infested with lice. Thogme used to give him whatever food and drink he had, bringing it to him discreetly at night to avoid making a show of his generosity. But one night the beggar was not in his usual place, and Thogme set out in search of him. Finding him at last as dawn broke, Thogme asked him why he'd gone away.

"Some people told me I was so disgusting that when they walked by, they could not even look at me, and they kicked me out," said the beggar.

Hearing this, Thogme was overwhelmed by compassion and wept. That evening he brought the beggar to his room, and gave the man his fill of food and drink. Then Thogme gave him his own new robes. Taking in exchange the beggar's rags, Thogme put them on and let the lice feed on his body.

It was not long before he looked as though he had been stricken by leprosy, or some other disease. He was so weakened and disabled by sickness that he had to stop teaching. His friends and disciples came to see him, wondering whether he had fallen seriously ill. They soon saw the condition he was in.

"Why don't you be a good practitioner again?" they admonished him.

Some quoted from the scriptures: "If your compassion is not totally pure, do not give your body away."

Others begged him, "For your sake and ours, don't carry on like this, get rid of these lice!"

But Thogme said, "Since time without beginning, I have had so many human lives, but they have all been in vain. Now, even if I were to die today, I will at least have done something meaningful. I will not get rid of the lice."

He kept feeding the lice for seventeen days, but they gradually died by themselves and he was free of them. He recited many mantras and *dharanis* over the dead lice, and made *tsa tsas*[15] with them. Everyone now marveled at the purity of his mind, his loving-kindness, and everywhere he became known as Gyalse Chenpo—"the Great Bodhisattva." He composed the following prayer, which truly reflected his thoughts:

> May whoever harms my body and my life
> Have a long life, with no illness or enemies,

And, having overcome all obstacles on the path,
Swiftly attain the dharmakaya, free of birth and
    death.

Once, on the way back from Sakya where he had gone to receive teachings from the Dharma Lord Sönam Gyaltsen,[16] he was
attacked by robbers. As soon as he reached Ngulchu, he said
many prayers to the Medicine Buddha, Tara, and other deities,
and dedicated them to the robbers. For their benefit he also made
offerings to the sangha and performed other virtuous actions. He
said that there had been one especially fierce robber in the gang,
and when he thought of the man's face, he felt boundless pity
and compassion.

There are countless examples of Gyalse Thogme's kindness.
When Thogme was teaching at Seryig, for example, someone
name Bulwa created a lot of misunderstanding, which greatly
disturbed Thogme. One day, after his return to Ngulchu, his at-
tendant announced that Bulwa had arrived.

Thogme's first reaction was to say to himself, "I'd rather he
hadn't come!" But instantly he thought, "Every day I make the
promise to return good for bad. Why should I be upset by
Bulwa's arrival? Even if he stays next to me for the rest of his life,
I shall let him do whatever he likes."

As soon as Thogme had finished his retreat, Bulwa came before him. Confessing his mischief, he vowed from then on to act
in accordance with the Dharma. Nevertheless, his constant and
unreasonable wants were a burden on everyone, and people told
Thogme that it would be better if Bulwa left.

But Thogme said, "He will improve, and what he does helps
me." He let Bulwa do whatever he wanted, and benefited him in
many ways. He taught Bulwa whatever he was able to understand, and gave him everything he needed.

Gyalse Thogme always brought happiness to all who made a
connection with him, even those who harmed him. Sometimes,
he would interrupt his own retreat for a few days to teach mind

training and *bodhichitta* practices to his many visitors. On these occasions there were often rainbows, a rain of flowers, and other marvelous signs, which filled people with joy and devotion.

At the age of sixty-seven, Gyalse Thogme decided to go see the most precious image of the Jowo, the Crowned Buddha of Lhasa.[17] He visited Lhasa, Phagmo Dru,[18] Samye, Gungthang, and many other places, giving teachings on compassion as he went. It was said that since Lord Atisha[19] had come to Tibet, no one had brought as much benefit to beings as Gyalse Thogme. Just to see his face was enough for people to feel overwhelming faith and an irrepressible urge to free themselves from samsaric existence.

After ten months he returned to Ngulchu, and then hurried on to Shalu Monastery when he learned that Butön Rinpoche[20] had fallen ill. As soon as Thogme offered long-life prayers and ceremonies, Butön Rinpoche's health improved. Everyone said that Thogme had taken Butön's sickness upon himself.

Back in Ngulchu, Gyalse Thogme remained in strict retreat. But every three months, until he died nine months later, he would emerge to give teachings on mind training and bodhichitta to the thousands of people who had flocked from all over the country to meet him. Most gave up concern for the affairs of this life. Devoting themselves to the practice of Dharma, they realized the true meaning of emptiness and compassion.

His compassion was so strong that he was able to help and transform not only human beings but animals, too. Mutual enemies, such as wolves and sheep and deer, forgot their cruelty and their fear. They would play peacefully together in his presence and listen with respect to his teachings.

Once, a hermit meditating on the inner channels and energies[21] encountered obstacles to his practice. Losing control of his mind, he began to run about naked. A female wild sheep came upon him; she circled him, threatening to butt him with her horns. When the hermit saw this, he recovered his self-control and realized what had befallen him. Hearing of the incident, Thogme teasingly said that this sheep was an expert in dispelling the obstacles of great meditators. When Thogme became sick, the same sheep showed many signs of distress. Three days after his passing, she leaped to her death below Thogme's hermitage. To be near Gyalse Thogme was like being on the Potala Mountain, the buddhafield of Avalokiteshvara.

Other great teachers, such as Khenpo Wanglo, used to say, "He is the Buddha in human form!" and would prostrate in the direction of Thogme's hermitage.

He was so serene, self-controlled, and kind that whoever stayed near him naturally became detached from worldly concerns. And then came the last months of his life:

> After giving help to all those he was to benefit,
> To dispel their belief that things could be permanent
> And for the sake of beings in other buddhafields,
> Although he was beyond all change, he manifested
> the signs of death.

He first showed signs of sickness to encourage his disciples to be diligent—by making them feel sad, and to show how sickness can be used on the spiritual path. He said that no treatment was likely to help, but to calm everyone, he took some medicine nonetheless, and let prayers and ceremonies be performed on his behalf. When Khenchen Changtse and the Dharma Lord Nishön organized a ceremony requesting that he remain in this world, his health improved, and he thus allowed everyone to accumulate merit through the great joy they felt. But not long afterward, he again showed signs of sickness.

When someone asked him if there were any way to prolong his life, Thogme said, "'If my being sick will benefit beings, may I be blessed with sickness! If my dying will benefit beings, may I be blessed with death! If my being well will benefit beings, may I be blessed with recovery!' This is the prayer I make to the Three

Jewels. Having complete certainty that whatever happens is the blessing of the Three Jewels, I am happy, and I shall take whatever happens on to the path without trying to change anything."

His close disciples begged him to consider whether medical treatment or anything else they could offer him would be of any benefit.

But Thogme said, "I have reached the limit of my years and my sickness is severe. Even the attentions of highly skilled physicians with ambrosia-like medicine would be unlikely to contribute much." And he added:

> If this illusory body, which I cling to as mine, is
>   sick—let it be sick!
> This sickness enables me to exhaust
> The bad karma I have accumulated in the past,
> And the spiritual deeds I can then perform
> Help me purify the two kinds of veils.[22]

> If I am in good health, I am happy,
> Because when my body and mind are well
> I can enhance my spiritual practice,
> And give real meaning to human existence
> By turning my body, speech, and mind to virtue.

> If I am poor, I am happy,
> Because I've no wealth to protect,
> And I know that all feuds and animosity
> Sprout from the seeds of greed and attachment.

> If I am rich, I am happy,
> Because with my wealth I can do more positive
>   actions,

> And both temporal and ultimate happiness
> Are the result of meritorious deeds.

If I die soon, that's excellent,
Because, assisted by some good potential, I am
    confident that
I shall enter the unmistaken path
Before any obstacle can intervene.

If I live long, I am happy,
Because without parting from the warm beneficial
    rain of spiritual instructions
I can, over a long time, fully ripen
The crop of inner experiences.

Therefore, whatever happens, I shall be happy!

And he continued, "I've been teaching these pith instructions to others, and I must practice them myself. As it is said, 'What is called sickness has no true existence whatsoever, but within the display of delusory phenomena appears as the ineluctable result of wrong actions. Sickness is the teacher that points out the nature of samsara and shows us that phenomena, manifest though they may, have no more true existence than an illusion. Sickness provides us with the grounds for developing patience toward our own suffering, and compassion for the suffering of others. It is in such difficult circumstances that our spiritual practice is put to the test.' If I die, I'll be relieved of the pains of my sickness. I can't recall any task that I've left undone, and what's more, I realize how rare an opportunity it is to be able to die as the perfect conclusion of my spiritual practice. That's why I'm not hoping for any cure for my illness. Nevertheless, before I die, you may complete all your ceremonies."

At this, his disciples declared that they would perform ceremonies lasting three years for him.

But Thogme answered simply, "If it's any use to you, I can bear three years of pain. But if not, what's the use of my living so long?"

But his disciples begged him. "Please remain for a long time!" they said. "We have no other wish than to continue to see your face and to hear your voice."

He said, "A ladle without a pot to ladle from can provide nothing. Yet, although I have no qualities, people's faith and the compassion of the Three Jewels have enabled me to benefit some beings. I hope that even after my death, my benefit to them will not diminish."

Again his disciples insisted. "Even if you continue to bring vast benefit to beings in other buddhafields," they said, "we ourselves will be deprived of our protector. Please stay longer."

"If I had no power at all to help," he said, "there would be no need for me to remain with you for a long time. My wish is to liberate all beings, so if I did have any power, how could I dare abandon those who rely on me? Yet, just as a doctor's prescription alone will not cure his patient, if you don't pray fervently to the Victorious Ones and apply their teachings, it's going to be difficult for them to protect you, let alone for me to do so. Therefore, practice correctly all the instructions you have received and you'll be able to help others, just as I have done. So you don't need to feel pain at the thought that we are going to be separated. Even if we part, rely upon the Three Jewels and pray to them—is there any refuge more supreme?"

When his close disciples requested that he grant a final audience to the many people who had come, he declined, saying that his emaciated face, sick body, and broken voice would only increase their grief. And then he gave a final piece of advice, concluding with these words:

> To keep the three vows,
> Give up all attachment and belief in things as truly
>   existing,
> And benefit others with your actions, words, and
>   thoughts,
> Is truly excellent practice.

When someone asked him which buddhafield he would go to in his next life, he said, "I'll happily go to a hell realm if that can help beings,[23] and I don't want to go to any buddhafield at all if that cannot help others. But I have no power to choose where to go, so I simply pray wholeheartedly to the Three Jewels to be reborn as someone who can benefit others. That is the only wish I have."

One morning at dawn, on the eighth day of the tenth month, Gyalse Thogme asked his disciples to help him sit upright and to turn his body around. He then folded his hands at his heart and prayed respectfully. And he wept, for a long time. The disciples asked him why he was weeping, and he replied that he had had some kind of vision. They asked him to say more about it. Tara had appeared, he told them, and since she was facing south, he had felt it improper to pray with his back to her, and he had therefore asked them to help him change position. Then, remembering the sufferings of beings, he had felt overwhelmed, and shed many tears.

Two days later he said happily, "Today, I was able to perform a great service for the Kashmiri Pandita, and he was extremely pleased."

"Where is he now?" they asked.

"In the Tushita Buddhafield," Thogme answered.

Gyalse Thogme had countless visions and auspicious dreams, and pure perception of his environment as a buddhafield never left him. It was clear, too, that he had full power over his life. Once, when his pulse had almost disappeared, he said that he was not going to go yet, and in fact he remained alive for three more months.

Then one day, when his pulse was better than ever, and everyone rejoiced, he said, "My pulse, like my mouth, is a clever talker, but this time I won't stay." He departed this world two days later.

On the nineteenth of that month, at dawn, he asked his

disciples to help him sit slightly more upright, and then said, "I feel extremely well like this, do not move my body at all."

From that morning until the next evening he remained seated in the lotus posture; his mind remained one-pointedly in equanimity, and within that state, he departed into bliss.

During that time his disciples had various visions and experiences. Some saw a host of celestial beings coming to invite him to Akanishta, the Unsurpassable Buddhafield; some saw *dakas* and *dakinis* inviting him to Amitabha's Buddhafield of Bliss, or to Arya Tara's Buddhafield of the Turquoise Array.

Between the moment his life ended and the time his cremation stupa was opened to gather the relics together, the earth shook,[24] rainbows appeared, and although the sky was completely clear, a fine flowerlike rain fell, and sounds were heard in the air. As his life came to an end, not only humans but animals, too, showed signs of despair, and even the earth mourned him— flowers withered, springs dried up, and the land lost its natural magnificence.

Nine days after his death, his cremation was performed by a number of spiritual masters who had come from all over the country, and the ceremonies continued for seven more days. Then the cremation stupa was opened, and the relics collected.

According to their karma, some disciples found precious pelletlike relics, some found tiny relics spiraling to the right, and some found bones on which one could see the shapes of various deities. The disciples took the relics home and set them in precious reliquaries and statues as objects of offering and reverence.

These excerpts are taken from Gyalse Thogme's life story, "written by the slothful Palden Yeshe at the mountain retreat of Pangkhan Gahden."[25]

The Root Text

The Thirty-Seven Verses on the Practice of a Bodhisattva

Namo Lokeshvaraya
Though he sees that in all phenomena there is no
   coming and going,
He strives solely for the sake of beings:
To the sublime teacher inseparable from
   Avalokiteshvara, the Protector of Beings,
I pay constant homage with respectful body, speech,
   and mind.

The perfect buddhas—source of happiness and
   ultimate peace—
Exist through having accomplished the sacred
   Dharma,
And that, in turn, depends on knowing how to
   practice it;
This practice of the bodhisattvas I shall therefore
   now explain.

1

Now that I have this great ship, a precious human
   life, so hard to obtain,

I must carry myself and others across the ocean of
    samsara.
To that end, to listen, reflect, and meditate
Day and night, without distraction, is the practice of
    a bodhisattva.

2

In my native land waves of attachment to friends
    and kin surge,
Hatred for enemies rages like fire,
The darkness of stupidity, not caring what to adopt
    or avoid, thickens—
To abandon my native land is the practice of a
    bodhisattva.

3

When unfavorable places are abandoned, disturbing
    emotions gradually fade;
When there are no distractions, positive activities
    naturally increase;
As awareness becomes clearer, confidence in the
    Dharma grows—
To rely on solitude is the practice of a bodhisattva.

4

Close friends who have long been together will
    separate,
Wealth and possessions gained with much effort will
    be left behind,
Consciousness, a guest, will leave the hotel of the
    body—
To give up the concerns of this life is the practice of
    a bodhisattva.

5

In bad company, the three poisons grow stronger,
Listening, reflection, and meditation decline,
And loving-kindness and compassion vanish—
To avoid unsuitable friends is the practice of a
   bodhisattva.

6

Through reliance on a true spiritual friend one's
   faults will fade
And good qualities will grow like a waxing moon—
To consider him even more precious
Than one's own body is the practice of a
   bodhisattva.

7

Whom can worldly gods protect
Themselves imprisoned in samsara?
To take refuge in the Three Jewels
Who never fail those they protect is the practice of a
   bodhisattva.

8

The Buddha taught that the unendurable suffering
   of the lower realms
Is the fruit of unvirtuous actions.
Therefore, to never act unvirtuously,
Even at the cost of one's life, is the practice of a
   bodhisattva.

9

Like dew on grass, the delights of the three worlds
By their very nature evaporate in an instant.

To strive for the supreme level of liberation,
Which never changes, is the practice of a
   bodhisattva.

10

If all the mothers who have loved me since
   beginningless time are suffering,
What is the use of my own happiness?
So, with the aim of liberating limitless sentient
   beings,
To set my mind on enlightenment is the practice of
   a bodhisattva.

11

All suffering without exception arises from desiring
   happiness for oneself,
While perfect buddhahood is born from the thought
   of benefiting others.
Therefore, to really exchange
My own happiness for the suffering of others is the
   practice of a bodhisattva.

12

If someone driven by great desire
Seizes all my wealth, or induces others to do so,
To dedicate to him my body, possessions,
And past, present, and future merit is the practice of
   a bodhisattva.

13

If, in return for not the slightest wrong of mine,
Someone were to cut off even my very head,
Through the power of compassion to take all his
   negative actions
Upon myself is the practice of a bodhisattva.

14

Even if someone says all sorts of derogatory things
  about me
And proclaims them throughout the universe,
In return, out of loving-kindness,
To extol that person's qualities is the practice of a
  bodhisattva.

15

Even if in the midst of a large gathering
Someone exposes my hidden faults with insulting
  language,
To bow to him respectfully,
Regarding him as a spiritual friend, is the practice of
  a bodhisattva.

16

Even if one I've lovingly cared for like my own child
Regards me as an enemy,
To love him even more,
As a mother loves a sick child, is the practice of a
  bodhisattva.

17

Even if my peers or my inferiors
Out of pride do all they can to debase me,
To respectfully consider them like my teachers
On the crown of my head is the practice of a
  bodhisattva.

18

Even when utterly destitute and constantly maligned
  by others,
Afflicted by terrible illness and prey to evil forces,

To still draw upon myself the suffering and
    wrongdoing of all beings
And not lose heart is the practice of a bodhisattva.

19

Though I may be famous, and revered by many,
And as rich as the God of Wealth himself,
To see that the wealth and glory of the world are
    without essence,
And to be free of arrogance, is the practice of a
    bodhisattva.

20

If one does not conquer one's own hatred,
The more one fights outer enemies, the more they
    will increase.
Therefore, with the armies of loving-kindness and
    compassion,
To tame one's own mind is the practice of a
    bodhisattva.

21

Sense pleasures and desirable things are like
    saltwater—
The more one tastes them, the more one's thirst
    increases.
To abandon promptly
All objects which arouse attachment is the practice
    of a bodhisattva.

22

All that appears is the work of one's own mind;
The nature of mind is primordially free from
    conceptual limitations.
To recognize this nature

And not to entertain concepts of subject and object
is the practice of a bodhisattva.

23

When encountering objects which please us,
To view them like rainbows in summer,
Not ultimately real, however beautiful they appear,
And to relinquish craving and attachment, is the
practice of a bodhisattva.

24

The various forms of suffering are like the death of
one's child in a dream:
By clinging to deluded perceptions as real we
exhaust ourselves.
Therefore, when encountering unfavorable
circumstances,
To view them as illusions is the practice of a
bodhisattva.

25

If those who wish for enlightenment must give away
even their own bodies,
How much more should it be true of material
objects?
Therefore, without expectation of result or reward,
To give with generosity is the practice of a
bodhisattva.

26

If, lacking discipline, one cannot accomplish one's
own good,
It is laughable to think of accomplishing the good of
others.

Therefore, to observe discipline
Without samsaric motives is the practice of a
   bodhisattva.

27

For a bodhisattva who desires the joys of virtue,
All who harm him are like a precious treasure.
Therefore, to cultivate patience toward all,
Without resentment, is the practice of a bodhisattva.

28

Merely for their own sake, even shravakas and
   pratyekabuddhas
Make efforts like someone whose hair is on fire
   trying to put it out:
Seeing this, for the sake of all beings,
To practice diligence, the source of excellent
   qualities, is the practice of a bodhisattva.

29

Knowing that through profound insight thoroughly
   grounded in sustained calm
The disturbing emotions are completely conquered,
To practice the concentration which utterly
   transcends
The four formless states[26] is the practice of a
   bodhisattva.

30

In the absence of wisdom, perfect enlightenment
   cannot be attained
Through the other five perfections alone.
Therefore, to cultivate wisdom combined with
   skillful means

And free from the three concepts[27] is the practice of
a bodhisattva.

31

If I do not examine my own defects,
Though outwardly a Dharma practitioner, I may act
contrary to the Dharma.
Therefore, continuously to examine my own faults
And give them up is the practice of a bodhisattva.

32

If, impelled by negative emotions, I relate the faults
Of other bodhisattvas, I will myself degenerate.
Therefore, to not talk about the faults of anyone
Who has entered the Mahayana is the practice of a
bodhisattva.

33

Offerings and respect may bring discord
And cause listening, reflection, and meditation to
decline.
Therefore, to avoid attachment
To the homes of friends and benefactors is the
practice of a bodhisattva.

34

Harsh words disturb the minds of others
And spoil our own bodhisattva practice.
Therefore, to give up rough speech,
Which others find unpleasant, is the practice of a
bodhisattva.

35

When emotions become habitual, they are hard to
　　get rid of with antidotes.
Therefore, with mindfulness and vigilance, to seize
　　the weapon of the antidote
And crush attachment and other negative emotions
The moment they arise is the practice of a
　　bodhisattva.

36

In short, wherever I am, whatever I do,
To be continually mindful and alert,
Asking, "What is the state of my mind?"
And accomplishing the good of others is the practice
　　of a bodhisattva.

37

Dedicating to enlightenment
Through wisdom purified of the three concepts
All merit achieved by such endeavor,
To remove the suffering of numberless beings, is the
　　practice of a bodhisattva.

Following the teachings of the holy beings,
I have arranged the points taught in the sutras,
　　tantras, and shastras
As *The Thirty-seven Verses on the Practice of a
Bodhisattva*
For the benefit of those who wish to train on the
　　bodhisattva path.

Since my understanding is poor, and I have little
　　education,

This is no composition to delight the learned;
But as it is based on the sutras and teachings of holy
beings
I think it is genuinely the practice of the
bodhisattvas.

However, it is hard for someone unintelligent
like me
To fathom the great waves of the bodhisattvas'
activities,
So I beg the forgiveness of the holy ones
For my contradictions, irrelevances, and other
mistakes.

Through the merit arising from this
And through the power of the sublime bodhichitta,
relative and absolute,
May all beings become like the Lord
Avalokiteshvara,
Who is beyond the extremes of samsara and
nirvana.

For his own benefit and that of others, Thogme, a teacher of scripture and logic, composed this text at Rinchen Phug, in Ngulchu.

Textual Outline of the *Thirty-seven Verses on the Practice of a Bodhisattva*

Introduction   43

Opening Verses   48

PART ONE: The Preparation   54

First, the need to give meaning to this human existence of yours, so rare and difficult to obtain   54

Second, abandoning your native land, the source of the three poisons   63

Third, living in solitary places, the source of all good qualities   65

Fourth, giving up the concerns of this life by reflecting on impermanence   68

Fifth, avoiding unsuitable friends, whose company creates conditions unfavorable to your progress   74

Sixth, relying on a spiritual teacher, whose presence creates conditions favorable to your progress   76

Seventh, going for refuge, the entrance to the Buddhist teachings   79

PART TWO: The Main Teachings,
Illuminating the Path   87

    First, the path for beings of lesser capacity   87

    Second, the path for beings of medium capacity   91

    Third, the path for beings of superior capacity   97

       1. The bodhichitta of intention   98

       2. The bodhichitta of application   106

          I. Relative bodhichitta   106

             A. The meditation practice of
exchanging oneself and others   106

             B. The post meditation practice of
using unfavorable circumstances on the path   116

                i. Using on the path the four things that
you do not want to happen   116

                   a. How to use loss on the path   116

                   b. How to use suffering on the path   119

                   c. How to use disgrace on the path   121

                   d. How to use disparagement on the path   123

                ii. Using on the path the two things that
are difficult to bear   125

                   a. How to use on the path being
wronged in return for kindness   126

                   b. How to use humiliation on the path   127

                iii. Using deprivation and prosperity on
the path   128

                   a. How to use deprivation on the path   128

                   b. How to use prosperity on the path   130

                iv. Using hatred and desire on the path   132

                   a. How to use objects of hatred on the path   132

                   b. How to use objects of desire on the path   135

II. Absolute bodhichitta   137

  A. The meditation practice of remaining in a
state free of conceptual elaborations without
any clinging   137

  B. The post meditation practice of abandoning
any belief in the objects of desire and aversion
as truly existing   146

    i. Abandoning any belief in the objects of
desire as truly existing   146

    ii. Abandoning any belief in the objects of
aversion as truly existing   147

3. The precepts for training in those practices   150

  I. Training in the six transcendent perfections   151

    A. Transcendent generosity   151

    B. Transcendent discipline   154

    C. Transcendent patience   156

    D. Transcendent diligence   160

    E. Transcendent concentration   164

    F. Transcendent wisdom   169

  II. Training in the four instructions taught in
the Sutra   175

    A. To examine oneself for one's own defects
and to give them up   175

    B. To give up speaking of a bodhisattva's
faults   178

    C. To give up attachment to a sponsor's
property   182

    D. To give up harsh speech   184

  III. Training in how to be rid of the negative
emotions   185

IV. Training in accomplishing others' good with
mindfulness and vigilance   190

V. Dedicating the merit to perfect enlightenment   193

CONCLUDING VERSES   196

1. How and for whom this text was composed   196

2. The unerring nature of these practices   199

3. A humble prayer for forgiveness   200

4. Dedicating the merit of having composed
this text   201

5. The colophon   202

FINAL ADVICE   203

The Commentary

INTRODUCTION

The Buddha's teachings describe a number of paths and vehicles. In different ways, all of them lead to liberation from samsara's sufferings and culminate in enlightenment. But it is the teachings of the Mahayana, or Great Vehicle, that are the most profound of all. And of these Mahayana teachings, numerous and vast though they are, the essential meaning can be found in the pith instructions of the great spiritual teachers, in a condensed form that is easy to put into practice. The particular pith instructions I will be explaining here deal with the bodhichitta—the determination to attain enlightenment for the benefit of others.

As on any occasion when teachings are to be given, we—both the teacher and his audience—should begin by saying prayers together to all the buddhas of the past, present, and future and by receiving their blessings. We should then pray for the blessings of all the great teachers of the Eight Great Chariots,[28] the principal Buddhist traditions brought from India to Tibet. You, as listeners, should make sure you have the proper motivation, which is to receive the teachings in order to be able to attain enlightenment for the sake of others. To generate such an attitude in everything you do is the basis of the bodhichitta.

Living beings are as limitless as space itself. But the lives we have all lived are limitless too—so over all those countless lives, we must surely have had all sorts of connections to every other living being. Indeed, every single being must have been your mother at least once. Down to the tiniest insect, what every living being wants and tries to do is to enjoy real happiness and freedom, and to avoid suffering. But the vast majority of them are completely unaware that happiness is the result of positive actions and that suffering is the result of negative ones. In their efforts to be happy, they spend all their time in negative actions, which therefore only brings them more suffering, the very opposite of what they intend. When you think about this state of affairs, a feeling of great compassion naturally arises in you.

On a practical level, however, the mere fact that you feel compassion for them is of no use whatsoever to all those beings. So, what can you do to actually help them? You now have a human existence with all its freedoms and advantages, and especially the immense fortune of having encountered and started to practice the supreme Dharma. You have met an authentic spiritual teacher and are in the process of receiving teachings that will enable you to reach buddhahood in a single lifetime. To make full use of this precious opportunity, you must not only listen to the teachings but also put them into practice. That way your feelings of compassion can be put to work, to the point that you will eventually be able to bring all living beings to enlightenment. As things are at present, however strongly you may want to help others, you are a beginner and lack the capacity to do anything much for them. The first step you need to take toward being really useful to others, therefore, is to perfect yourself, by training and transforming your mind.

The way you are now, your mind is powerfully influenced by the clinging attachment you have to friends, relatives, and anyone who brings you satisfaction, and by your hostile feelings toward whoever seems to go against your wishes and toward all those who prevent you from acquiring wealth, comfort, and pleasure and whom you therefore regard with aversion as enemies. In your delusion, you do whatever you can to benefit yourself and those you like, and try to overcome and eliminate all those you consider enemies with such aversion that you can hardly bear even to hear their names. Over countless lifetimes you have been dragged into samsara, this vicious ocean of existence, and carried away by these strong currents of attachment and aversion. Attachment and aversion are the very cause of samsara, the very reason for our endless wandering in the circle of existence.

Consider carefully what you mean by friends and enemies. When you look into it, it is obvious that there are no such things as permanent, enduring friends or enemies. Those you think of as friends have not always been so. Indeed, they may well have been your enemies in the past, or they could become your enemies in the future. There is nothing certain about it. Why should you be so compulsively attached to particular people? Are not all your relationships temporary? In the end, whatever may happen during your life, the time will come for you to die. Then you will have no choice but to part from everyone, regardless of whether you feel attachment or aversion for them. But everything you have done in your lifetime, all those actions motivated by attachment and aversion, will have created within you a force that will then propel you to the next life, in which you will experience their result.

So, if you want to travel the path to buddhahood, give up attachment to friends and relatives, and hatred for enemies. Regard all beings with impartial equanimity. If people now seem to be either friends or enemies, it is just the result of past connections and actions. To ascribe any solid reality to those feelings of attachment and aversion, arising as they do from mistaken and confused perceptions, is just delusion. It is like mistaking a rope, lying in your path in the twilight, for a snake—you might feel afraid, but that does not mean your fear has any real basis. The rope never was a snake.

Why do you feel attachment and aversion, and where do they

come from? Fundamentally, their origin lies in the idea you have of being a truly existing individual. Once that idea is present, you develop all kinds of concepts, such as "my body," "my mind," "my name." You identify with these three things, and whatever seems agreeable to them, you cling to it. Whatever is unpleasant or repugnant to them, you want to be rid of it. The slightest suffering, such as being pricked by a thorn or being hit by a spark from the fire, upsets you. If someone wrongs you, you retaliate by doing them as much harm as possible. The minutest good action you might do for others fills you with pride. As long as this self-cherishing attitude remains deeply anchored in your being, there is no way you will be able to reach enlightenment. The idea of being a truly existing individual is ignorance at its most basic level, from which all the other negative emotions arise.

Even when you find yourself in the best of situations, you never feel it is enough. You always want more. You give little thought to others' wishes and desires, and only want favorable circumstances for yourself. If you do the slightest favor for someone, you feel you have done something quite extraordinary. That you are so preoccupied with your own happiness and welfare, and neglect the welfare and happiness of others, is the reason you are wandering in samsara. As Shantideva[29] says:

> All the joy the world contains
> Has come through wishing happiness for others.
> All the misery the world contains
> Has come through wanting pleasure for oneself.

Should you be fortunate enough to have recognized that the only lasting, true happiness is that of buddhahood, and that actions with samsaric motives just result in suffering, you must apply yourself to help everyone recognize this. If you train and tame your mind, all clinging to notions of "friend" and "enemy" will vanish, and you will perceive everyone as your parents, brothers, and sisters.

The view of the bodhisattvas—those engaged in practicing the Mahayana path—is to let go of the whole idea of a truly existing self. Once that preoccupation with one's self is no longer present, there can be no hatred, selfish attachment, pride, jealousy, or ignorance.

The different teachings of the Buddha can be divided into two major approaches at different levels: the Basic Vehicle, or Hinayana, and the Great Vehicle, or Mahayana. The two do not contradict each other. However, when practiced correctly, the Mahayana naturally includes the teachings of the Hinayana. Within the Mahayana are countless profound instructions, but the essence of them all is that you need to train your mind—to rid it of attachment and hatred, to dispel everything that obscures it from perceiving clearly, and to dedicate the results of all your positive actions to the benefit of all beings.

The mind set on enlightenment, the bodhichitta, is to consider that whatever you do—whether you do a single prostration, recite just one rosary of mantras, or give rise to a single good thought—is for the sake of all living beings. This is the most precious wish, to attain buddhahood solely for the benefit of others.

Of all the vast and profound teachings on bodhichitta, the essence is to be found in this text, the instructions known as *The Thirty-seven Verses on the Practice of a Bodhisattva* by Gyalse Ngulchu Thogme, who was Avalokiteshvara himself appearing in the form of a spiritual teacher in fourteenth-century Tibet. There is no doubt that if, while studying and reflecting on the precepts explained here, you manage to give rise to genuinely altruistic thoughts, the bodhichitta will effortlessly form within you. And once the bodhichitta is properly established in your mind, you will possess the very root of all the teachings of the Sutrayana, Mahayana, Mantrayana, Mahamudra, and Great Perfection.

Constantly check your actions and intentions against each

verse of this text, one by one, and any practice you engage in will progress and bear fruit with the greatest of ease. Permeate your mind with these teachings day by day, month by month, and without difficulty you will naturally awaken and develop within you all the qualities of a bodhisattva, just as a bee flying from flower to flower sips nectar from each, and from that nectar produces honey.

OPENING VERSES

The text begins with a short homage in Sanskrit:

Namo Lokeshvaraya

Namo means "I pay homage"; *loka* signifies the world or universe; *ishvara,* "the all-powerful master," here in the vocative case (*-aya*). Thus the first line means, "I pay homage to you, the Lord of the Universe."

The Lord of the Universe referred to here is Avalokiteshvara. Avalokiteshvara is compassion itself, appearing in the form of a deity. Aware of the suffering of all living beings, he is known in Tibetan as Chenrezi, which means "he who sees all." He continually turns the wheel of the Mahayana teachings throughout the buddhafields of the ten directions, and manifests in whatever form is appropriate to help beings: as a buddha, a bodhisattva of the tenth level, a deity, a spiritual teacher, or even as an ordinary person or an animal.

Great bodhisattvas like Avalokiteshvara manifest in our world for the benefit of living beings. Unlike ordinary beings, they are not driven to take birth by the force of their past actions. Rather, they simply appear to those who have pure faith and are ready to be set on the path of liberation, in the same way that the sun and moon are naturally reflected wherever there is still, clear water. Bodhisattvas may take the form of spiritual friends, or any other guise that may help those to whom they appear.

Next comes a more expanded homage:

> Though he sees that in all phenomena there is no
>   coming and going,
> He strives solely for the sake of beings:
> To the sublime teacher inseparable from
>   Avalokiteshvara, the Protector of Beings,
> I pay constant homage with respectful body, speech,
>   and mind.

The spiritual master, with perfect wisdom, sees that the nature of all phenomena is beyond such concepts as coming and going, eternalism and nihilism, existence and nonexistence, oneness and diversity. He sees the true condition of all things and, out of great compassion, works solely for the sake of all beings, showing them the path of the Mahayana.

The sublime spiritual master is inseparable from Avalokiteshvara, the embodiment of the compassion of all the buddhas. Although he manifests in infinite ways for the sake of beings, and displays countless different forms, Avalokiteshvara's nature never changes. Fully enlightened, he has actualized primordial wisdom. His mind is the nondual, unchanging enlightened mind of all the buddhas—the absolute, dharmakaya.

Avalokiteshvara, as I have said, appears in our universe not, as is the case for ordinary beings, as a result of his past karma and obscuring emotions, but to benefit beings. In India he manifested as a bodhisattva who requested Buddha Shakyamuni to turn the wheel of Dharma. In Tibet, in the seventh century, he appeared as the great King Songtsen Gampo[30] in order to establish Buddhism in the Land of Snows. In our time, His Holiness the Dalai Lama and Gyalwa Karmapa are emanations of Avalokiteshvara. Guru Padmasambhava[31] is also an emanation of Avalokiteshvara, and has himself manifested countless forms throughout his miraculous, self-liberated lives. Guru Padmasambhava and Avalokiteshvara continue to appear in infinite forms dedicated to the benefit of all living beings. This unceasing flow of activity will continue until not a single being remains in samsara. Some sutras in the *Tripitaka*—the collection of the Buddha's discourses—such as the *Sutra Designed as a Jewel Chest,* and the *Sutra of the White Lotus of Compassion,*[32] contain detailed accounts of Avalokiteshvara's life of perfect liberation.

Avalokiteshvara is the expression of the infinite compassion that dwells in the heart of all the buddhas. He is known by many other names, too, such as "King of the Sky," "Bountiful Lasso," "He Who Dredges the Depths of Samsara," "Greatly Compassionate Transformer of Beings," "Ocean of Victorious Ones," "Khasarpani," "Lion's Roar," "Unwinding in Ultimate Mind," and "Sovereign of the Universe."[33] As human beings, if we develop devotion and faith in Avalokiteshvara, we can receive his blessings and realize all his enlightened qualities.

The six syllables of Avalokiteshvara's mantra—*Om Mani Padme Hum*—are a manifestation of Avalokiteshvara himself. Whenever anyone, even an ignorant wild animal, sees these six syllables or hears the sound of the mantra, the seed of liberation is sown in his being and he is protected from rebirth in the lower realms of existence. The syllables of Avalokiteshvara's mantra, even when written by an ordinary human hand, are not ordinary syllables, but have been consecrated by Avalokiteshvara's wisdom mind. These syllables are made of his blessings; they have the power to liberate.

Just as space provides room for the mountains and continents to exist, the wisdom and compassion of Avalokiteshvara and all buddhas allow beings to realize liberation. The compassion of buddhas is not limited or preferential—it is not bound by like and dislike, or by partiality for one over another. Their compassion is all-encompassing, like the sky. Just as a mother knows whether her child is well or hungry, in danger or feeling cold, Avalokiteshvara is ever aware of beings who need to be freed from the lower realms of samsara; Avalokiteshvara is ever aware of who can be set on the path of the Mahayana, and of who is ready to be guided to Amitabha's Buddhafield of Bliss. Avalokiteshvara's compassion knows no barrier or delay. His compassionate activity is effortless and spontaneous. Even a fresh summer breeze is the activity of the buddhas.

Unlike that of ordinary beings, the buddhas' activity does not require any effort or purposeful aim. Just as water naturally has the quality of moistening things and dissolving dirt, so, too, every minute action of Avalokiteshvara's, even a gesture of his hand, brings others toward liberation. This is the result of powerful prayers and aspirations that Avalokiteshvara made before attaining enlightenment. Liberation from samsara would not be possible without the infinite compassion and wisdom of the buddhas. Consider your root teacher—the one who unerringly shows you what to do and what not to do—as inseparable from Avalokiteshvara, and pay homage with great devotion and respect.

After this offering of homage, Gyalse Thogme expresses his intention to expound the precepts of a bodhisattva:

> The perfect buddhas—source of happiness and
>   ultimate peace—
> Exist through having accomplished the sacred
>   Dharma,
> And that, in turn, depends on knowing how to
>   practice it;
> This practice of the bodhisattvas I shall therefore
>   now explain.

Through knowing and applying these precepts you will gradually see the truth of the Buddha's teachings and you will progress on the path.

A truly good, altruistic mind is the source of temporary happiness—good health, long life, wealth—as well as of ultimate bliss, which is liberation from samsara and attainment of unchanging enlightenment. All the sorrows of samsara, wars, famines, illnesses, and natural calamities arise from hatred and the other inner poisons. When injurious thoughts prevail and people think of nothing but harming each other, the general welfare of the world declines daily. If people's minds are permeated with the wish to help others, the general welfare of the world steadily increases.

In order to realize temporary and ultimate happiness, you first need to arouse the motivation of the bodhichitta, the mind set on attaining enlightenment for the sake of all beings, which is rooted in compassion. You must then combine means and wisdom: the practice of the *paramitas*, the transcendent perfections, with the realization of emptiness. As Nagarjuna says in the *Ratnamala*:

> If you aspire to enlightenment, the root of it
> Is bodhichitta as firm as Mount Meru,
> All-pervasive compassion,
> And nondual wisdom.

When the Buddha was a bodhisattva traveling the path to omniscience, he was even reborn as birds and as wild animals to expound the Dharma to fellow creatures. He encouraged them to give up harming one another and to develop loving-kindness and the wish for enlightenment. By the strength of his pure and altruistic mind, harvests in the surrounding countryside were always bountiful, the inhabitants were free of illness, and not a single being was reborn in the lower realms. It is important to appreciate the inconceivable strength and effect of a single thought of benefiting another.

A buddha has developed this altruistic mind to its ultimate extent; he has conquered the archenemies of beings—ignorance, anger, desire, pride, and jealousy. When the Buddha was seated under the bodhi tree, an army of twenty-one thousand demons showered him with a rain of weapons to distract and prevent him from attaining enlightenment. But the Buddha just meditated on love and compassion, and by the power of his meditation, the rain of weapons turned into a shower of fresh, fragrant flowers.

He has such power because his body, speech, and mind are totally united and in harmony with the truth of Dharma, and are permeated with compassion. The Dharma dwells in the Buddha's heart, and through his compassion it arises and is expressed to others as instruction that shows the path to liberation. The Buddha naturally manifests as a guide to lead all those who are blinded by ignorance out of the cycle of existence. His compassion is such that if one person were attacking him and another, simultaneously, making offerings to him, the Buddha would feel neither the slightest animosity toward the first person, nor the least special attraction toward the second.

Those who practice the Dharma of the Mahayana in accordance with the Buddha's intention are known as bodhisattvas.[34] If you practice the teachings of the Mahayana, you can reach the level of the great bodhisattvas Avalokiteshvara and Mañjushri, in the best case, or become like the Buddha's two main disciples Shariputra and Maudgalyayana, who were gifted with insight and miraculous powers.[35] Even if you are unable to practice to the full in this life, you will at least be reborn among the principal disciples of the future Buddha, Maitreya.

The buddhas being those who have totally conquered the enemies of ignorance and the other emotions, they are often referred to by the epithet "Victorious Ones," while bodhisattvas, in many texts, including the Tibetan original of the root verses of these teachings, are called "children of the Victorious Ones."[36] Who, then, are the children of the buddhas? In the case of Buddha Shakyamuni, the child of his body was his physical son, Prince Rahula. The children of his speech were all those who heard him teach and attained the level of *arhat*[37]—the great beings such as Shariputra, Maudgalayana, the sixteen arhats and others, who became the holders of his teachings. Above all, the children of the Buddha's mind are the great bodhisattvas such as

Avalokiteshvara and Mañjushri, who carry out their noble intention to bring all beings to enlightenment. For, just as a great monarch with a thousand children would choose the one with the most perfect qualities to be his heir, so, too, a buddha regards as his authentic heirs the bodhisattvas who have perfected the union of wisdom and compassion.

The teachings of the Dharma have great power, but unless you practice them properly, that power will remain merely as a potential that is never expressed. If one has a tool and does not use it, not much will be accomplished. An unused tool is not particularly beneficial in itself. But if you truly put the teachings into practice, as the Dharma takes birth and grows in your mindstream, all your faults will naturally diminish and all your positive qualities will spontaneously blossom, just as the sun, as it rises higher in the morning, gradually spreads increasing light throughout the world.

One can learn about the practice of a bodhisattva in many ways. It is always necessary, though, to hear the teachings, reflect upon them, and to assimilate them through meditation. Pith instructions such as *The Thirty-seven Verses on the Practice of a Bodhisattva* contain the essence of all the bodhisattva teachings on discipline, concentration, and wisdom. If you can assimilate and actualize these teachings, you will easily travel the path toward liberation.

PART ONE: THE PREPARATION

This section explains how to enter the path, while part 2 contains the instructions on how to actually follow the path according to one's capacities, whether inferior, middling, or superior.

The preparation is covered in seven topics.

First, the need to give meaning to this human existence of yours, so rare and difficult to obtain

1

Now that I have this great ship, a precious human
life, so hard to obtain,
I must carry myself and others across the ocean of
samsara.
To that end, to listen, reflect, and meditate
Day and night, without distraction, is the practice of
a bodhisattva.

At the moment, you are fortunate enough not to have taken
birth in one of the eight states in which there is no freedom to
practice the Dharma, and moreover to be endowed with the ten
advantages conducive to Dharma practice.

The eight states in which there is no freedom to practice the
Dharma are (1) to be born in a hell realm, (2) to be born as a tortured spirit, or *preta*, (3) to be born as an animal, (4) to be born
among barbarians, (5) to be born as a long-lived god, (6) to hold
erroneous views, (7) to be born in a dark *kalpa* in which no buddha has appeared, and (8) to be born with impaired sense faculties.

Of the ten advantages conducive to Dharma practice, five
pertain to the individual. These are (1) to be born as a human
being, (2) to be born in a central place where the Dharma flourishes, (3) to be born with all one's faculties intact, (4) not to have
a lifestyle that is in conflict with the Dharma, and (5) to have
faith in the teachings.

The remaining five advantages depend upon circumstances
outside yourself. They are (6) a buddha has appeared in this
world, (7) he has taught the Dharma, (8) the Dharma has remained and still exists in your time, (9) you have entered the
Dharma, and (10) you have been accepted by a spiritual teacher.

Longchen Rabjam[38] also details eight intrusive circumstances that cause you to drift away from Dharma, and eight incompatible propensities that limit your natural potential to
attain freedom.[39]

The eight intrusive circumstances that cause you to drift away from Dharma are (1) to be greatly disturbed by the five poisonous emotions; (2) to be extremely stupid, and thus easily led astray by unsuitable friends; (3) to fall prey to the devil of a mistaken path; (4) to be distracted by laziness even though you have some interest in Dharma; (5) to lead a wrong way of life, and be afflicted by negative karma; (6) to be enslaved or controlled by others; (7) to practice for mundane reasons, such as just to be protected from danger or out of fear that you might lack food or other basic necessities; and (8) to practice a hypocritical semblance of Dharma in the hope of wealth or fame.

The eight incompatible propensities that limit your natural potential to attain freedom are (1) to be fettered by your family, wealth, and occupations so that you do not have the leisure to practice the Dharma; (2) to have a very corrupt nature that drives you to depraved behavior, so that even when you meet a spiritual teacher it is very hard to turn your mind to Dharma; (3) to have no fear of samsara's sufferings, and therefore no feeling of disillusionment with samsara, or determination to be free from it; (4) to lack the jewel of faith and therefore have no inclination whatsoever to meet a teacher and undertake the teachings; (5) to delight in negative actions and have no compunction about committing them, thereby turning your back on the Dharma; (6) to have no more interest in Dharma than a dog in eating grass, being therefore unable to develop any positive qualities; (7) to have spoiled your *pratimoksha* vows and Mahayana precepts, and thus to have nowhere else to go but the lower realms of existence, where there is no leisure to practice the Dharma; and (8) having entered the extraordinary path of the Vajrayana, to break *samaya* with your teacher and vajra brothers and sisters, and thus be parted from your natural potential.

If you possess the freedoms and favorable conditions, and can avoid these sixteen additional conditions, you will be free of any hindrances to your practice, and will be able to reach enlightenment. Having this precious human life is like having a well-rigged ship on which to sail across the ocean to an island of trea-sures. As Shantideva says in *The Way of the Bodhisattva:*

> Cross the sea of emotions
> On the boat of human existence.

You have not obtained this precious human existence just by chance. It is the result of having heard the Buddha's name in a past life, having taken refuge in him, accumulated virtuous ac-tions, and developed some wisdom. There is no certainty that you will obtain this vessel again. If you fail to practice the Dharma in this life, it is certain that you will not obtain a human existence in the next life. To neglect such an opportunity would therefore be very foolish. Do not waste it. Practice day and night.

The very first of the ten advantages is to have taken birth as a human being. Consider the number of beings throughout sam-sara. To give some simple comparative numerical images, if the number of beings in the hell realms was like the number of par-ticles of dust on the face of the earth, the number of pretas would be like the number of grains of sand in the Ganges, the number of animals like the number of millet grains in a barrel of *chang,*[40] and the number of demigods like the number of snowflakes in a blizzard. But the number of both human and celestial beings would be like no more than the number of dust particles on a fingernail. And there are far fewer human beings than celestial beings—human beings are like the stars at daybreak.

Improbable though the chances were that you have been born as a human being, you can easily see how much more against all odds it is that not only have you been born in a place where the Dharma exists, but also that you take an interest in Dharma—and even more so that you actually put it into prac-tice. That is extremely rare. Look at the small number of individ-uals interested in practicing the Dharma. Look at how many countries there are in the world, and at those where the Dharma is a living tradition. Even in one such country, how many beings are inspired to practice, and among them how many will actually bring their practice to fruition? Most beings fritter their lives away in meaningless, selfish, trivial activities.

Nevertheless, you might think, "I'll continue my ordinary activities until I'm fifty years old, but then I will dedicate myself to the Dharma." Such ideas show an alarming lack of discernment and ignore the fact that death comes without warning. As it is said,

> The time of death is uncertain;
> The cause of death is unpredictable.

How many of those alive in the world tonight will be dead by dawn? To have a human existence is like possessing great riches; it should be put to use right away. Right now is the time to practice Dharma. As Gyalse Thogme himself said:

> He who in autumn does not provide for the coming winter
> Is considered a fool.
> The Dharma alone will help us when we die, and we know that death is certain—
> So not to practice it now is utterly foolish.

Every day, remind yourself that if you do not study and reflect upon the teachings, meditate, and recite prayers and mantras, at the moment of death you will be helpless. Death is certain. If you wait for the moment of death to begin your practice, it will be too late.

Think about why you are engaging in practice. Wishing to obtain a long life free from illness, or hoping to increase your wealth and influence are petty aims. Practice to free yourself and all others from the suffering that is samsara.

To thoroughly appreciate the necessity of practicing the Dharma, it is important to be aware of the extent of suffering throughout samsara. From the bottom to the top of samsara, there is nothing but suffering. Samsara is said to be pervaded by three kinds of suffering: suffering upon suffering, the suffering of change, and the all-pervasive suffering of the composite.

The lower realms are mainly afflicted by "suffering upon suffering"—a ceaseless round of sufferings, one on top of another: the heat and cold of the hells; the thirst and hunger of tortured spirits; and the mental darkness, stupidity, and fear of the animal realm.

The higher realms are particularly subject to "the suffering of change." Among human beings there are four root sufferings: birth, old age, sickness, and death. These four powerful currents of existence are strong enough to carry us helplessly away—there is no way we can reverse their flow. Additionally, we suffer when we do not get what we want, whether food, clothing, wealth, or influence; when we get what we do not want, such as criticism, physical illness, or unpleasant circumstances; when we cannot be with the people we love; and when we have to be with people we dislike. In fruitless self-centered attempts to achieve happiness, most human beings commit predominantly negative actions. Unfortunately, all that is generated is more suffering and confusion. The demigods, or *asuras*, suffer from constant fighting and jealousy. The higher gods suffer from the change they endure when their long celestial life of bliss and enjoyment ends, and they fall again into the lower realms.

The formless realms are characterized by the latent, "all-pervasive suffering of the composite." Beings remain in states of deep, blissful contemplation, but once the good karma that caused and therefore underlies this peaceful condition is exhausted, they will again have to experience the anguish of samsara. They have not dispelled ignorance and have therefore not eradicated the five poisons.

When buddhas look at samsara with the eyes of their omniscience, they do not see it as an enjoyable place. They are acutely aware of the sufferings of beings, and they see how senseless are the pointless, temporary goals that beings try so hard to attain. It is important to become more and more clearly convinced that the only thing worth achieving is supreme enlightenment. Contemplating the sufferings of samsara, you will naturally develop a strong wish to be liberated from it. Rather than meaninglessly wasting your energy, you will concentrate on practicing the Dharma.

Even to hear the teachings is something very rare, which only happens once in aeons. That you have met the Dharma now is not just coincidence. It results from your past positive actions. Such an opportunity should not be wasted. If your mind is in accord with Dharma, you will not experience any problems with the things of this life; while if you are constantly preoccupied with your ordinary pursuits, your problems will increase, and nothing will be accomplished. As Longchen Rabjam said:

> Our activities are like children's games.
> If we're doing them they won't end; they'll end if we
>   stop.

Determination to be free from samsara, based on disillusionment, is the foundation of all Dharma practice. Unless you have made a clear decision to turn your back on samsara, then however many prayers you recite, however much you meditate, however many years you remain in retreat, it will all be in vain. You may have a long life, but it will be without essence. You may accumulate great wealth, but it will be meaningless. The only thing that is really worth doing is to get steadily closer to enlightenment and farther away from samsara. Think about it carefully.

Contemplate death and the sufferings of samsara, and you will not want to waste a single moment in pointless distractions and activities, such as trying to get rich, defeating your enemies, or spending your life protecting and furthering the interests of those to whom you are attached. You will only want to practice the Dharma.

A bedridden patient only thinks about getting well again. He or she has no wish to remain sick forever. Likewise, a practitioner who yearns to leave the miseries of samsara behind will make use of all the ways in which that can be done, such as taking refuge, generating the mind set on attaining enlightenment for the sake of others, undertaking positive actions, and so on, with a firm determination to get out of samsara constantly in mind.

It is not enough to wish from time to time that you could be free of samsara. That idea must pervade your stream of thinking day and night. A prisoner locked in jail thinks all the time about different ways of getting free—how he might climb over the walls, ask powerful people to intervene, or raise money to bribe someone. So, too, seeing the suffering and imperfection of samsara, never stop thinking about how to gain liberation, with a deep feeling of renunciation.

When some great teachers of the past reflected on the rarity of human existence, they did not even feel like sleeping; they could not bear to waste a single moment. They put all their energy into spiritual practice.

When the Buddha first turned the wheel of Dharma, he taught the Four Noble Truths. The First Noble Truth is that there is suffering, and it should be recognized. The Second Noble Truth is that suffering has a cause, which therefore needs to be given up. That cause is the *klesha*s, the negative emotions or afflicting mental factors. Although there are many such obscured states of mind, the five principal obscurations are desire, aggression, ignorance,[41] pride, and jealousy. The Third Noble Truth is that there is a path that leads beings away from suffering; this path therefore needs to be followed. The Fourth Noble Truth is that suffering can thus be brought to cessation. Through the Four Noble Truths, the Buddha urged us to renounce worldly concerns and strive for liberation from samsara.

In our search for the means to be free from samsara, the first step is to listen to the teachings, which explain the different methods of so doing. In addition to the precious knowledge that is thus acquired, simply hearing the sound of the Dharma being taught—even the sound of the conches and gongs that call the community to gather for teachings—has inconceivable blessings and benefits, the Buddha said, and can liberate beings from rebirth in the lower realms. Through listening to the teachings, even those who lack the faculties to understand their meaning thoroughly will at least gain some notion of the Dharma's qualities. Even a general idea of how to practice the Dharma is already precious.

The second step is to reflect on what you have heard and try to find the essential meaning in it. Examine your own mind to see whether it is really as the teachings describe or not, and whether you can keep it focused on an object of meditation.

Third, once you have a clear idea of the essential meaning of the Dharma, you must try to realize that meaning through your inner experience, and assimilate it into your being. This is called meditation.

As you progress through these three steps, spiritual qualities will naturally arise, and you will see the truth of the teachings. Those qualities will bloom spontaneously because the buddha nature within you is being revealed. The buddha nature, or *tathagatagarbha,* is present in all beings, but is hidden by obscurations, in the same way that buried gold is hidden by the earth under which it lies. As you listen to, reflect, and meditate on the Dharma, all the inherent qualities of your buddha nature will be actualized. When a field has been carefully prepared and planted with seeds, and all favorable conditions are present, such as temperature, moisture, and warmth, the seeds will germinate and grow into crops.

The scriptures and texts of the Dharma include many profound and detailed teachings. They cover a wide variety of subjects, such as the five traditional sciences.[42] Many people, however, will not be able to hear, reflect, and meditate in detail on all of those texts. In the present text, however, the very essence of all the teachings is laid bare and conveyed in the form of instructions on how a bodhisattva should practice.

Using these instructions, devote yourself entirely to practice. Reflect on their meaning again and again, and try your best to apply them. Eventually, you may wish to go to a solitary mountain retreat to meditate deeply upon them.

It is said that there is nothing, however difficult, that cannot become easy through familiarization. If you persevere in the practice of these instructions, you can be sure of achieving results.

> *Second, abandoning your native land, the source of the*
> *three poisons*

2

> In my native land waves of attachment to friends
>   and kin surge,
> Hatred for enemies rages like fire,
> The darkness of stupidity, not caring what to adopt
>   or avoid, thickens—
> To abandon my native land is the practice of a
>   bodhisattva.

The meaning of leaving behind your native land is to leave behind the emotions of attachment, hatred, and the obscuring ignorance that permeates both. These three poisons, generally speaking, are most active in the relationships you establish with family and friends in your own homeland. There, it is all too easy for the protection of those to whom you are attached, and the increasing of their wealth and happiness, to become your main preoccupation. If you feel any hesitation at all in this constant pursuit of ordinary goals, it is simply about how best to achieve them—should you continue whatever you are currently doing, or turn your efforts in some new and more profitable direction? You end up engaging in meaningless activities without end, frittering away what is left of your precious life. In the same way, conflict arises much more easily in such circumstances. Hatred is often engendered by arguments, feuds, and distorted beliefs that can be perpetuated through a family or district for generations. In truth, even if you live to be seventy or more, you can never hope to overcome all your adversaries and totally gratify your close ones.

Getting the better of competitors and looking after your own interests and friends are what many people would consider a useful and intelligent way to spend your life. But acting with those ends in mind could only make sense if you were completely unaware of the consequences that are bound to follow. Not to see how pointless it would be to waste your life with such goals is simply ignorance.

So, rather than stay near the people and things that are liable to arouse your attachment and resentment, go to a completely unknown place where there is nothing that will engender negative emotions. Your mind will not be disturbed, and you will be able to devote your time and energy to the practice of Dharma. As it is said:

> Go hundreds of miles away
> From places of dispute;
> Don't stay for an instant
> Where disturbing emotions prevail.

And, as Longchen Rabjam said:

> Ordinary worldly activities
> Are like a swamp that engulfs an elephant seeking
>   cool.

> Affectionate relatives and friends
> Are like jailers detaining you in samsara.

> The pleasures of this life
> Are like a bone being gnawed by a toothless old dog.

Entanglement in desire or aversion toward sensual
    experiences
Is like honey into which an insect falls.

Seized by fear, throw them all away!

Once you have left home, country, family, friends, and
worldly work behind, you will have nothing to cling to. You will
feel as free as the birds and wild animals. If, however, in your new
and initially unfamiliar surroundings, you begin to forge new attachments, you will soon find once again that you are unable to
practice the Dharma. Like the moon, which is always on the move,
do not remain in one place too long. As time goes on, it will become obvious through your practice of the Dharma that hatred
toward anyone is a mistake. You will have nothing but good
thoughts and intentions toward all beings. So, too, the pointlessness of becoming attached to anyone and anything will also become obvious, and you will see that all objects of attachment are
like things perceived in dreams, like phantasmagoric illusions.

Third, living in solitary places, the source of all good
qualities

3

When unfavorable places are abandoned, disturbing
    emotions gradually fade;
When there are no distractions, positive activities
    naturally increase;
As awareness becomes clearer, confidence in the
    Dharma grows—
To rely on solitude is the practice of a bodhisattva.

When you live in a solitary place, your negative emotions
gradually diminish, and your self-control and moderation increase. Gyalse Thogme himself said:

In a solitary place,
There are no enemies to defeat,
No relatives to protect,
No superiors to look up to,
No servants to be looked after.
So, apart from taming your mind,
What else will you have to do there, Mani-reciters?[43]

Undisturbed by friends and relatives, undistracted by the need to earn a living through business or cultivating the land, you will be able to concentrate one-pointedly on deep spiritual practice and thus make spiritual progress with your body, speech, and mind. Your mind will become self-controlled, serene, clear, and filled with certainty about the truth of the teachings. This is why all the sages of the past lived in the wilderness, in solitary, mountainous places conducive to spiritual practice. As Shantideva said:

And so, revolted by our lust and wanting,
Let us now rejoice in solitude,
In places where all strife and conflict cease,
The peace and stillness of the greenwood.[44]

And it is also said:

Unattached to gain, be like the wind, like a bird.
Dwelling in the wilderness, be like a shy animal.
Acting rightly, you will remain unperturbed.

If you wish to concentrate entirely on the Dharma instead of being constantly tossed hither and thither by waves of attachment and aversion, give them up and go to a solitary place. Turn your mind inward, identify your defects, rid yourself of them, and develop all your inherent good qualities. Be content with just enough food for sustenance, just enough clothing to protect yourself, and your practice will progress from day to day, month to month, and year to year.

Once you are free from all distracting conditions, your practice will bring you progress along the path. That is why all the yogins of the past wandered like beggars from one solitary place to another. Even a single month in a quiet and lonely place will be enough for your animosity to be replaced by a wish to benefit others, and your attachment to friends by a strong feeling of impermanence and impending death.

As Lord Atisha said: "Until you have attained stability, distractions harm your practice. Dwell in forest and mountain solitudes. Free of upsetting activities, you will be able to devote yourself entirely to practicing the Dharma, and you will have no regrets at the time of death."

And Drom Tönpa[45] said: "This decadent age is not a time for ordinary beings to help others externally, but rather a time to live in solitary places and train their own minds in the love and compassion of bodhichitta."[46]

Such is the strength of delusion and habitual tendencies that practicing Dharma might initially seem very hard; but these difficulties will gradually subside. Once you have understood the essential point of the teachings, you will experience no hardship or difficulty with the practice. Your efforts will bring you joy. It is like developing any skill—as you master the important points, it becomes progressively easier, you gain increasing confidence, and your capacity and endeavor keep on growing.

Whatever meditation or reflection you have done, it will never be wasted. The benefit it brings will be present in your mindstream at the time of your death, and will help you be reborn in a place where the Dharma flourishes, near an authentic spiritual teacher. Life after life, you will evolve from a mediocre into an average practitioner, and from an average practitioner into an excellent one. The essence of learning is reflection, and the essence of reflection is meditation. As you go deeper and deeper into the meaning of the teachings, the wondrous qualities of the Dharma will become ever clearer, like the sun appearing ever brighter the higher you fly.

The sign that you have fully assimilated your learning of the Dharma is that you become peaceful by nature. The sign that you have assimilated your meditation is that you are free of obscuring emotions. As learning leads to reflection and reflection transforms into meditation, your eagerness for the deluded activities of this life will relax, and you will yearn for the Dharma instead.

Anything you do that is in accord with the Dharma, however small or trivial it may seem, will be beneficial. As the *Sutra of the Wise and the Foolish* says:

> Do not take lightly small good deeds,
> Believing they can hardly help;
> For drops of water one by one
> In time can fill a giant pot.

Similarly, even if you practice only for an hour a day with faith and inspiration, good qualities will steadily increase. Regular practice makes it easy to transform your mind. From seeing only relative truth, you will eventually reach a profound certainty in the meaning of absolute truth.

The main hindrance to the growth of such qualities is distraction. Distraction can occur in every single moment. If you let time flow pointlessly by, at the time of death you will regret that you have not practiced the Dharma. But by then it will be too late, and your regret will not help at all. Now is the time to go to a secluded place and put the instructions you have received from your teacher into practice. Each instant of your life will then become precious and meaningful, leading you farther away from samsara and closer to liberation.

Fourth, giving up the concerns of this life by reflecting on impermanence

4

Close friends who have long been together will
    separate,
Wealth and possessions gained with much effort will
    be left behind,
Consciousness, a guest, will leave the hotel of the
    body—
To give up the concerns of this life is the practice of
    a bodhisattva.

Ordinary, worldly concerns bring only suffering and disappointment in this life and the next. The appearances of samsara are highly unstable, ever changing, and impermanent, like lightning as it flashes across the night sky. To reflect on the impermanence of all phenomena helps turn your mind toward the Dharma. As it is said:

Whatever is born will die,
Whatever is gathered will disperse,
Whatever is accumulated will come to exhaustion,
Whatever is high will fall.

In our delusion, we see things as being permanent and truly self-existing. But in reality phenomena are impermanent, and devoid of any true substantial existence. We want to believe that our friends, partner, wealth, and influence will all endure, but by nature they are bound to change. It is therefore senseless to be so preoccupied with them.

The impermanence of composite phenomena is apparent throughout the universe. Look, for example, how the seasons change here on earth. In summer, luscious green foliage abounds everywhere and the landscape looks like paradise. By autumn, the grass has dried and yellowed, flowers have turned to fruit, and the trees begin to lose their leaves. In winter, the land can be white with snow, which later melts as the warmth of spring arrives. The sky may be covered with clouds in the morning, and clear in the afternoon; rivers may run dry or overflow; the apparently solid earth may shake and tremble; and the land may slip and slide. Not a single stable phenomenon can be found anywhere in the world outside.

The same is true of people. We change with every passing moment. We change minute by minute, from youth to old age, and from old age to death. Our opinions, ideas, and plans are constantly changing and evolving. It is never certain that a project once begun will ever be completed, nor is it certain to unfold in the way we intended. As Longchen Rabjam says:

> We would like to stay forever with those we love,
> But we will surely part from them.
> We would like to stay in a pleasant place forever,
> But we will surely have to go.
> We would like to enjoy comforts and pleasure
>   forever,
> But we will surely lose them.

Look at the number of people you have known since you were very young—how many are still alive? For the moment, you may still be with parents, friends, a partner, and so on. But you cannot escape the fact that at death you will be taken away from them like a hair removed from butter—not a bit of butter remains attached to the hair.

The timing of your death is uncertain, and the circumstances that will bring it about are unpredictable. Like a frog in the mouth of a snake, you are already in Death's mouth. Death may strike at any moment, without warning, and result from all sorts of causes and circumstances. Some people die young, some old, some from sickness, some in war, or because of a sudden violent accident such as falling off a cliff. Some die in their sleep, some while walking, some while eating. Some die serene, some wracked by attachment for their relatives and possessions. We all have to die, no matter how. Jigme Lingpa said:

> People who have sweltered in the summer's heat
> Rejoice at the clear, cool light of the autumn
>   moon—
> But are not frightened at the thought
> That a hundred days of their lives have passed, and
>   gone.

Life is as evanescent as dew on the tip of a blade of grass. Nothing can stop death, just as no one can stop the lengthening shadows cast by the setting sun. You might be extremely beautiful, but you cannot seduce death. You might be very powerful, but you cannot hope to influence death. Not even the most fabulous wealth will buy you a few more minutes of life. Death is as certain for you as for someone stabbed through the heart with a knife.

At present you find it hard to bear the minor discomfort of a prickly thorn or the heat of the sun. But what about the anguish you will have to face at the time of death? Dying is not like a fire going out, or like water soaking away into the earth. Consciousness continues; when you die, your consciousness has to abandon your body, accompanied only by the karmic impressions left by your previous positive and negative actions. It is then forced to wander in the different pathways of the *bardo*, the transitory state between death and a new existence. The bardo is a frightening, unknown place, sometimes incredibly dark and opaque, without an instant of peace. During your time in the bardo, you will sometimes hear terrifying noises or see horrific things. Like a criminal taken to the execution ground, you may be pushed and pulled by messengers of Yama, the Lord of Death, shouting, "Kill him!" and "Bring him here!" It is not a place of comfort and ease.

The terrible sufferings of the bardo are followed by the sufferings of the next life, whatever that may be. The suffering you will have to undergo is the unfailing result of negative actions committed in the past. Neglecting the Dharma, you have indulged in negativity over countless lifetimes. As the Buddha pointed out in the *Sutra of the Sublime Dharma of Clear Recollection*,[47] if you were to heap up all the limbs from the innumerable lifetimes you have lived, even just those in which you were reborn as an ant, the pile would be higher than the highest mountain on earth. If you were to collect all the tears you have shed in past lives when your aims were not realized, they would form an ocean bigger than all the oceans of the earth put together.

Once a Khampa came to see Drubthop Chöyung, one of Lord Gampopa's[48] foremost disciples, and, offering him a length of cloth, requested teachings. Several times, despite his insistent pleas, Drubthop Chöyung put him off. But again the Khampa insisted, and finally the master took the man's hands in his, and said, three times, "I will die, you will die." And then he added, "That's all my guru taught me; that's all I practice. Just meditate on that. I promise there is nothing greater."

Gyalwa Götsangpa said:

Meditate on death and impermanence
And you will sever ties to your homeland,
Entangling attachments to your relatives,
And craving for food and wealth.

The thought of death turns your mind toward the Dharma; it inspires your endeavor; and finally, it helps you to recognize the radiant clarity of the dharmakaya. It should always remain a major subject of your meditations.

When you think about samsara, if you feel as if you were aboard a sinking ship, as if you had fallen into a pit of deadly snakes, or as if you were a criminal about to be handed over to the executioner, these are sure signs that you have discarded the belief in the permanence of things. It is the authentic understanding of impermanence dawning in your mind.[49] As a result, you will no longer get entangled in discrimination between friends and enemies. You will be able to cut through the dense weave of meaningless distractions. Your endeavor will be strong, and everything you do will be oriented toward the Dharma. Your good qualities will bloom as never before.

The body is the servant of the mind; it can act positively or negatively. You can use this body as an instrument to achieve liberation, or as something that will plunge you deeper into samsara. Do not waste your time. Take advantage of the opportunity you now have to meet spiritual teachers and practice the Dharma. In the past, practitioners achieved enlightenment by listening to the teachings on impermanence and death, by remembering them and reflecting on them, and by integrating them into their being through meditation. As it is said:

> We ought to fear death now,
> And thus become fearless at the time of death;
> But instead we are careless now,
> And when death arrives we will beat our breast in
>   anguish.

Lord Atisha said:

> Leave everything behind and go.
> Do nothing,
> Crave nothing.

Do not be overly concerned with the ordinary affairs of this life. Just concentrate on the Dharma. Start the day by arousing the wish for enlightenment. In the evening, examine everything you have done during the day, confess whatever was negative, and dedicate whatever was positive to the benefit of all beings. Make a promise to do better the next day.

The Brahman Upagupta set aside a black pebble each time

he had a negative thought, and a white pebble each time he had a virtuous thought. To start with, he mostly accumulated black pebbles. But gradually, by maintaining mindfulness and vigilance, he soon found himself collecting only white pebbles.

Fifth, avoiding unsuitable friends, whose company creates conditions unfavorable to your progress

5

In bad company, the three poisons grow stronger,
Listening, reflection, and meditation decline,
And loving-kindness and compassion vanish—
To avoid unsuitable friends is the practice of a
     bodhisattva.

A crystal, when placed on a piece of cloth, takes on the color of that cloth, whether white, yellow, red, or black. In the same way, the friends with whom you keep company the most often, whether suitable or unsuitable, will greatly influence the direction your life and practice take.

Bad company, in this context, refers to two different kinds of relationship: with false spiritual teachers and with unsuitable friends.

If the teacher in whom you place your confidence is someone whose views and conduct are erroneous, you will ruin this life and future ones, completely missing the path to liberation. When a faithful disciple starts a relationship with such an impostor, failing to recognize him as such, all the merit he has accumulated, as well as his entire life, will be wasted. As the great Guru Padmasambhava said, "Not to examine the teacher before committing yourself is like drinking poison."

As for "unsuitable friends," what is meant here is those who have the effect on you of increasing your three negative emotions—hatred, attachment, and stupidity—and who encourage you to commit negative actions. When you are with certain people, you may find that your defects and emotions only increase, and this shows that those people might not be true friends. There is a saying that "When you are with a turbulent person, you will be carried away by distractions; when you are with a greedy person, you will lose everything you have; when you are with a comfort-craving person, you will be preoccupied with petty things; when you are with an overactive person, your concentration will be scattered."

An unsuitable friend is one who is fond of distractions, totally immersed in ordinary worldly activities, and who does not care in the least about achieving liberation—a friend who has no interest or faith in the Three Jewels. The more time you spend with such a person, the more the three poisons will permeate your mind. Even if you do not initially agree with their ideas and actions, if you spend a lot of time with unsuitable friends, you will eventually be influenced by their bad habits. Your resolve to act positively will decline, and you will waste your life. Such people will prevent you from spending any time studying, reflecting, and meditating—which are the roots of liberation. And they will make you lose whatever qualities you may have developed, especially compassion and love—which are the very essence of the teachings of the Great Vehicle. An unsuitable friend is like a bad captain who steers his ship onto the rocks. Such people are your worst enemy. You owe it to yourself to stay away from them.

In contrast, being with people who embody or aspire to gentleness, compassion, and love will encourage you to develop those qualities so essential to the path. Inspired by their example, you will become filled with love for all beings, and come to see the inherent negativity of attachment and hatred. Authentic spiritual friends are those who have received teachings from the same teacher as yourself and, detached form worldly concerns, are devoting themselves to practice in secluded places. In the company of such friends, you will naturally be influenced by their good qualities, just as birds flying around a golden mountain are bathed in its golden radiance.

*Sixth, relying on a spiritual teacher, whose presence
creates conditions favorable to your progress*

6

Through reliance on a true spiritual friend one's
    faults will fade
And good qualities will grow like a waxing moon—
To consider him even more precious
Than one's own body is the practice of a
    bodhisattva.

To achieve liberation from samsara and attain the omniscience of enlightenment would be impossible without following an authentic, qualified spiritual teacher. Such a teacher always acts, speaks, and thinks in perfect accord with the Dharma. He shows you what you have to do to progress successfully on the path, and what obstacles you will have to avoid. He encourages you to concentrate on practicing the Dharma above all, and to do only what is virtuous and beneficial. He helps you give up all unsuitable conduct without hypocrisy, and he reminds you to be aware of impermanence, and to stop clinging to samsara.

An authentic teacher is like the sail that enables a boat to cross quickly over the ocean. If you trust his words, you will easily find your way out of samsara—and that is why the teacher is so precious. It is said, "The merit of offering a drop of oil to a single pore of the teacher's body surpasses the merit derived from making countless offerings to all the buddhas."

When Lord Buddha was a bodhisattva, his spiritual master put to the test his determination to receive just four lines of the precious teaching. Since his master had told him to do so, the bodhisattva without any hesitation pierced a thousand holes in his body, inserted a thousand wicks, and set them alight.

All accomplished practitioners of the past attained enlightenment by following a spiritual teacher. They would start their search by listening to accounts of the doings of different masters.

When the stories they heard about a teacher were particularly inspiring, they would examine his qualities[50] from a distance before committing themselves. Once they had complete confidence in him, they would go into his presence, serve him, and one-pointedly put whatever instructions he gave them into practice.

You will not be able to attain enlightenment by relying only on your own ideas and being totally independent. It is true that *pratyekabuddhas*[51] are said to be able to achieve liberation by themselves, but the fact that they have no spiritual teacher in their present life does not mean they did not have one in the past. Pratyekabuddhas, indeed, attend spiritual teachers and receive their teachings over countless lives. For each and every practice of sutra and tantra, an explanation from a qualified teacher is necessary.

If you now long to meet an authentic teacher, it is because of your inclination toward the Dharma from the past. Jetsun Milarepa, having heard no more than Marpa's name, could not rest until he actually met him.[52] The teacher stands at the juncture of the path, the point where you could either go up or down. You should receive teachings from him, and allow his instructions to mature through direct experience.

There are three main ways to fulfill the wishes of the teacher. The best way is to put his instruction into practice, and spend your whole life experiencing the essence of the teachings and attaining realization. The second-best way is to serve him with devoted body, speech, and mind. As you serve your teacher, your being will be transformed by his readily apparent qualities, just as a piece of ordinary wood in a sandalwood grove will gradually be permeated by the scent of the surrounding trees. The third way to please the teacher is to make material offerings to him.

Someone who cannot help harboring many doubts, or whose character is not very refined, may find himself developing erroneous views of the teacher if he stays in close proximity to him. If this is the case, it is better to receive the teacher's instruction and go to practice elsewhere. Staying near an enlightened teacher is said to be like staying near a fire. If you have enough faith and confidence in him, he will burn away your ignorance and obscurations. But if your faith and confidence are inadequate, you will be burned yourself.

Carefully applying your teacher's instructions, you will be able to progress on the path without hindrances, like a blind person who finds a perfect guide to lead him past a dangerous precipice. But without the advice of an authentic teacher, trying to practice in a solitary place will not help you; there will be little to distinguish you from the wild birds and animals.

Even a few words of instruction from the guru can bring you to enlightenment. Therefore, pay attention, and assign great value to each and every word of his teachings. Reflect on their meaning, and meditate upon them. Always check to see whether or not the way you have understood the teachings and put them into practice works as an antidote to your inner confusion. Keep your devotion constant and unwavering—the teacher is the jewel that fulfills all wishes.

Once someone said, "Atisha, give me your teachings!" Atisha replied:

> Ha! Ha!
> That sounds so nice!
> But to give you the pith instructions
> I need one thing from you:
> Faith! Faith!

Faith is the major prerequisite for the path. If you have no faith, even following the Buddha himself will not help you. Progress on the Mahayana path depends on the teacher, so until you reach the ultimate goal, never separate from him. He is the one who will enable you to realize the truth of unborn emptiness.

If you have faith in the teacher, you will receive the blessing of his enlightened body, speech, and mind. Never tire of gazing at the teacher, as a true master is rare in this world, and it is rarer still to be able to see one. Constantly visualize him on the crown of your head, and pray to him with yearning devotion.[53] This is the most profound and essential practice in the sutras and tantras. To follow a teacher is the root of all accomplishment. If you see your teacher as the real buddha, enlightenment is not far off.

To cherish the teacher more than yourself, and more than anyone else, is the practice of a bodhisattva.

Seventh, going for refuge, the entrance to the Buddhist teachings

7

Whom can worldly gods protect
Themselves imprisoned in samsara?
To take refuge in the Three Jewels
Who never fail those they protect is the practice of a
   bodhisattva.

The previous six verses have explained the preliminaries for developing bodhichitta. You are aware of the importance and the rarity of the human life you now have, and you realize the stark immediacy of death. You feel a great disillusionment with this world, and have decided to rid yourself of distracting conditions and misleading influences, and to try to tame your mind according to the instructions of an authentic teacher. Now, you are ready to cross the threshold of the Dharma and take refuge in the Three Jewels.

People naturally search for refuge, for someone or something to protect them from sorrow and torment. Some people turn to the powerful with the hope of achieving wealth, pleasure, and influence. Others seek protection through natural forces, such as the stars or mountains. Some seek aid through the power of spirits. But none of these mistaken objects of refuge are free from ignorance and samsara, and they therefore cannot provide ultimate refuge. Their compassion, if they have any, is partial and limited.

True refuge can only be provided by something that is itself totally free—free from the bonds of samsara and free from the limited peace of a one-sided nirvana. This quality of true refuge is to be found only in the Three Jewels—the Buddha, Dharma, and Sangha—with their absolute wisdom, unbiased compassion, and unimpeded ability.

The first of the Three Jewels is the Buddha. The qualities that characterize the Buddha can be seen in terms of three aspects, or dimensions, called *kaya*s ("bodies") in Sanskrit—the dharmakaya, the absolute body; the sambhogakaya, the body of perfect endowment; and the nirmanakaya, the manifestation body. These three are all aspects of one essence.

The dharmakaya is the absolute, inconceivable, empty expanse of wisdom. The enlightened wisdom mind of the Buddha is imbued with awareness, compassion, and ability. Beyond all conceptual elaboration, its expression is the five primordial wisdoms. The sambhogakaya is the natural display of these five primordial wisdoms, arising as the five certainties—the perfect teacher, the perfect teachings, the perfect time, the perfect place, and the perfect retinue. The sambhogakaya remains by nature unchanging and unceasing throughout past, present, and future, beyond both growth and decline. Buddhas manifest as the nirmanakaya according to the different needs and capacities of beings, and thus the nirmanakaya appears in countless different forms.

For a bodhisattva on one of the ten *bhumi*s, or levels, the buddhas manifest in the sambhogakaya aspect. For ordinary beings of great merit and fortune, buddhas manifest as supreme nirmanakayas, such as the Buddha Shakyamuni. For beings of lesser merit, buddhas appear in human form as spiritual friends. For those without faith in the Three Jewels, they appear in countless helpful forms, such as animals, wheels, bridges, boats, fresh breezes, medicinal plants, and so on. They manifest constantly to benefit beings through their limitless activity.

These three aspects of the buddhas' nature are not three separate entities. It is not as if they were three different persons. Of these three aspects, it is only the dharmakaya buddha that is the ultimate refuge. But to actualize the dharmakaya refuge, we have to rely on the teachings given by the nirmanakaya buddha.

In our present age, the supreme nirmanakaya aspect is Buddha Shakyamuni. He is the fourth of the 1,002 buddhas who will appear during this kalpa, or aeon. On the eve of their enlightenment all of these buddhas made vast aspirations to benefit beings. The Buddha Shakyamuni made five hundred great prayers that he would be able to help beings in this decadent and difficult age, and all the other buddhas praised him as being like a white lotus—a lotus grows and flourishes in the mud but remains unstained by it.

Without ever actually moving from the dharmakaya, Buddha Shakyamuni appeared as a prince in India. He displayed the twelve deeds of a buddha, and achieved enlightenment under the bodhi tree at Bodhgaya. On the sambhogakaya level, he manifests as Mahavairochana to an infinite retinue of bodhisattvas.

The buddhas are aware of your faith and devotion, and know the very moment you take refuge. Do not think that the buddhas are far away in distant, absolute realms where your prayers and aspirations go unheard and unheeded. Buddhas are as ever present as the sky.

The second of the Three Jewels is the Dharma, the teachings the Buddha gave on how the enlightenment he had realized can be attained through practice. In this world, the Buddha Shakyamuni taught three categories of teachings, called the *Tripitaka,* or Three Baskets: the *vinaya,* or discipline; the *sutras,* or condensed instructions; and the *abhidharma,* or cosmology and metaphysics. He gave these teachings from different points of view at different times and places, known as the Three Turnings of the Wheel of Dharma. In the first turning, he taught relative truth; in the second, a blend of relative and absolute truth; and in the third, the ultimate, irrevocable truth.

The third of the Three Jewels, the Sangha, is the community of the Buddha's followers. It includes the eight great bodhisattvas, the sixteen arhats, the seven patriarchs that succeeded the Buddha, and all those who teach the Buddha's teachings, along with those who practice them.

The Buddha is the one who shows you the path to enlightenment. Without him you would have no choice but to remain in the darkness of ignorance. You should therefore see the Buddha as the teacher. The Dharma is the path, the unmistaken way that leads directly to enlightenment. The Sangha is composed of the companions who accompany you along this extraordinary path. It is always good to have traveling companions who can help you avoid dangers and pitfalls and ensure that you arrive safely when you are in distant and unfamiliar lands.

According to the Mantrayana, the Three Jewels also have inner aspects. These are the Three Roots, which are the Teacher, the meditation deity or Yidam, and the feminine wisdom principle or Dakini. Roots are the basis of all growth: if the root is strong and of good quality, the tree will grow, and fruit will ripen easily. The Teacher is the root of all blessings, the Yidam is the root of all accomplishments, and the Dakinis together with the Dharma-protectors are the root of all activities. Although the terms are different, the Three Roots correspond to the Three Jewels. The Teacher is the Buddha, the Yidam is the Dharma, and the Dakinis and Dharma-protectors are the Sangha.

The Teacher can also be considered the very embodiment of all Three Jewels. His mind is the Buddha, his speech the Dharma, and his body the Sangha. He is therefore the source of all blessings that dispel obstacles and enable us to progress on the path.

On the ultimate level the dharmakaya is the Buddha, the sambhogakaya is the Dharma, and the nirmanakaya is the Sangha. All are one in the Teacher, the Buddha in actuality.

The motive for taking refuge can be of three different levels, according to an individual's capacity. These different levels of motive define the three vehicles. Those with a limited attitude, as in the Hinayana, or Basic Vehicle, seek refuge from fear of the suffering that pervades the three realms of samsara. Those who have a vaster attitude, the bodhisattvas of the Mahayana, go for refuge from fear of selfish attitudes, with the vast motivation of helping all other beings as well as themselves to be free from samsara. Practitioners of the Vajrayana go for refuge from fear of delusion, in order to free all other beings and themselves from the delusion of samsara and the chains of entangling emotions; they go for refuge in order to recognize their innate buddha nature.

Similarly, there are differences in the duration of refuge. Hinayana practitioners take refuge for the duration of their present life. In the Mahayana, this is seen as inadequate, and bodhisattvas take refuge until they and all beings have attained the enlightenment of perfect buddhahood.

A king whose predominant concern was the welfare of his subjects would be considered a noble king, while a king who looked after his own welfare and comfort at the expense of his subjects would be judged shameless. Likewise, you should not take refuge with a narrow-minded concern to attain enlightenment for yourself alone. Throughout your past lives you have been connected with all beings, and at some time or other all of them must have been your loving parents. You should take refuge for their benefit. When you take refuge, consider that all these beings are taking refuge along with you, even those who do not know of the Three Jewels.

Taking refuge is the gateway to all of the Buddha's teachings, and thus to the practice of all the vehicles. Just as you have to step through the door to enter a house, every practice in the Sutrayana, the Mantrayana, or the ultimate vehicle of the Great Perfection, has refuge as its threshold. If you visualize deities and recite mantras without full confidence in the Three Jewels, you will not attain any accomplishments. In the teachings of the Great Perfection, recognizing the true nature of all phenomena is the ultimate refuge, through which you will actualize the three kayas.

Faith is the prerequisite for refuge, and its very essence. Taking refuge does not just mean reciting a refuge prayer. It must come from the depth of your heart, from the marrow of your bones. If you have that complete confidence in the Three Jewels, their blessings will always be present in you, like the sun and moon being instantly reflected in clear, still water. Without being concentrated by a magnifying glass, dry grass cannot be set alight by the rays of the sun, even though they bathe the whole earth evenly in their warmth. In the same way, it is only when focused through the magnifying glass of your faith and devotion that the all-pervading warm rays of the buddhas' compassion can make blessings blaze up in your being, like dry grass on fire.

As faith develops, four successive levels of faith can be distinguished. When you meet a teacher, hear the scriptures, learn of the extraordinary qualities of the buddhas and bodhisattvas, or read the life stories of great masters of the past, a vivid feeling of joy arises in your mind as you discover that there are such beings. This is the first kind of faith, vivid faith.

When thinking of the great masters fills you with a deep longing to know more about them, to receive teachings from them, and to develop spiritual qualities, this is the second kind of faith, eager faith.

As you reflect on the teachings, practice, and assimilate them, you develop complete confidence in their truth, and in the Buddha's boundless perfection. You come to realize that even though the Buddha displayed the *parinirvana*, he did not die like an ordinary person, but rather is always present in the absolute expanse of the dharmakaya. You clearly understand the law of cause and effect, and the need to act in accord with it. At this stage, you are free from doubt. This is the third kind of faith, confident faith.

When your confidence is so well established that it can never waver, even at the cost of your life, this is the fourth kind of faith, irreversible faith.

To take refuge in a genuine way, you should have these four kinds of faith, especially irreversible faith. Faith and devotion make you a perfect container for the nectar of blessings that pour from the teacher, so that your good qualities steadily grow like the waxing moon. Devotion is as precious as having a skilled hand that can accomplish all crafts. It is like a great treasure that fulfills all needs, the panacea that cures all illness. Entrust your heart and mind to the Three Jewels like throwing a stone into deep water.

Without faith, taking refuge would be pointless. It would be like planting a burned seed, which will never sprout no matter how long it remains in perfect conditions in the ground. Without faith, you will never be able to develop any positive qualities. Even if the Buddha were to appear in person right in front of you, without faith you would fail to recognize his qualities, and you may even conceive erroneous views about him—as some heretic teachers did in his time. You would then miss the opportunity of being benefited by him.

After having taken refuge, you must observe its precepts carefully. There are three things to be avoided, and three things to be done.

The three things to be avoided are as follows. (1) Having taken refuge in the Buddha, you should not take refuge in worldly gods and powerful people of this world. (2) Having taken refuge in the Dharma, you should give up all forms of violence, whether in thought, word, or deed. (3) Having taken refuge in the Sangha, you should not willingly share the lifestyle of those who live in a totally wrong way, nor distrust the karmic law of cause and effect.

The three things to be done are as follows. (1) Having taken refuge in the Buddha, you should respect any representation of the Buddha, including paintings and statues, even those in disrepair, and keep them in elevated places. (2) Having taken refuge in the Dharma, you should respect all the scriptures; this even extends down to a single letter of the alphabet, since letters are the support of the Dharma. Never step over books; the Buddha himself said that in this decadent age he would manifest in the form of scriptures. (3) Having taken refuge in the Sangha, you should respect members of the monastic community and all fellow Dharma practitioners.

To obtain the Dharma, bodhisattvas have endured countless hardships. In many of his former lives as a bodhisattva, the Buddha took birth as a king in remote countries where there were few teachers. He would search the whole countryside for someone who knew even four lines of authentic teaching. To test the bodhisattva king's determination, buddhas would manifest as wandering hermits. In order to receive from them even four lines of teaching, such as:

> Abandon evildoing.
> Practice virtue well.
> Master your own mind.
> This is the Buddhas' teaching,

the king would readily give up his queen, his heirs, and the whole of his kingdom, and, putting these four lines into practice, attain realization.

Sacrifices on such a scale are not always easy to make, but you can certainly remember the Three Jewels in all your activities throughout the day, no matter whether you are happy or sad. If you see a beautiful landscape, flowers, or anything wonderful and inspiring, offer it mentally to the Three Jewels. When good circumstances or events arise, see them as the blessing and kindness of the Three Jewels. Regard all sicknesses and obstacles, without complaint, as blessings in disguise that will enable you to purify your past negative karma. When confronted with great danger, or with terrifying situations, call upon the Three Jewels for assistance. At that very moment, the blessings of the Three Jewels will grant you protection. When you practice taking refuge in this manner, refuge will become an inherent part of your stream of consciousness.

Take refuge from the core of your heart, for the sake of all beings, from now until they all attain enlightenment. This is the true way of a bodhisattva.

Part Two: The Main Teachings, Illuminating the Path

After the seven topics of the preparation comes the second section, the main teachings, which explain the paths for beings of lesser, medium, and superior capacity.

First, the path for beings of lesser capacity

This consists of rejecting negative actions out of fear of the suffering that permeates the three lower realms of existence.

8

The Buddha taught that the unendurable suffering
    of the lower realms
Is the fruit of unvirtuous actions.
Therefore, to never act unvirtuously,
Even at the cost of one's life, is the practice of a
    bodhisattva.

Once you have taken refuge in the Three Jewels, it is important to behave in accordance with their teachings. Whatever happens, keep trying to do more and more positive, beneficial actions, and always avoid doing anything negative. Actively engage in the ten virtues; and abstain from the ten non-virtues. This means not only, for instance, to abstain from killing, but also to protect life, to ransom the lives of animals about to be butchered, to set captive fish free, and so on.

There are four black dharmas to avoid, and four white dharmas to keep to. The four black dharmas are (1) to deceive those worthy of respect, (2) to cause sadness by bringing doubt into someone's mind about the value of his virtuous actions, (3) to criticize and denigrate holy beings, and (4) to be dishonest about your faults and qualities and to cheat others.

The four white dharmas are (1) not to tell a lie, even at the risk of your life; (2) to respect and praise the bodhisattvas; (3) to be free of deceit, and benevolent toward all beings; and (4) to lead all beings on the path to enlightenment.

Confess every negative action you commit, even in a dream. Do not be confused about how to act in everyday situations. Try to keep your actions in accordance with the instructions given by your teachers. It is said that Lord Atisha never let a day go by without confessing whatever negative actions he may have committed. Once confessed, a negative action is relatively easy to purify.

Someone who has done many negative actions, even if rich and powerful, will inevitably sink into the lower realms of samsara. Someone who has done many positive actions, even the humblest of beggars, will be led by all the buddhas from the bardo to the Western Buddhafield of Bliss, or be reborn in the higher realms. As it is said:

> Good and evil actions
> Bring their results without fail.
>
> What happens at death
> Accords with what you have done.
> If your actions have been wholesome and virtuous,
> There will be happiness and birth in higher realms.
> If your actions have been unwholesome and
>   negative,
> There will be suffering and birth in lower realms.
>
> Right now, while you can choose
> To be happy or to suffer,

Do not indulge yourself in negative actions
But strive as best you can
To do good and virtuous deeds, both great and
    small.

There is no such thing as even a single act that vanishes, leaving nothing behind. The imprint created by a negative action, such as killing, will never disappear until you either experience its inevitable result or counteract it with a positive antidote.[54] While, on the one hand, even offering a single flower to the Three Jewels, or reciting a single *Mani* mantra, brings inconceivable merit, so too, on the other hand, even the most seemingly insignificant negative action has a negative result—and should thus be purified straight away.

All the teachings of the Buddha say that every action has a result. This is the infallible law of karmic cause and result.

Some people hold the opinion that actions bring no karmic result, even for a murderer who has killed thousands of people. The hell realms cannot really exist, they would argue, because no one has ever returned from there to tell us about it. They dismiss the infallibility of the cause and effect of actions as just an invention, and deny that there can be any such thing as past and future lives. But they are simply wrong. For the moment, surely, instead of believing in your own limited perceptions, why not rely on the Buddha's wisdom? The Buddha sees the past, present, and future lives of all beings. You can have confidence in the Buddha's words. For example, the buddhas have praised the benefits of reciting a single *Mani* mantra; but if you nevertheless feel doubt about those benefits, or think that the results will take aeons to appear, you are only making your own realization that much more distant.

Doubt and hesitation are the main obstacles to achieving the common and supreme accomplishments. If you doubt the teacher, you will not be able to receive his blessings. If you doubt the teachings, no matter how much time you spend studying and meditating, your efforts will remain mostly sterile.

Always try to accomplish even the smallest beneficial action without any reservation or hesitation, and avoid even the most insignificant negative actions. As the great master Padmasambhava said:

> Although my view is higher than the sky,
> My attention to actions and their effects is finer than
>   flour.

When your realization of emptiness becomes as vast as the sky, you will gain an even greater conviction about the law of cause and effect, and you will see just how important your conduct really is. Relative truth functions inexorably within absolute truth. A thorough realization of the empty nature of all phenomena has never led anyone to think that positive actions do not bring happiness, or that negative actions do not bring suffering.

All phenomena appear from within emptiness as a result of the coming together of illusory causes and conditions. The infinite display of phenomena can arise only because everything is empty in nature. As Nagarjuna said:

> Only by things being empty
> Can things be possible at all.

The presence of space makes it possible for the whole universe to be set out within it, and yet this does not alter or condition space in any way. Although rainbows appear in the sky, they do not make any difference to the sky; it is simply that the sky makes the appearance of rainbows possible. Phenomena adorn emptiness, but never corrupt it. If you have a thorough understanding of the way phenomena appear through dependent arising, it will not be difficult for you to understand the view of emptiness while remaining in meditation. On arising from such a meditation and entering the path of action, you will recognize clearly the direct relationship between actions and their results.

This will enable you to discriminate easily between positive and negative actions.

Your view can, and should be, as high as possible—there is no danger in this, since enlightenment is the total realization of the absolute view. But at the same time your behavior should be as grounded as possible in an awareness of cause and effect. If you lose this basic attitude regarding actions, if you forget all common sense and use the loftiness of the view as an excuse for putting into action whatever comes into your mind, you are engaging in mundane activities contrary to the Dharma, just like ordinary worldly people. And if you let your emotions lead your practice astray in that way, you are likely to sink in the swamp of samsara.

A spacious view and a thorough, careful attitude regarding your activities are never contradictory. The more careful you are in whatever you do, the easier it is to realize emptiness; the more profound your view, the clearer your understanding will be of the relationship between cause and effect.

Never confusing what should be done with what should be avoided is the practice of a bodhisattva.

Second, the path for beings of medium capacity

This involves detaching yourself from samsaric pleasures, and redirecting your efforts toward liberation.

9

Like dew on grass, the delights of the three worlds
By their very nature evaporate in an instant.
To strive for the supreme level of liberation,
Which never changes, is the practice of a
    bodhisattva.

Once you have understood the union of emptiness and the dependent arising of phenomena, you will see clearly how deluded and deceiving the ways of the world really are, and, like an old man forced to play children's games, you will find them very tiresome.

Once you have realized the utter foolishness of spending your life attached to friends and scheming to subdue your enemies and competitors, you will find it tedious. Once you have been struck by the pointlessness of letting yourself be forever influenced and conditioned by your habitual tendencies, you will become sick of it. Once you know that it is sheer delusion to be preoccupied by thoughts of the future, and to lose your mindfulness and vigilance in the present moment, you will weary of it.

All those illusory goals and ambitions—even if you could ever manage to follow them through and bring them to some kind of conclusion, would that lead to a lasting result? You will recognize that there is nothing permanent in any of them. You might be the heir to a throne, but it is obvious that no king has ever maintained his power indefinitely—if nothing else, death will snatch it away. You might be the most formidable general, but you will never subdue all of your country's enemies, no matter how many wars you wage. You might have tremendous power, influence, fame, and wealth, but it is all meaningless and hollow.

Worldly enjoyments are pleasurable in the beginning, but as time goes on they become an increasing source of torment. If you wrap a strip of wet leather around your wrist, it is fine at first, but as the leather dries and shrinks, it tightens painfully. What a relief it is to cut it away with a knife!

If you turn your mind to Dharma, and practice genuinely, even for as little as an hour a day, through life after life you will gradually purify your defilements and free yourself from samsara. This is meaningful. As Guru Padmasambhava said:

> However industrious you may be,
> There is no end to worldly activities;
> But if you practice the Dharma
> You will swiftly conclude everything.

However nice they may seem,
Samsaric affairs always end in disaster;
But the fruits of practicing the Dharma
Will never deteriorate.

Since beginningless time you have collected and
    encouraged
Karma, negative emotions, and habitual tendencies,
Which force you to wander in samsara.
If you continue like that, when will liberation arrive?

If you only see all this at the moment of death,
It's rather too late—
When the head's already been severed,
What use is any medicine?

Recognizing the suffering of samsara,
Turn toward the peace of nirvana.

If you recognize delusion for what it is, you will see that
there is nothing worthwhile in this ordinary world, nothing in
the whole of samsara.[55] Even the highest gods of this world, such
as Brahma and Indra, whose bodies emanate light that can illuminate the whole sky, who possess priceless jewels and ornaments, and who enjoy matchless power and prosperity, have no
choice but to fall back into the lower states of samsara when the
karma that brought them to their exalted position becomes exhausted.

Realized beings see the higher realms of existence as no better than the hell realms. Beings of lesser capacity see the suffering of the lower realms and wish to be reborn in the higher
realms. Beings of medium capacity see that everything throughout samsara is unsatisfactory and ends in suffering. They see
samsara as like a big house on fire, within which there is nowhere
to stay.

Recognizing the nature of samsara, you will feel weary of it, and such weariness will inspire you to strive toward liberation—and by striving for it, you will attain it. Samsara will never just disappear on its own. You have to want to get rid of it actively yourself.

If you acknowledge the suffering of samsara, you will recognize that the source of suffering lies in your obscuring emotions and the negative actions they engender, and that the source of your obscuring emotions lies in your clinging to the idea of self. If you can rid yourself of that clinging, suffering will cease. Liberation means freeing yourself from the ties of your emotions and negative actions. The way to free yourself from them is to practice the Dharma—to train in discipline; in concentration; and in *prajña,* the wisdom that allows you to realize the nonexistence of the individual self and phenomena. Discipline is the basis of concentration; concentration is the basis of wisdom. If you practice the Dharma properly, even for as little as an hour a day, the results of countless lifetimes and kalpas of negative actions can be purified.

As you practice the Dharma steadily, even in quite a modest way, you will gradually be able to progress farther and farther on the path to liberation. Eventually, you will attain a true bliss that can never diminish.

As Gyalse Thogme said:

> You won't accomplish
> Both the Dharma and the aims of this ordinary
>   life—
> If that's your wish,
> No doubt you're deceiving yourself.

And he also said:

> There is no greater obstacle to Dharma practice
> Than to be obsessed by the achievements of this life.

Realizing this, great practitioners of the past like Milarepa left home, went to live in solitary places, and meditated in caves with hardly any clothes to wear or food to sustain themselves. Yet Milarepa and others attained total realization of the skylike dharmakaya, the absolute nature, ultimate enlightenment. That realization was their only possession. This is why Jetsun Milarepa, who spent his time sitting on a rock wearing nothing more than a simple cotton cloth, is respected throughout the world as a prime example of an authentic spiritual practitioner, even by nonreligious people. When Jetsun Milarepa was leaving for his homeland, his teacher, Marpa, said to him, "Son, if you don't give up concern for this life, and try to mix Dharma with the affairs of this life, your Dharma is gone. That's all. Son, think about the suffering of samsara."

Milarepa himself once gave this advice in the form of a song about the attributes of the "devil":

Relatives' demonstrations of affection
Are the devil's entreaties to keep postponing your
     practice:
Don't trust them—sever all ties!

Food and wealth are the devil's spies:
If you become addicted to them, everything will go
     wrong—
Give up all such inclinations!

Sense pleasures are the devil's noose:
There's no doubt they'll ensnare you—
Cast all craving far away!

Young companions are the devil's daughters:
They're sure to bewitch and beguile you—
Beware of them!

Your native land is the devil's prison:
It is hard to escape from—
Run away, now!

In the end, you will have to go, and leave everything
    behind—
So leave it now! It makes more sense to do so!

Son, if you listen to my words, and put them
    into practice,
You will enjoy the fortune of the sublime
    Dharma.

To give up all concern for the ordinary things of this life is a very deep teaching. If I tell someone whose mind is unprepared for it that everything is empty by nature, he won't be able to accept it. He will think, "The old man is crazy!" Ordinary people find the teachings on emptiness unfathomable. In the same way, if I tell people these days, whether religious or lay, to give up worldly affairs, they will think, "The old man is delirious!" The real meaning of what I am saying will not penetrate their minds. Yet it is true that if you keep strong ties to pleasure, acquiring things, fame, and praise, then however much you may study, meditate, try to integrate high teachings, or even become a teacher yourself, it will be of no help to you at all.

Those who savor the sheer joy of Dharma practice through having given up all concern for this life are extremely rare. If I start teaching about turning away from relatives, possessions, house, land, and other enjoyments of this life, people start to look like donkeys that have been hit on the head with a stick. Their faces darken, they feel uncomfortable and uneasy, and would rather not listen at all.

Tsangpa Gyare[56] said that in order to renounce the world, you need to keep eleven pledges:

Not to conform to the attitudes of ordinary people,
   but to stay alone.
To leave your native land far behind.
To feel that you have had enough of sensual
   pleasures.
To maintain the humblest possible condition,
   thereby being free from caring what others think.
To keep a spy posted in your mind—the meditation
   on ridding your mind of attachment to loved
   ones.
Not to not pay attention to what people say;
   whatever they may say, simply leave it be and let
   them say what they will.
Not to feel distress, even if the winds carry away all
   that is dear to you.
To have nothing to regret in this life, as though you
   were a dying beggar.
To continually recite the mantra "I need nothing!"
To keep the reins of your destiny firmly in your own
   hands.
To remain enveloped by the cloud of authentic
   practice.

When people come into contact with those who have re-
nounced this world, wear religious robes, and spend their lives in
study and contemplation, they respect them as authentic members of the sangha, and offer them as much help as they can.

This natural respect is a clear manifestation of the goodness
inherent in the Dharma.

Third, the path for beings of superior capacity

*This consists of meditating on emptiness and compassion in
order to attain liberation beyond both samsara and nirvana. This
section has three parts:*

1. The bodhichitta of intention, which is the evocation of supreme bodhichitta
2. The bodhichitta of application, which is the meditation and practice of the two aspects of bodhichitta
3. The precepts for training in those practices.

1. The bodhichitta of intention

10

If all the mothers who have loved me since
  beginningless time are suffering,
What is the use of my own happiness?
So, with the aim of liberating limitless sentient
  beings,
To set my mind on enlightenment is the practice of
  a bodhisattva.

The absolute nature of everything is primordially pure, free of all conditions, and beyond any concepts of existence and nonexistence. But within relative truth, self and others, suffering and happiness, manifest in infinite ways. These appearances are devoid of any true existence, yet beings believe them to be true and thus wander, deluded, in samsara.

The bodhichitta of intention, of aspiration, has two aspects: compassion, which is directed toward beings; and wisdom, which is directed toward enlightenment. Neither aspect by itself, neither the mere wish to benefit beings nor the mere wish to attain enlightenment, expresses bodhichitta. On the one hand, if you do not aim at attaining ultimate enlightenment, then however strong your wish to benefit beings may be, you will never go beyond ordinary kindness and compassion. On the other hand, if you wish to attain enlightenment for your own sake alone, you will never go beyond the limited nirvana of Hinayana practitioners. Both aspects are indispensable. This is expressed in the *Ornament of True Realization:*

> Bodhichitta is to aspire to enlightenment
> For the benefit of others.

The infinite number of beings who, in your successive lives since time without beginning, have been your parents have loved you and cared for you to the point of being ready to give up their own lives for your sake. It would be heartless of you to forget their indescribable kindness and to ignore their suffering; and it would thus be heartless, too, to practice the Dharma for your own liberation, ignoring the bondage of others.

Are you really going to abandon all these beings immersed in so much suffering? A son who is prosperous and happy, and lives comfortably and eats good food while his parents go about in rags, destitute, hungry, and with no roof over their heads would be seen by everyone as a figure of shame and contempt. But is that any different from failing to care for all beings of the six realms, who have all been your loving parents at one time or another? If you harbor such self-centered attitudes and do not strive for the happiness of others, you will be a figure of shame for all great beings, and will have strayed from the path of the Mahayana. As Gyalse Thogme himself said:

> If you don't take the suffering of all beings squarely
>   on your shoulders,
> What's the use of receiving the supreme Mahayana
>   teachings?

Just as all the buddhas and bodhisattvas of the past aroused the bodhichitta, making the wish to bring all beings to enlightenment, so now you in your turn should generate great compassion and arouse the bodhichitta. The essence of the Dharma is the Mahayana teachings, and the essence of the Mahayana is the bodhichitta. Once the bodhichitta takes birth in your being, you are a true child of the buddhas, and the buddhas will always look on you with great happiness. In all your lives to come you will meet Mahayana teachers and benefit others. Your activity will join the oceanlike activity of all the bodhisattvas, who are full of compassion and appear in infinite forms, even as birds and wild animals, to benefit beings in infinite ways. Such an enlightened attitude benefits the whole country around you.

A bodhisattva benefits all beings equally, without discriminating between enemies and friends. Giving food, clothes, and the like to others can only bring them temporary and limited relief; it does not help them at the moment they die, nor after their death. But if you can establish all beings in the Dharma, you will help them in a way that is both immediately beneficial and beneficial for their future lives. Practicing the Dharma enables them to free themselves from samsara and achieve enlightenment—so that is the way to truly repay your parents' kindness. Any other way is not enough.

Do not hoard for your own benefit all your learning, possessions, and whatever else you may have accomplished. Instead, dedicate everything to all beings, and make the wish that they may all be able to listen, reflect, and meditate on the Dharma. Simply to express such a prayer is highly beneficial. Anything done with pure intention, even the wish to relieve beings from their headaches, has great merit. So the merit is all the more if you pray to free all beings from samsara. Since the number of beings is infinite, the merit of such a prayer is infinite, too.

Whether you are practicing the generation or perfection phase, Mahamudra, or Ati Yoga, as long as your practice is permeated with bodhichitta, it is naturally a Mahayana practice. But without the bodhichitta, your practice can only stagnate.

To have a thorough understanding of absolute wisdom is very difficult for ordinary people. That is why it is necessary to progress stage by stage along the path. To advance in the right direction, your practice should always observe what are called the three supreme points: (1) start with an attitude based on the bodhichitta, in other words with the wish to undertake the practice to attain enlightenment for the sake of all beings; (2) while you are engaged in the main part of whatever practice you are doing, be free of concepts and distractions; and (3) at the end, conclude the practice with a dedication. Practicing like this will turn even the modest practice of some small positive action into a cause for enlightenment, and the dedication will protect the merit you have gained through that practice from being destroyed as a result of your anger and other negative emotions.

1. Starting with the wish to benefit others is a perfect preparation for any practice you are about to undertake, and a skillful way to ensure that your practice will reach fruition and not be swept away by a torrent of unfavorable circumstances and obstacles.

2. For the main part of the practice, being concentrated and free of concepts and distractions has several different levels to it. Basically, it means being free of all forms of attachment—and especially of pride. No matter how learned, disciplined, or generous you might be, as long as you feel conceited and proud about such things and at the same time contemptuous of other people, nothing positive can come of your practice. The twofold accumulation of merit and wisdom is indeed the way to buddhahood, but if it is adulterated with clinging, arrogance, and condescension, it cannot bear fruit.

More particularly, being free of attachments and concepts also means being free of any clinging to whatever practice you may be doing as having some intrinsic reality. Consider the example of making offerings to the bodhisattvas. Bodhisattvas appear in the form of spiritual friends for those who have faith, or as blessings, sacred scriptures, statues, and so on; but these manifestations are like dreams, or magical illusions, devoid of any intrinsic existence. So indeed is everything else in the phenomenal world, so that not only the object of your offerings but also the offerings you are making are all illusory. Any result of the offering is also an illusion—which does not mean that there is no result, but rather that the result is not a solid, concrete entity. What sense does it make to be full of attachment and pride regarding the results of your illusory actions? When a bodhisattva performs a beneficial action, he is totally free from clinging to the concepts of a subject who acts, an object who benefits from the action, and the action itself. That total absence of clinging makes the merit infinite.

3. Dedicate all the merit and positive actions you have done or will do throughout the past, present, and future, so that all beings, especially your enemies, may achieve enlightenment. Try to dedicate the merit in the same way that the great bodhisattvas do. Any merit they dedicate within the infinite expanse of their wisdom is inexhaustible. Dedication is like putting a drop of water in the ocean. The ocean is so vast that a drop once dissolved into it can never dry up.

Not a single prayer vanishes. Dedicating the merit of every positive action you do with a pure mind will continuously bear positive fruit until you attain enlightenment. As *The King of Aspirations for Excellent Conduct* says:

> Until all beings are free from negative emotions,
> May my prayers never come to exhaustion.

The attitude of a bodhisattva must be extremely vast, constantly keeping in mind the infinity of beings and the wish to establish them all in buddhahood. If your mind is vast, the power of your prayers is unlimited, too. If your mind is narrow and rigid, your accumulation of merit and the purification of your obscurations will also be very limited.

Do not let yourself be discouraged by such thoughts as that it is not worth dedicating what you see as your miserable accumulation of merit because it could hardly benefit anyone; or by the idea that for you helping others is just talk since you will never really be able to benefit them. If you keep your mind open and vast, the effectiveness of your bodhichitta will increase, and so too will the benefit and merit of all your words and deeds.

In your daily life and practice you must keep developing the excellent mind of enlightenment. You will find inspiration in the quintessential, profound prayers of the bodhisattvas found in the oceanlike collection of Mahayana scriptures, such as:

> May the bodhichitta, precious and sublime,
> Arise where it has not yet come to be;
> And where it has arisen may it never fail
> But grow and flourish ever more and more.

And,

> May all beings find happiness;
> May all the lower realms be emptied forever;
> May all the bodhisattvas' prayers
> Be perfectly accomplished.

And,

> Wherever the sky ends,
> There ends the number of beings.
> Wherever beings' destinies and emotions end,
> Only there end my prayers.

The three supreme points include the whole practice and attitude of the Mahayana. That is why Mahayana teachers expound them over and over again. But just hearing them explained is not enough. You must assimilate and integrate them into your being. Day after day, check whether you are really acting in accord with them. If not, feel regret, and try to correct yourself. Do not allow your mind to become distracted and merely follow its inclinations.

If you become aware that you have succeeded to some extent in blending your mind with the Dharma, dedicate the merit to all beings, and aspire to do so more and more. If you constantly check your defects, eradicate those you already have, and prevent new ones from taking root; and at the same time try constantly to increase your positive qualities by allowing new ones to arise, and increasing those you already have, you will gradually progress along the five paths and levels that lead to buddhahood: the path of accumulating, the path of joining, the path of seeing, the path of meditation, and the path beyond learning.

Until you realize emptiness, you must never part from the enlightened attitude of bodhichitta. When you realize emptiness perfectly, no effort will be needed for unconditional compassion to manifest, since compassion is the expression of emptiness.

Just as you yourself wish to be happy, so, too, you should wish the same for others. Just as you yourself wish to be free from suffering, so, too, you should wish the same for all beings. "May all beings be happy, free from suffering, and the cause of suffering. May they reach perfect happiness, remain in it, and live in equanimity. May they maintain love for all others without discrimination." This wish is called the bodhichitta.

The bodhichitta will grow effortlessly if you have this pure attitude of mind. A good mind has a natural, intrinsic power to benefit others. Whatever merit arises from this vast attitude, instead of feeling that you own it, dedicate it to all beings, as infinite as space is vast. Stay free from any grasping at the reality of subject, object, and action, and the day will come when your body and speech become the servants of your mind and everything you do and say will spontaneously benefit others.

At present, like a blade of grass that bends whichever way the wind blows, you are vulnerable to many gross and subtle emotions. Trying to help others under those circumstances is unlikely to be of much benefit for them, but is quite likely to be a cause of distraction for you.

To hope for a harvest without sowing seeds is to ask
   for famine;
To hope to benefit others prematurely is to ask for
   trouble.

If you continue to gain stability in your practice, if you continue to work on your attitude and develop unconditional altruism, the bodhichitta will grow. Gradually, you will become able to put your love and compassion into action in a way that truly does benefit others.

The bodhichitta has such tremendous power that the moment it arises, you enter the noble family of bodhisattvas. If you have bodhichitta, you are immune to negative forces, and when they manifest, they have no way to cause harm or to create obstacles.

This is illustrated by a story from the life of Jigme Gyalwai Nyugu,[57] the root teacher of Patrul Rinpoche.[58] Once, a vindictive spirit decided to take Jigme Gyalwai Nyugu's life. Full of harmful thoughts, the spirit arrived at the entrance to Gyalwai Nyugu's cave. He saw a serene old man sitting with his eyes closed, entirely peaceful, full of love and compassion, his head encircled with white hair. The sight was enough for the spirit's bad thoughts to disappear in an instant. He was awestruck as he contemplated the old man. The bodhichitta was born within him, and he made the promise never to take another's life again. After this, whenever an opportunity to harm someone arose, the image of the serene white-haired old man would instantaneously appear in his mind. The spirit lost all his power to harm.

When Lord Atisha was at Bodhgaya in India, paying his respects on the eastern side of the Diamond Throne, he saw two beautiful celestial women in the sky before him.

The younger said to the elder, "If one wants to swiftly become enlightened, what is the best method?"

The elder one said, "Train yourself in arousing bodhichitta."

The young woman was Arya Tara, and the elder one Chandamaharoshana,[59] the Great Frowning One.

If bodhichitta has not yet arisen in you, pray that it will arise. And if it has arisen, pray that it will increase. If the merit of arousing bodhichitta were to take physical form, not even the whole of space would be vast enough to contain it.

2. The bodhichitta of application

Bodhichitta has two aspects, relative and absolute. Absolute bodhichitta is the realization of emptiness attained by bodhisattvas on one of the supreme levels, or bhumis. Until that realization dawns, the emphasis should be placed on relative bodhichitta, which, in essence, is the altruistic mind, the profound wish to benefit others and to be free of all selfish aims. If relative bodhichitta is practiced correctly, absolute bodhichitta will be naturally present mixed in with it, and will eventually be fully realized.

I. Relative bodhichitta

Relative bodhichitta itself has two stages, the aspiration to benefit others, and the putting of that aspiration into action. The difference between the two is like the difference between wishing to go somewhere and actually setting out on the journey. The practice of relative bodhichitta consists of (A) the meditation practice of exchanging oneself and others, and (B) the postmeditation practice of using unfavorable circumstances on the path.

A. The meditation practice of exchanging oneself and others

11

All suffering without exception arises from desiring happiness for oneself,

While perfect buddhahood is born from the thought
of benefiting others.
Therefore, to really exchange
My own happiness for the suffering of others is the
practice of a bodhisattva.

At present, when you feel happy yourself, you are probably quite satisfied. Other people may not be feeling happy, but you do not really consider that to be your problem. And when you yourself feel unhappy, you are too preoccupied with being rid of whatever it is that is upsetting you to care, or even remember, that others might be feeling unhappy, too. All this is completely deluded.

There is a way to train yourself to see things from a wider perspective. It is a practice called exchanging oneself and others, and consists of trying to put others in your place, and put yourself in theirs. The idea is, on the one hand, to imagine that you are giving away to all beings whatever good things may happen to you, however small they may be—even a spoonful of good food; and on the other hand, to remember the unbearable sufferings that others are going through, and make up your mind to take all those sufferings upon yourself with the same readiness a mother feels when she takes upon herself the suffering of her child. Indeed, when you reflect that all beings must have actually been your kind parents at one time or another, and that surely you therefore owe it to them to do as much for them as you possibly can, you will be able to bear happily whatever hardships you may have to endure to help others. When you can actually take other people's suffering upon yourself, rejoice that you have fulfilled your aims; never think they did not deserve so much help or that you have now done quite enough for them.

By sincerely training in the meditation practice of exchanging suffering with happiness, you will eventually become capable of actually taking on others' illness and curing them, and of giving them your happiness in reality. Moreover, those with harmful intentions, even evil spirits who try to steal people's life force, will be powerless to harm either you or anyone else if you exchange their suffering and hatred with your happiness and peace.

There are some extraordinary pith instructions that explain in more detail how to make this practice more effective. First, it is important to start by arousing a deeply felt warmth, sensitivity, and compassion for all beings. To do so, begin by thinking about someone who has been very kind and loving to you; in most cases, this could be your own mother. Remember and reflect on her kindness—how she gave you life, how she suffered the discomforts of pregnancy and the pain of childbirth, how she looked after you as you grew up, sparing no effort. She was ready to make any sacrifice for you and to put your welfare before her own.

When you feel strong love and compassion, imagine, step by step, that she is undergoing the sufferings of the six realms. In the hell realm, she is repeatedly and brutally killed and revived; she is tossed into a boiling cauldron of molten bronze; she suffers in agony before your very eyes. Then imagine that she has been reborn as a starving spirit, just skin and bones, and has not even so much as caught sight of food for twelve years. She stretches her hands out to you, imploring you, "My child, do you have anything you can give me to eat?" Imagine her reborn as an animal, a terrified doe being chased by hunters and their dogs. In panic, she leaps off a high cliff to escape them but falls with unbearable pain, shattering all her bones; still alive, but unable to move, she is finished off by the hunters' knives.

Continue to imagine her undergoing, in quick succession, situation after situation of suffering. An intense feeling of compassion will irresistibly well up in your mind. At that moment, turn that intense compassion to all beings, realizing that each one of them must surely have been your mother many times, and deserves the same love and compassion as your mother of this present life. It is important to include all those whom you now consider enemies or troublemakers.

Reflect deeply about everything that all these beings are going through as they wander endlessly in samsara's vicious cycle of suffering. Think about old, infirm people unable to care for themselves, about all those who are sick and in pain, people who are desperate and impoverished, lacking even the most basic necessities, about people suffering famine and starvation, the pangs of hunger and thirst, those who are physically blind—and about those who are spiritually destitute, starved of the nourishment of Dharma, and blind to any authentic vision of truth. Think about all those who suffer as slaves to their own minds, constantly maddened by desire and aggression, and about those who harm one another without respite. Visualize all these sentient beings as a crowd in front of you, and let all the different forms that their suffering takes arise vividly in your mind.

With an intense feeling of compassion, begin the practice of sending and receiving. Start by focusing on your most hated enemy, or someone who has caused much trouble and difficulty for you. Consider that as your breath goes out, all your happiness—all your vitality, merit, good fortune, health, and enjoyment—is carried out to him on your breath in the form of cool, soothing, luminous white nectar. Make the following prayer: "May this truly go to my enemy and be entirely given to him!" Visualize that he absorbs this white nectar, which provides him with everything that he needs. If his life was to be short, imagine that now it is prolonged. If he needs money, imagine that now he is wealthy; if he is sick, that now he is cured; and if he is unhappy, now imagine him so full of joy that he feels like singing and dancing.

As you breathe in, consider that you take into yourself, in the form of a dark mass, all the sickness, obscurations, and mental poisons your enemy may have had, and that he is thereby completely relieved of all his afflictions. Think that his sufferings come to you as easily as mountain mist wafted away by the wind. As you take his suffering into you, you feel great joy and bliss, mingled with the experience of emptiness.

Do the same for the infinity of beings you are visualizing before you. Send them all of your happiness and take on their suffering. Repeat this, again and again, until it becomes second nature to you.

You can use this precious, vital practice at any time and in all circumstances, even while engaged in the activities of ordinary life, whether you are sick or well. It can be practiced both in and out of meditation sessions. By constantly practicing the exchange of self and others, you will reach the very core of the practice of compassion and the bodhichitta.

Sometimes, visualize that your heart is a brilliant ball of light. As you breathe out, it radiates rays of white light in all directions, carrying your happiness to all beings. As you breathe in, their suffering, negativity, and afflictions come toward you in the form of dense, black light, which is absorbed into your heart and disappears in its brilliant white light without a trace, relieving all beings of their pain and sorrow.

Sometimes, visualize yourself transformed into a wish-fulfilling jewel, radiant and blue like a sapphire, a little larger than your own body, on top of a victory banner. The jewel effortlessly fulfills the needs and aspirations of whoever addresses a prayer to it.

Sometimes, visualize that your body multiplies into infinite forms of yourself, which go to the hells and throughout the six realms of samsara, immediately taking on all the sufferings of each and every being they encounter, and giving away all your happiness to them.

Sometimes, visualize that your body transforms into clothes for all those who are cold and need clothing, into food for all those who are hungry, and into shelter for all who are homeless.

Sometimes, visualize that you are calling all the spirits who harm beings in various ways. You give them your flesh to eat, your blood to drink, your bones to gnaw at, and your skin to wear. With compassion, consider that bodhichitta takes birth in their minds as they happily revel in all of these offerings.[60]

As Shantideva says in *The Way of the Bodhisattva*,

May I be a guard for those who are protectorless,
A guide for those who journey on the road.
For those who wish to go across the water,
May I be a boat, a raft, a bridge.

May I be an isle for those who yearn for landfall,
And a lamp for those who long for light;
For those who need a resting place, a bed;
For all who need a servant, may I be their slave.

May I be the wishing jewel, the vase of plenty,
A word of power, and the supreme healing;
May I be the tree of miracles,
And for every being the abundant cow.

Like the earth and the pervading elements,
Enduring as the sky itself endures,
For boundless multitudes of living beings,
May I be their ground and sustenance.

The exchange of self and others can also be used as a way of dealing with your negative emotions. If you allow the negative emotions to express themselves in the ordinary way, you cannot hope to progress on the path. If you do not skillfully deal with them, either by getting rid of them or pacifying them, they will lead to the boundless suffering of the lower realms. Overcoming them will allow you to progress on the path to buddhahood. In the sutras there are many instructions on how to deal with the emotions by rejecting them. Here, we consider how to work with them through compassion. Take desire as an example.

Desire is the compulsive attraction and attachment we feel toward a person or an object. Start by considering that if you tame your own desire, you will be able to reach enlightenment in order to best help beings and to establish them all in buddhahood. Then think about someone you do not like. Arousing great compassion for that person, add all his desires to your own, and think that as you take them, he becomes free of them. Progressively take all beings' desires, whether manifest or latent, upon yourself, and as you do so, think that all beings become free from desire and achieve enlightenment. This is the way to meditate on taking negative emotions according to relative truth.

To meditate according to absolute truth, arouse in yourself an overwhelming feeling of desire. Fuel it by adding the desires of all beings, to make a great mountain of desire. Then look right into it. You will see that desire is nothing but thoughts; it appears in your mind but does not itself have even the tiniest particle of independent existence. And when you turn the mind inward to look at itself, you become aware that the mind, too, is without any inherent existence in either past, present, or future. The nature of the mind is as insubstantial as the sky.

Using these same methods, you can meditate on anger, pride, jealousy, and ignorance, as well as on anything else that obscures the mind.

As you practice this core practice of the bodhisattva path, you should try to see very vividly all your happiness going to others, and all their sufferings coming to you. Think that it is actually happening. Of all the practices of the bodhisattvas, this is the most essential. There is no obstacle that can disrupt it. Not only will it help others, but it will bring you to enlightenment, too.

There was a true bodhisattva called Langri Thangpa,[61] who constantly meditated on this practice of exchanging self and others. He prayed many times to be reborn in hell when he died in order to help all the beings there who were undergoing such intense suffering. But his prayer was not fulfilled, for as his life came to an end, visions of Dewachen, Amitabha's Buddhafield of Bliss, arose in his mind and he knew that he was going to be reborn there, instead. He immediately prayed to be able to take as many beings with him as possible. So strong was his wish that a vast number of beings poured after him into the buddhafield.

The main disciple of the great pandita Atisha, Drom Tönpa,[62] was a dedicated practitioner of bodhichitta. When

Atisha was afflicted by a very powerful illness in his hand, he said to Drom Tönpa, "You have a good heart. Put your hand on mine; the power of your compassion will help to remove the pain."

Mara, the demon king, asked the Buddha, "If someone repeats my name, it brings them neither benefit nor harm, but if they repeat Mañjushri's name even once, they will be relieved of their suffering. Why?"

The Buddha said, "That power comes from the strength of the compassion and loving-kindness that great bodhisattvas such as Mañjushri have generated."

The great master Padmasambhava, Guru Rinpoche, is an emanation of Avalokiteshvara and the very embodiment of compassion. His dedication to others is so potent that even now, in this degenerate age, simply to remember him or invoke his name instantly cuts through obstacles, adverse circumstances, and evil influences, rendering them powerless, and brings the blessings of his body, speech, and mind. When Guru Rinpoche arrived in Tibet, he subdued all the negative forces, such as the Twelve Sisters, the Twenty-one Upasakas, and many others who were creating obstacles to the establishment of Dharma. He was able to do so not because he was motivated by anger, but by the power of his compassion and bodhichitta.

Some people may have the idea that these teachings on compassion and exchanging self and others are part of the "gradual path" teachings of the sutras, and are not nearly as effective as the more advanced "direct path" teachings of the Great Perfection or the Great Seal. That is a complete misunderstanding. Only if you have developed the love and compassion of relative bodhichitta can absolute bodhichitta—the very essence of the Great Perfection and the Great Seal—ever take birth in your being.

If the teachings of Longchen Rabjam and Jigme Lingpa[63] have become so widespread and have been of benefit to so many people, it is because the minds of these two great teachers were constantly pervaded with compassion and bodhichitta. Jigme Lingpa's great disciple, Dodrup Jigme Trinle Öser,[64] went to

Kham, the eastern provinces of Tibet, and helped thousands of people there by transmitting the teachings of the *Longchen Nyingthig*, the *Heart Essence of the Vast Expanse*[65] to them. He later wrote to Jigme Lingpa, "This could only happen because I had meditated for so long in mountain solitudes on compassion."

The exchange of yourself and others can be approached step by step. The first stage is to see yourself and others as equally important—others want to be happy and want not to suffer, just as you do. So you should wish happiness for others in the same way that you wish it for yourself, and wish that they may avoid suffering, just as you do. The second stage is the exchange of yourself and others; you wish that others may have your happiness and that you may take their suffering. There is a third stage, which is to cherish others more than yourself, like the great bodhisattvas who, meeting a blind person, would have no hesitation in giving him their own eyes. At that point, all selfish preoccupation has completely disappeared and you are solely concerned with the welfare of others. Keep right on with this practice until it becomes a reality.

Shantideva says in *The Way of the Bodhisattva*:

> All the joy the world contains
> Has come through wishing happiness for others.
> All the misery the world contains
> Has come through wanting pleasure for oneself.
>
> Is there need for lengthy explanation?
> Childish beings look out for themselves,
> While buddhas labor for the good of others:
> See the difference that divides them!

It is from the constant wish to benefit others that the thirty-two major and eighty minor marks of a buddha, manifestations of his everlasting bliss and perfection, arise. It is also due to the power of compassion and bodhichitta that the Buddha Amitabha can lead beings to be reborn in his buddhafield simply by their hearing his name.

The Buddha, who loved all beings like his only child, said:

> To benefit beings is to benefit me;
> To harm beings is to harm me.
> Just as a mother rejoices when someone is helpful to
>   her child,
> My heart gladdens when someone is helpful to any
>   being.
> Just as a mother is distressed when someone harms
>   her child,
> My heart is distressed when someone harms any
>   being.

To have love and compassion for all beings as if each one was your only child is by far the best way to repay the Buddha's kindness, and to help them is the most supreme offering to the Buddha. As he himself said:

> Incense, flowers, lamps, and so on are not the best
>   offering to the Buddha;
> The best offering to the Buddha is to benefit all
>   beings.
> Therefore to make offerings to the Buddha, benefit
>   all beings—
> Your offering will delight all buddhas and make all
>   beings happy.
> There is no other way to please the Victorious Ones
>   than to bring all beings to happiness.

To have overflowing love and unbearable compassion for all beings, therefore, is the best way to fulfill the wishes of all the buddhas and bodhisattvas. As a beginner you may not be able to help beings outwardly very much, but you should meditate constantly on love and compassion until your whole being is imbued with them. The training of exchanging suffering and happiness is something to practice, not just for one session or for one day but over the days, months, and years, until the bodhichitta fully blooms from within you. The core text of the teachings on bodhichitta is Shantideva's *The Way of the Bodhisattva.* When the great yogi Patrul Rinpoche was studying it, he did not learn more than two or three verses a day, because he was meditating on them and integrating their meaning thoroughly. He was constantly struck by how wonderful and profound a teaching it was, and felt sad each time he reached the end of the text. He always had it with him, till the end of his life.

B. THE POSTMEDITATION PRACTICE OF USING UNFAVORABLE CIRCUMSTANCES ON THE PATH

To continue the practice of relative bodhichitta into daily life, it is necessary to make use of the adverse circumstances that one is bound to meet as fuel for spiritual practice. In the postmeditation stage, the practice is the training related to the bodhichitta of application.

Adverse circumstances are considered under four headings: (i) four things that you do not want to happen, (ii) two things that are difficult to bear, (iii) deprivation and prosperity, and (iv) hatred and desire.

i. Using on the path the four things that you do not want to happen

These four things are (a) loss, (b) suffering, (c) disgrace, and (d) disparagement.[66]

A. HOW TO USE LOSS ON THE PATH

12

> If someone driven by great desire
> Seizes all my wealth, or induces others to do so,
> To dedicate to him my body, possessions,

> And past, present, and future merit is the practice of
> a bodhisattva.

To have wealth and property is normally thought of as desirable, but attachment to them is actually an obstacle on your spiritual path. So someone who deprives you of your money and possessions is, in fact, freeing you from the fetters these things have created in your mind, and is preventing you from falling to the lower realms. You should feel nothing but gratitude. If you own nothing at all, you are free. No enemies or thieves will bother you. As the saying goes:

> If you have no wealth, thieves won't break in.
> If you carry no bags, robbers won't lie in wait.

It is important to remember that if you lose everything you possess, it can only be the karmic result of your having deprived others of their possessions in the past. There is therefore no reason to feel angry with anyone other than yourself. Seen from that point of view, is it not you who are attracting enemies with your wealth, fame, and rank? If there were no target, there would be nothing at which to shoot arrows. As a result of negative actions in your past lives, you have set yourself up as a target at which the arrows of suffering are now being shot.

A great bodhisattva never has angry thoughts toward anyone who harms him. Instead, his main concern is for that person's welfare. In each of the Buddha's past lives as a bodhisattva, he met an incarnation of the same person, who constantly tried to make difficulties for him. In return, the Buddha always tried his best to help that person. In his lifetime as Shakyamuni, when he became the fully enlightened Buddha, the person was reborn as his cousin, Devadatta. Even though Devadatta tried to harm the Buddha, and even tried to kill him on several occasions, the Buddha repeatedly said that he did not see Devadatta as an enemy, but rather as a kind teacher who had taught him how to act as a bodhisattva.

Once, in a previous life, the Buddha was born as a snake that was eventually stoned to death by a band of children. Although he could have killed them by simply looking at them, he kept his mind filled with compassion and died praying to be able to benefit them in the future through this connection.

Whatever harm others may inflict on you, always pray that all beings' suffering may come to you and not to them. Make the wish that you will always be able to serve them, and that their minds will be ever full of joy. In the same way that, in the Guru Yoga practice, you meditate on the teacher visualized above the crown of your head, so, too, meditate here on all beings as though you were carrying them on your head, and pray to be able to dispel their suffering and bring them happiness. As we have already seen, there is no greater offering to the buddhas than that.

To feel compassion for someone who is harming you is such an effective way of purifying your obscurations, freeing yourself from anger, and developing the positive side of your nature that, in fact, the harm that the person has done to you will carry you along the bodhisattva's path. As it is said, therefore, "I take refuge in whoever harms me, as he is the source of all happiness."

In the beginning, this may seem difficult to put into practice. But to have a truly good heart is something for which everyone has the capacity. Take all the suffering of the person harming you into your heart, and send him your own happiness, with great compassion. With the same attitude, you can also offer a water *torma*, the burned offering of *sur*, and the visualization practice of giving away your body as an offering to the Three Jewels, a present to the Dharma protectors, a gift to suffering sentient beings, and repayment of your karmic debts to harmful spirits and obstacle makers.[67]

For all these practices, it is important to have a thorough grounding in the practice of the four boundless attitudes. They are as follows: boundless love, the wish that all others may have happiness; boundless compassion, the wish that they may all be free from suffering; boundless joy, the wish that all those who already have some happiness may keep and increase it; and boundless impartiality, the recognition that beings are all equally deserving of love, compassion, and joy, and not more or less so just because of the good, bad, or nonexistent relationship you may have with them in the narrow perspective of the present.

In the morning, your first thought should be the commitment to do whatever you can during the day to help others and bring all beings to ultimate happiness. In the evening, dedicate to all beings the merit that you have gathered during the day. If anyone has tried to harm you, make the wish that they be free from all animosity and vindictive feelings, and that all their positive aspirations may be fulfilled.

To bring about a true change in your attitudes is hard at first. But if you understand the meaning behind this mind training, and keep on trying to apply it, you will find that it helps you in every difficult situation, just as a well-designed vehicle can travel any distance quickly, and with ease.

B. HOW TO USE SUFFERING ON THE PATH

13

If, in return for not the slightest wrong of mine,
Someone were to cut off even my very head,
Through the power of compassion to take all his
    negative actions
Upon myself is the practice of a bodhisattva.

Whatever someone may be about to inflict on you—even beheading you or some other terrible suffering—it is important to remember that this is the result of your own past actions. You must have done the same to others in a previous life. Do not get angry. Let your enemy do whatever he wants to get satisfaction. Be full of compassion for him. Drom Tönpa said:

> Should someone chop my body into a thousand
>   pieces,
> May I not be the least bit upset,
> But straightaway put on the armor of patience.

In return for harm, a bodhisattva tries to give help and benefit. If you see someone doing something negative, think of all the suffering he is accumulating for himself and pray that, rather than his being reborn in the lower realms, the results of his negative actions may come upon you instead; and dedicate to him the results of your own positive actions.

To practice in such a way also helps to eradicate your belief in a truly existing self. For, finally, your true enemies are not some ruthless people in power, some fierce raiders or merciless competitors who constantly harass you, take everything you have, or threaten you with legal proceedings. Your real enemy is your belief in a self.

That idea of an enduring self has kept you wandering helplessly in the lower realms of samsara for countless past lifetimes. It is the very thing that now prevents you from liberating yourself and others from conditioned existence. If you could simply let go of that one thought of "I," you would find it easy to be free, and to free others, too. If you overcome the belief in a truly existing self today, you will be enlightened today. If you overcome it tomorrow, you will be enlightened tomorrow. But if you never overcome it, you will never gain enlightenment.

This "I" is just a thought, a feeling. A thought does not intrinsically possess any solidity, form, shape, or color. For example, when a strong feeling of anger arises in the mind, with such force that you want to fight and to destroy someone, is the angry thought holding a weapon in its hand? Could it lead an army? Might it burn anyone like a fire, crush them like a stone, or carry them away like a raging river? No. Anger, like any other thought or feeling, has no true existence. It cannot even be definitely localized anywhere in your body, speech, or mind. It is like wind in empty space. Instead of allowing such wild thoughts to determine what you do, look at their essential emptiness. For example, you might find yourself suddenly face-to-face with someone you think wants to harm you, and a strong feeling of fear would arise. But once you realized that the person, in fact, had only good intentions toward you, your fear would disappear. It was just a thought.

Similarly, even though you have spent many lifetimes believing in the reality of this "I," once you realize that it has no inherent existence, your belief in it will easily disappear. It is only because you are unaware of its true nature that the idea of "I" has such power to affect you. Without that belief in a self, anger, desire, fear, and so on can no longer arise. Look at the actual nature of harm itself: it is ungraspable, like a drawing made on the water's surface. When you truly experience that, resentment vanishes of its own accord. As soon as the fiery waves of thoughts subside, everything becomes like empty sky, which has nothing to gain and nothing to lose.

"I" is merely a label you have given to a transient combination of concepts and attachments to your body, speech, and mind. It is not an absolute, eternal, indestructible truth, like the dharmakaya nature of the buddhas. Use any practice you do to dissolve this idea of "I" and the self-oriented motivations that accompany it. Even if you do not succeed in the beginning, keep trying.

c. How to Use Disgrace on the Path

14

Even if someone says all sorts of derogatory things
   about me
And proclaims them throughout the universe,
In return, out of loving-kindness,
To extol that person's qualities is the practice of a
   bodhisattva.

If someone defames and disgraces you, that is simply the result of having criticized and dishonored others in the past, especially bodhisattvas. Instead of feeling angry with such people, you should feel grateful to them for giving you the opportunity to purify your past misdeeds. In all circumstances, it is important to act in accordance with the teachings—but especially at such moments. What is the point of having received teachings if you do not apply them? Unfavorable circumstances are the best opportunity you will have to put the teachings into practice.

Once a pure monk of Ratreng Monastery was blamed for the theft of a lost plate. He went to see his abbot and asked him, "I am not at fault, what should I do?" The abbot advised him, "Accept the blame, offer tea to all the monks, and eventually your innocence will be proved." The monk did so. That night he had many good dreams indicating a great purification of his being. Soon after, the plate was found, and the monk was cleared of the accusation. Informed of the matter, the abbot concluded, "This is the right way to behave!"

So, remember that whether you have a good reputation or a bad one, it has no objective reality at all. It is not worth caring about. The great teachers of the past never bothered about such things. They always answered slander and disparagement with kindness, and with patience.

Langri Thangpa was one such master. Once, in the region of the cave where he was meditating, there was a couple whose children always died in infancy. When yet another child was born to them, they consulted an oracle, who said that the child would survive only if they claimed that he was the son of a spiritual master. So the wife took her baby boy up to Langri Thangpa's cave and set him down in front of the sage. She said, "Here is your son," and went away. The hermit said nothing about it apart from simply asking a devoted woman he knew to feed and care for the child. Sure enough, Langri Thangpa being a monk, gossip spread about him having fathered a child. A few years later, the parents of the boy came with large offerings, and respectfully said to him, "Please forgive us. Although you were not in the least at fault, we let ill rumor spread about you. The child has survived due only to you kindness." Serene as always, Langri Thangpa gave the boy back to his parents without a word.

Some people spend all their energy, and even risk their lives, to achieve fame. Fame and notoriety are both no more than an empty echo. Your reputation is an alluring mirage that can easily lead you astray. Discard it without a second thought, like the snot you blow from your nose.

D. HOW TO USE DISPARAGEMENT ON THE PATH

15

Even if in the midst of a large gathering
Someone exposes my hidden faults with insulting
    language,
To bow to him respectfully,
Regarding him as a spiritual friend, is the practice of
    a bodhisattva.

If you want to be a genuine follower of the Buddha, never retaliate when you are harmed. Always remember the four principles of positive training,[68] which are as follows: (1) if someone abuses you, do not abuse him in return; (2) if someone gets angry with you, do not get angry with him in return; (3) if someone exposes your hidden faults, do not expose his in return; and (4) if someone strikes you, do not strike him back.

If someone criticizes you, picking on your most sensitive points, or angrily insults you with the most offensive language, do not return like for like, no matter how difficult it is to bear. Practice patience, and never give way to anger. Take it positively, and use it as a chance to let go of your own pride. Practice generosity and compassion by giving the victory to others and being happy to lose. Allowing others to win is a characteristic of all Buddhist paths. In fact, what is there to be won or lost? From an absolute viewpoint, there is not the slightest difference between winning and losing.

Many Buddhist teachers were abused, treated as criminals, and beaten when the Chinese communists came to Tibet. Instead of feeling hatred, they prayed that the negative actions of all beings would be purified through the vindictive attacks against them. Like them, when you are insulted and humiliated, pray that, using the connection you have established with those insulting you, you may be able to bring them all to liberation.

There should be no insult or humiliation that is too great for you to bear. If you were ever to feel it was justifiable to respond vindictively, the exchange of bitter words and recriminations that ensue would be bound to inflame and escalate the anger on both sides. This is how people start to fight and kill each other. Murders and wars all begin with just one angry thought. As Shantideva says,

> No evil is there similar to anger,
> No austerity to be compared with patience.

Never give way to anger, therefore. Be patient—and, moreover, be grateful to someone who humiliates you, as they are giving you a precious opportunity to strengthen your understanding and practice of bodhichitta. The great Jigme Lingpa said:

> Ill treatment by opponents
> Is a catalyst for your meditation;
> Insulting reproaches you don't deserve
> Spur your practice onward;
> Those who do you harm are teachers
> Challenging your attachment and aversion—
> How could you ever repay their kindness?

Indeed, you are unlikely to make much spiritual progress if you lack the courage to face your own hidden faults. Any person or situation that helps you to see those faults, however uncomfortable and humiliating it may be, is doing you a great service. As Lord Atisha says,

> The best spiritual friend is one who attacks your
>   hidden faults.
> The best instructions are the ones that hit your
>   hidden faults.
> The best incentives are enemies, obstacles, and the
>   sufferings of illness.

And the Kadampa master Shawopa[69] used to warn his disciples as they came to see him, saying, "I only show people their hidden defects. If you can avoid getting annoyed, stay; but if not, go away!"

Of the eight ordinary concerns, therefore, even from the relative point of view there are many ways of eliminating the distinction between the good and the bad, those you want to happen and those you do not. From the point of view of absolute truth, there is not the slightest difference between gain and loss, pleasure and pain, fame and disgrace, praise and disparagement. They are all equal, all empty by nature. As Shantideva says,

> Thus, with things devoid of true existence,
> What is there to gain, and what to lose?
> Who is there to pay me court and honors,
> And who is there to scorn and to revile me?
>
> Pain and pleasure, whence do these arise?
> And what is there to give me joy and sorrow?

ii. Using on the path the two things that are difficult to bear

The two things that are difficult to bear are: (a) being wronged in return for kindness, and (b) humiliation.

A. How to use on the path being wronged in return for kindness

16

Even if one I've lovingly cared for like my own child
Regards me as an enemy,
To love him even more,
As a mother loves a sick child, is the practice of a
bodhisattva.

If you do something good for others, it is a mistake to expect anything in return, or to hope that people will admire you for being a bodhisattva. All such attitudes are a long way from the true motivation of bodhichitta. Not only should you expect nothing in return; you should not be disturbed in the slightest when people respond ungratefully. Someone for whom you have risked your very life may return your kindness with resentment, hatred, or harm. But just love him all the more. A mother with an only child is full of love for him no matter what he does. While she is suckling him, he may bite her nipple and badly wound it, but she will never get angry or love him any less. Whatever happens, she will continue to care for him as best as she can.

Many people do not have the good fortune that you enjoy of having met a spiritual teacher, and thus cannot find their way out of delusion. They need your help and your compassion more than anyone else, no matter how badly they may behave. Always remember that people who harm you are simply the victim of their own emotions. Think how good it would be if they could be free of those emotions. When a thoughtless child wrongs a thoughtful adult, the adult will not feel resentment, but will try with great love to help the child to improve.

To meet someone who really hurts you is to meet a rare and precious treasure. Hold that person in high esteem, and make full use of the opportunity to eradicate your defects and make progress on the path. If you cannot yet feel love and compassion for those who treat you badly, it is a sign that your mind has not been fully transformed and that you need to keep working on it with increased application.

A true bodhisattva never hopes for a reward. He responds to the needs of others spontaneously, out of his natural compassion. Cause and effect are unfailing, so his actions to benefit others are sure to bear fruit—but he never counts on it. He certainly never thinks that people are not showing enough gratitude, or that they ought to treat him better. But if someone who has done him harm later changes his behavior, is set on the path, and achieves liberation, that is something that will make a bodhisattva rejoice wholeheartedly and be totally satisfied.

B. HOW TO USE HUMILIATION ON THE PATH

The next section considers how we may deal with receiving humiliation in return for kindness.

17

Even if my peers or my inferiors
Out of pride do all they can to debase me,
To respectfully consider them like my teachers
On the crown of my head is the practice of a
    bodhisattva.

Someone with your own ability or status, or an inferior without any good qualities, might—despite being treated politely and considerately by you—criticize you contemptuously out of pure conceit and arrogance, and try to humiliate you in various ways. When such things happen, do not be angry or upset, or feel badly treated.

Instead, see and respect such people as kind teachers showing you the path to liberation. Pray that you may be able to do them as much good as possible. Whatever happens, do not wish for a moment to take your revenge. The capacity to patiently bear scorn and injury from those who lack your education, strength, and skill is particularly admirable. To remain humble while patiently bearing insults is a very effective way of countering your ingrained tendency to be interested only in your own happiness and pleasure.

Never be proud, but instead take the most humble position and regard everyone as being above you, as though you were carrying them on your head. It is said, "Carrying all beings above one's head is the torch and banner of the bodhisattvas."

The great teacher Drom Tönpa Gyalwai Jungne would circumambulate even a dog on the side of the road, in recognition of the buddha nature that, like all beings, it possessed.

iii. Using deprivation and prosperity on the path

A. HOW TO USE DEPRIVATION ON THE PATH

18

Even when utterly destitute and constantly maligned
    by others,
Afflicted by terrible illness and prey to evil forces,
To still draw upon myself the suffering and
    wrongdoing of all beings
And not lose heart is the practice of a bodhisattva.

Countless people in this world are deprived of everything—food, clothing, shelter, affection. They can hardly keep themselves alive. Many people are victims of ill treatment or are stricken by serious illness. When you yourself suffer such torments, wish with compassion and courage to take the difficulties and anguish of all beings upon yourself and to give them whatever happiness you may have. Try to provide others with whatever they need in reality. Reflect on the positive qualities of suffering.

Suffering, in fact, can be helpful in many ways. It spurs your motivation, and as many teachings point out, without suffering there would be no determination to be free of samsara. Sadness is an effective antidote to arrogance. Patrul Rinpoche says,

I don't like happiness, I like suffering:
If I am happy, the five poisons increase.
If I suffer, my past bad karma is exhausted.

I don't value high positions, I like low ones.
If I am important, my pride and jealousy increase;
If I am lowly, I relax and my spiritual practice grows.
The lowest place is the seat of the saints of the past.

And Kharak Gomchung[70] said:

Difficulties are our spiritual teachers;
Obstacles are a spur to Dharma practice:
Suffering is a broom to sweep away our evil deeds,
Do not regard them with dislike.

It is indeed when difficult times and circumstances arise that the difference between genuine practice and its mere semblance is revealed.

There are negative spirits who thirst to take life. The best way to stop them from harming you and others is not to combat them with anger but to satisfy them by repeatedly making visualized offerings of your body. Until you are ready to give your life and body for the sake of others in reality, which is not the case at present, you can at least do it mentally. As your mind grows used to altruistic love and compassion, your words and actions will naturally reflect that attitude.

Once, five rakshasas, ogre-like beings who live on flesh and blood, arrived in a country that was new to them and set out on a killing rampage. They started by attacking sheep, trying to kill everything in sight with their weapons and sharp teeth and claws, but to no avail—they were unable to kill a single animal, and could not even wound them. The beings of this country seemed invulnerable, as if they were made out of rock. So their anger gave way to surprise. They asked some shepherds, "Why is it that we cannot kill any of your sheep?" The shepherds told them that the kingdom was ruled by a monarch called The Strength of Love. He spent all his time in the highest tower of his palace, absorbed in deep meditation on compassion and love. Such was the strength of his love that there were no famines, no sicknesses or plagues, and no living being in his kingdom could ever be killed.

The five rakshasas went to see the king. They told him that in order to survive, they needed to eat flesh and blood, but they could not find any in his kingdom. The king said, "I would like to provide you with sustenance, but I cannot allow you to harm anyone. As you need flesh and blood to sustain your own lives, however, I shall give it to you myself." Piercing his body with a spear, he gave them his own flesh and blood. As soon as they tasted the blood of the bodhisattva king, they suddenly experienced a deep meditative state of love. They vowed never to harm any being from that moment onward.

This story illustrates the power and strength of love. *The Ornament of the Mahayana Sutras* mentions the eight supreme qualities that arise from meditating upon love.[71] Patrul Rinpoche said that to meditate on love pacifies all calamities and troubles in the surrounding countryside. Jetsun Milarepa, too, said that to treat human beings like celestial beings is to offer a treasure to ourselves; if we wish only good for others and are full of love, it opens up a mine of perfections, and all our aspirations will naturally be accomplished.

B. HOW TO USE PROSPERITY ON THE PATH

19

Though I may be famous, and revered by many,
And as rich as the God of Wealth himself,

> To see that the wealth and glory of the world are
>   without essence,
> And to be free of arrogance, is the practice of a
>   bodhisattva.

A bodhisattva sees that wealth, beauty, influence, prosperity, family lineage—in fact, all the ordinary concerns of this life—are as fleeting as a flash of lightning, as ephemeral as a dewdrop, as hollow as a bubble, as evanescent as the skin of a snake. He is never conceited or proud, no matter what worldly achievements and privileges may come to him.

However much wealth you may gather, it will eventually be taken away, either by robbers, by people in power, or, finally, by death. If your descendants inherit it, there is no certainty that it will do them any real good; they are likely to use it to get the better of their enemies, influence their relatives, and so on, accumulating negative actions that will propel them to the lower realms of existence.

Jetsun Milarepa always taught his lay disciples that the best way for them to accomplish the Dharma was to be generous to those in need. Even a small act of generosity done with an altruistic mind accumulates great merit. If you have power and wealth, make it meaningful; use it for the sake of the Dharma and to benefit beings, as did the three great religious kings of Tibet.[72] To be miserly, on the other hand—whether you are rich or poor at present—is to sow the seeds of rebirth among the tortured spirits, who are deprived of everything.

Pray to be able to follow the example of the great bodhisattvas, who, because of their past generosity and accumulated merit, were born as powerful monarchs with fabulous wealth, using their riches to help the poor and to alleviate famine and sickness. In addition to caring for the physical welfare of their people, they taught them to avoid the ten negative actions[73] and to perform the ten positive ones. As a result of their compassionate activity, not a single being in their kingdoms would be reborn in the lower realms. Good harvests, prosperity, and general happiness abounded.

Think, "May the needs of all beings, even the smallest insect, be fulfilled." Use your wealth and possessions in the best possible way to help others. Whenever possible, try to provide others with their everyday needs of food, clothing, shelter, and so on. At the same time, make the wish to be able to fulfill their ultimate needs by giving them the sublime gift of the Dharma.

iv. Using hatred and desire on the path

A. HOW TO USE OBJECTS OF HATRED ON THE PATH

20

If one does not conquer one's own hatred,
The more one fights outer enemies, the more they
   will increase.
Therefore, with the armies of loving-kindness and
   compassion,
To tame one's own mind is the practice of a
   bodhisattva.

Once you overcome the hatred within your own mind, you will discover that in the world outside, there is no longer any such thing as even a single enemy. But if you keep giving free reign to your feelings of hatred and try to overcome your outer adversaries, you will find that however many of them you manage to defeat, there will always be more to take their place. Even if you could subjugate all the beings in the universe, your anger would only grow stronger. You will never be able to deal with it properly by indulging it. Hatred itself is the true enemy, and cannot be allowed to exist. The way to master hatred is to meditate one-pointedly on patience and love. Once love and compassion take root in your being, there can be no outer adversaries. As *The Hundred Verses* says,

If you kill out of anger,
Your enemies will be never-ending;
If you kill anger,
That will kill your enemies once and for all.

In one of his past rebirths, the Buddha was a giant ocean turtle. One day, while he was far from any land, he saw that a ship
carrying some merchants had been wrecked and was sinking.
The merchants were about to drown, but the turtle rescued them
by carrying them the long way to the nearest shore on his back.
After carrying them to safety, he was so exhausted that he fell
asleep on the beach. But while he slept, eighty thousand flies
began to eat their way into his body. The turtle awoke in great
pain, and realized what had happened. He saw that there was no
way to be rid of all the flies; if he plunged into the sea, all of them
would die. So, being a bodhisattva, he stayed where he was and
let the flies eat away his body. Filled with love, he made the
prayer, "Whenever I attain enlightenment, may I, in turn, con-
sume all these insects' negative emotions and actions, and their
belief in true existence, and thus lead them to buddhahood." As
a result of this prayer, when the Buddha turned the wheel of
Dharma for the first time in Varanasi, the former flies had been
reborn as the assembly of eighty thousand fortunate celestial beings who were present. Had the turtle killed the insects in anger
by diving into the sea, however, there would have been no end to
his sufferings. The result of killing a single being out of anger is
to be reborn in the hell realms for the duration of five hundred
human lives, or a great kalpa.

Never get angry, even with someone who has deliberately
and maliciously harmed you. As we have already seen, you
should be grateful to such a person for helping you to purify past
negative actions, to increase your determination to be free from
samsara, and to develop love and compassion.

These days, famines, conflicts, wars, and other upheavals are
increasing all over the world. This is because people allow their

emotions to run wild, and act under their power. Were hatred, pride, jealousy, desire, and stupidity to decrease, not only conflicts but also epidemics and natural calamities in the world would decrease as well, like the smoke disappearing when a fire is extinguished. People would naturally turn their minds toward the Dharma.

It is a crucial point of the teachings to become conscious that attachment, aversion, and ignorance are your oldest enemies, and that once you have overcome them, there are no further enemies in the world outside. The time will come when you see very clearly and precisely how this is so. If you do not understand this point, and act carelessly, your emotions can get completely out of control. In anger, you could be prepared to sacrifice your life in war, and you could go so far as to kill everyone on the face of the earth in one blinding instant without any regret. Such things can happen when anger is allowed to take over the mind and gather its full force.

Examine anger itself, and you will find that it is nothing but a thought. If that angry thought disappears, it will not lead to an action done in anger, with its negative karmic results. Trample on anger with realization, and it dissolves like a cloud in the sky; and as it dissolves, the notion of "enemy" will vanish with it.

Anger and the other emotions will keep coming up in the mind of an ordinary person, yet they can all be neutralized with the right antidotes, for they are completely empty in essence. It is important to realize that all outer torments come from harboring these poisons within your mindstream. As Geshe Potowa[74] said,

> If you see anyone as an enemy and think of others in terms of close and distant, you will not attain buddhahood. So generate love and compassion impartially for all sentient beings, as infinite in number as space is vast.

Turn your mind inward and apply the right antidotes, with

pure motivation. You will be able to transform yourself in accordance with the Dharma, and to act in the way of the bodhisattvas.

B. HOW TO USE OBJECTS OF DESIRE ON THE PATH

21

Sense pleasures and desirable things are like
    saltwater—
The more one tastes them, the more one's thirst
    increases.
To abandon promptly
All objects which arouse attachment is the practice
    of a bodhisattva.

Whatever comfort, wealth, beauty, and power you enjoy today is the result of some minor good actions in a past life. However much of them you have, it is the characteristic of ordinary people never to feel satisfied. You may have more wealth than you actually need, you may have triumphed over many opponents, you may have close relationships with friends and relatives, but it is never enough; even if coins of gold were to rain down on you from the sky, it would probably not be enough.

When craving for all sorts of desirable things[75] becomes so ingrained in your mind, trying to satisfy your wants is like drinking saltwater—the more you drink, the more you feel thirsty.

The destructive power of dissatisfaction is illustrated by the story of King Mandhatri,[76] who had accumulated a lot of merit in a past life and was reborn as a universal monarch. He gradually ascended the different levels of god realms, eventually reaching the celestial Heaven of the Thirty-three. There he was able to share the throne with Indra, the god of the gods, who had a life span of many kalpas, could enjoy the fruits of the wish-fulfilling tree, drink the nectar of ambrosial lakes, and illuminate the whole universe with the light emanating from his body. King Mandhatri could have continued to enjoy such exquisite happiness. But he conceived the idea of killing Indra in order to make himself even more powerful and become the greatest being in the universe. This thought came to him just as his merit was exhausted, and he died wretchedly, falling back into the ordinary world.

Looking at life in the great cities of ancient and modern times, you can see how people feverishly accumulate ever-increasing amounts of wealth, but still die without having satisfied their craving. As Lord Atisha said,

> Abandon desire for everything,
> And stay without desire.
> Desire does not bring happiness,
> It cuts off liberation's very life.

To know how to be satisfied with what you have is to possess true wealth. The great saints and hermits of the past had the ability to be content with whatever they had, and with however they lived. They stayed in lonely places, sheltering in caves, sustaining their lives with the very barest of necessities.

When you know how to judge what is enough for you, you will no longer be tormented by wants, desires, and needs. Otherwise, as the saying goes, "Craving is like a dog—the more it gets, the more it wants." The followers of the Buddha—the arhats and the *shravakas*—possessed only their saffron Dharma robes and a begging bowl. They spent their lives absorbed in deep concentration. That was how they freed themselves from samsara. They did not hanker after wealth, fame, or position, which they saw as utterly meaningless and left behind without a second thought, like spittle in the dust. Nowadays, people chase busily after externals and are preoccupied by what they can get. As a result, learning, reflecting, and meditating have declined, and with them the Buddha's teachings themselves.

Learning, reflecting, and meditating are, in fact, the only things of which you can never have enough. Not even the most learned sages—such as Vasubandhu,[77] who knew 999 important treatises by heart—ever thought they had reached the ultimate extent of learning; they were aware that there was still an ocean of knowledge to acquire. The bodhisattva Kumara Vasubhadra studied with one hundred fifty spiritual masters, yet no one ever heard him say that he had received enough teachings. Mañjushri, sovereign of wisdom, who knows all that can be known, travels to all the buddhafields in the ten directions throughout the universe, ceaselessly requesting the buddhas to turn the Wheel of the Mahayana for the sake of beings.

Be satisfied, therefore, with whatever you have by way of ordinary things—but never with the Dharma. If your ordinary desires and dislikes are insatiable, on the other hand, and you have no wish for the Dharma, you can only sink lower and lower.

II. Absolute bodhichitta

The practice of absolute bodhichitta consists of (A) the meditation practice of remaining in a state free of conceptual elaborations without any clinging, and (B) the postmeditation practice of abandoning any belief in the objects of desire and aversion as truly existing.

A. THE MEDITATION PRACTICE OF REMAINING IN A STATE FREE OF CONCEPTUAL ELABORATIONS WITHOUT ANY CLINGING

22

All that appears is the work of one's own mind;
The nature of mind is primordially free from
    conceptual limitations.
To recognize this nature
And not to entertain concepts of subject and object
    is the practice of a bodhisattva.

The many different perceptions of everything around you in this life arise in your mind. Look at your relationships with others, for example. You perceive some people in a positive way—friends, relatives, benefactors, protectors; while there are others whom you perceive as enemies—those who criticize and defame you, beat, fool, or swindle you. The process starts with the senses, through which the mind perceives various forms, sounds, smells, tastes, and feelings. As it becomes aware of those objects outside, it categorizes them. Those that it finds pleasant it is attracted to, while those that it finds unpleasant it tries to avoid. The mind then suffers from not getting the pleasant things it wants and from having to experience the unpleasant things it wants to avoid. It is always busy running after some pleasant situation or other that it really wants to enjoy, or trying to escape some unwanted one that it finds difficult and unpleasant. But these experiences of things as pleasant or unpleasant are not functions intrinsically belonging to the objects you perceive. They arise only in the mind.

Take as an example the process of perceiving visual form. The object is a particular form in the outer world, the organ that senses it is the eye, and that which perceives the image and categorizes it is consciousness. If you see a beautiful person, a dear relative, or a sacred statue, you feel glad. If you see something ugly, or some ill-intentioned person come to ridicule or attack you, you feel upset, anxious, or angry. All these perceptions arise in the mind itself. They are triggered by the object perceived, but they do not themselves exist in that object, nor do they originate anywhere else outside the mind.

Generally, mind is the slave of its own biased perceptions. Dividing everything into pleasant or unpleasant, it constantly tries to experience what is pleasant and to get rid of what is not—blind to the fact that this is not the way to achieve happiness and avoid suffering. Blind ignorance drives the mind constantly to generate feelings of like and dislike. You engage in endless ordinary worldly activities with no more durability than drawings on water. Preoccupied entirely by these distractions, you exhaust your life and squander this precious human existence with all the freedoms and advantages that you now enjoy.

The mind thus contrives everything, so the only thing to do is to master the mind. As Tilopa taught Naropa:[78]

> It is not what you perceive that binds you,
> It is your clinging to it that binds you.
> Cut through your clinging, Naropa!

If you master your mind, it will remain naturally concentrated, peaceful, and aware. You will even be able to wander around in a crowd without being distracted and carried away by desire or aversion. But if you have no mastery over your mind and are influenced and conditioned by your habitual tendencies, even in the quiet of an isolated retreat your thoughts will follow one upon another like ripples on water. Memories of past events will well up vividly in your mind—as will plans, decisions, and speculation about your future. You will spend your whole time running after thoughts and concepts, a lot of mental activity with no benefit at all for your practice.

A mind that has been brought under control is indeed the only true source of happiness. But to master your mind, you need to know more about how it works. So, what is this mind?

When you see a pleasant form, a friend or a relative, a feeling of happiness arises, and you think, "What a joy to meet them!" This is mind, in one aspect. Another aspect of the mind is the feeling of outrage and fury that might arise when you see someone who dislikes you and accuses you of stealing or being dishonest. All such reactions are just thoughts, but once they arise in your mind, they can expand and give rise to further thoughts, becoming very powerful. Once hatred arises, it may increase to the point where you are ready to kill. Once attachment and desire are kindled, you may soon be ready to do anything and give every penny you have to get whatever it is you desire so much, whether it is a woman or a man or some other object. Look at what is happening, and you will see that it is all just thoughts, and nothing more. Everything you perceive is like that.

At present you are seeing me sitting here, and you are thinking, "He is teaching the Dharma, I had better listen to what he is saying." These are thoughts, too. You think there is something solid in front of you because you have perceived an object, and various different feelings are arising in relation to it.

The process begins, as I have said, with sense perception. There is one consciousness that perceives visual forms, another consciousness that perceives sounds, another that perceives taste; and there are consciousnesses that perceive smell and physical feelings. But these are not yet what we call thoughts. They are merely basic perceptions. Then, when you come into contact with something, a train of thoughts is triggered. If, for instance, you have just heard someone praising you, you start to feel elated, and to think how your reputation is increasing. Or if someone has just insulted you, you start to feel annoyed. These are just thoughts. To put it simply, the mind is just this random collection of thoughts.

Past thoughts are dead. The countless thoughts that have arisen in your mind since sunrise have all gone. Future thoughts have not yet arisen, and what they will be is utterly unpredictable. Who knows what you are going to think about from now until midnight? So you are left with only the present thought as something you could investigate.

Let us examine such a present thought. You may be thinking, for example, "I am cold." Is that thought in your skin, or in your bones or nerves; or is it perhaps in your heart, or in your brain or liver? Or is it anywhere else? If you think there is something somewhere, then does it have any shape? Is it square, round, or triangular? Does it have a color—is it red, blue, black, yellow, or what? Or is it just like a rainbow in the sky that has suddenly appeared because of the conjunction of various circumstances?

No matter how much you look, there is nothing that you can point your finger at and say, "Here is the thought!" And the reason you cannot do it is because the nature of thought is empty. There is nothing but emptiness.

When a rainbow appears vividly in the sky, you can see its beautiful colors, yet you could not wear it as clothing or put it on as an ornament. It arises through the conjunction of various factors, but there is nothing about it that can be grasped. Likewise, thoughts that arise in the mind have no tangible existence or intrinsic solidity. There is no logical reason why thoughts, which have no substance, should have so much power over you, nor is there any reason why you should become their slave.

The endless succession of past, present, and future thoughts leads us to believe that there is something inherently and consistently present, and we call it "mind." But actually, as I said before, past thoughts are as dead as a corpse. Future thoughts have not yet arisen. So how could these two, which do not exist, be part of an entity that inherently exists?

It is hard to imagine a present thought that is not connected to either past or future. On the other hand, how is it that a present thought can rely on two things that do not exist? Could there be points of mutual contact where past, present, and future thoughts are joined together? If the present thought was in contact with the past thought, for example, then either that present thought must actually be a past thought, or else the past thought would have to be in the present. The same is true for the meeting of present and future thoughts. Either the present thought is actually still part of the future or else the future thought is already a present thought.

When you look at the mind, it seems superficially that past thoughts lead to present thoughts and present thoughts to future ones. But if you examine these thoughts more closely, you will see that none of them truly exist. To formulate the existence of something that has no existence at all is called delusion. It is only your lack of awareness and your grasping that make thoughts seem to have some kind of reality. If thoughts had any inherent existence in the absolute nature of mind, they should at least have a form, or be located somewhere. But there is nothing.

However, that nothingness is not just a blank emptiness like empty space. There is an immediate awareness present. This is called clarity. If someone gives you an apple, you are cheerful; if a bee stings you, you feel pain. This is the clarity aspect of mind. This clarity of mind is like the sun, illuminating the landscape and allowing you to see mountain, path, and precipice—where to go and where not to go.

Although the mind does have this inherent awareness, to say there is "a mind" is to give a label to something that does not exist—to assume the existence of something that is no more than a name given to a succession of events. One hundred and eight beads strung together, for example, can be called a rosary, but that "rosary" is not a thing that exists inherently on its own. If the string breaks, where did the rosary go? Likewise, the thought "I" is the very cause that makes you wander in samsara. But if you examine it closely, there is no such thing as an "I." It is a mistaken belief in something that does not exist. Once that concept "I" is rooted in your mind, it grows and ramifies into a number of associated beliefs, such as in "my body," "my mind," "my name."

Your body is composed of the five aggregates, and your mind of the various kinds of consciousnesses. Your name, or the idea "I," is the label affixed to the momentary association of these two.

Examine first the concept "body." If you single out the skin, the flesh, and the bones of your body one by one, and then ask yourself if the body is dwelling in the skin, if flesh could be the body, or if you can call the bones the body, what will you find? The farther you take your investigation, all the way down to the atomic particles, the less you can point to the "body"—or to any other material object, for that matter—as a discrete entity. "Body" is merely a name given to a conglomeration of different things to which, once they are separated, that label no longer applies.

The same is true of the mind. What you call "my mind" is something you believe to have a certain continuity. But, as we have just seen, past, present, and future thoughts and feelings can have no veritable point of mutual contact. It is not possible to conceive of an entity that is an amalgam of thoughts of which some have already ceased, some have not yet happened, and some exist in the present.

As for your name, you hold on to your identity as if it had some autonomous existence—as if it truly belonged to you. But if you examine it carefully, you will find that it has no intrinsic reality—as is the case with the name of anything. Take the word *lion*, for instance. It is made up of the letters *l, i, o,* and *n*. Take those four letters apart, and there is nothing left; the name has vanished.

Once you recognize these three concepts of "body," "mind," and "name" as being empty, there is no longer anything left of the so-called I. The "I" is purely an invention, an imposture conjured up by delusion. Someone with eye disease might see all kinds of objects apparently floating in the sky—lights, lines, and spots— when in truth there is nothing there. Similarly, because we have the disease of believing in an "I," we see that "I" as an inherently existing entity.

In essence, the mind is what is aware of everything—it is a clarity that perceives all external objects and events. But try to find it, and it turns out to be as impossible to grasp and as elusive as a rainbow—the more you run after it, the farther away it appears to recede; the more you look at it, the less you can find. This is the empty aspect of the mind. Clarity and emptiness are inseparably united in the true nature of mind, which is beyond all concepts of existence and nonexistence.[79] As the Great Master of Oddiyana said:

Like a precious jewel buried under a poor man's
    house,
Primordially pure awareness has always been present
    in the dharmakaya.
It is because it is not recognized that the delusion of
    samsara takes place.
By being introduced directly to that awareness and
    recognizing it,
One realizes the wisdom of primordial space—
    and this is known as buddhahood.

Once you have been able to recognize the empty nature of mind, attachment and desire will not arise when your mind sees something beautiful, and hatred and repulsion will not develop whenever it comes across anything horrible or unpleasant. Since these negative emotions no longer arise, the mind is no longer deceived or deluded, karma is not accumulated, and the stream of suffering is cut.

If you throw a stone at the nose of a pig, it will immediately turn around and run away. Likewise, whenever a thought develops, recognize it as being empty. That thought will immediately lose its compelling power and will not generate attachment and hatred—and once attachment and hatred are gone, realization of the perfectly pure Dharma will unfold naturally from within.

Indeed, try as you might, there is no way you will ever be rid of your attachment and hatred as long as you keep believing that they arise because of the external objects or circumstances to which they are connected. The more you attempt to reject external phenomena, the more they will spring back at you. Hence, therefore, the importance of recognizing the empty nature of your thoughts and simply allowing them to dissolve. When you know that it is mind that both creates and perceives samsara and nirvana, and also, at the same time, that the nature of mind is emptiness, then mind will no longer be able to delude you and lead you around by the nose.

Once you have recognized the empty nature of mind, to allow love to arise for someone who is harming you becomes easy. But without that recognition, it is very hard to stop anger from arising instead, is it not? Look into it, and you will see that mind is what does positive actions, and mind is what makes circumstances negative. Because the Buddha entirely understood the empty nature of mind and remained in the *samadhi* of great love, the weapons the Maras showered upon him were transformed into a rain of flowers. If, instead, the Buddha had allowed the thought "The Maras are trying to kill me" to stoke him into an outburst of anger, he would certainly have been vulnerable to those weapons, and suffered greatly from the wounds they would have inflicted.

Letting the mind become peaceful and staying in a meditative state of stillness free from many thoughts is called *shamatha,* or sustained calm. Recognizing the empty nature of mind within that state of calm is called *vipashyana,* or profound insight. Uniting shamatha and vipashyana is the essence of meditation practice. It is said:

> Looking at the mind
> There is nothing to see.
> Seeing nothing, we see the Dharma,
> The source of all buddhas.

As the great Kadampa teachers[80] used to say:

> I will hold the spear of mindfulness at the gate of
>   the mind,
> And when the emotions threaten,
> I, too, will threaten them;
> When they relax their grip, only then will I relax
>   mine.

In truth, if you cannot tame your own mind, what else is there to tame? What is the use of doing many other practices? The aim of the whole Buddhist path, both the Basic and the Great Vehicles, is to tame and understand the mind.

In the Basic Vehicle, you realize that the world is pervaded by suffering, so you try to control your own craving and grasping in order to be able to progress on the path to liberation from that suffering. In the Great Vehicle, you let go of your grasping to the idea of "I," to the truly existing self, and become solely concerned with the welfare of others. You also recognize the essential indivisibility of emptiness and phenomena, or absolute bodhichitta, seeing that it is because phenomena are empty by nature that they can appear unobstructedly, just as empty space allows the whole universe, with its continents and mountains, to take shape.

B. THE POSTMEDITATION PRACTICE OF ABANDONING ANY BELIEF IN THE OBJECTS OF DESIRE AND AVERSION AS TRULY EXISTING

i. Abandoning any belief in the objects of desire as truly existing

23

When encountering objects which please us,
To view them like rainbows in summer,
Not ultimately real, however beautiful they appear,
And to relinquish craving and attachment, is the
practice of a bodhisattva.

It is easy to think that if only you could get enough of the things you want—relatives, friends, possessions, or whatever—you would be completely happy. The problem is that, in practice, if you let the mind follow its natural propensities, what it wants may turn out to be a lot. A person who has one friend wants a hundred; a general with a hundred soldiers under his command would like a thousand.

Moreover, the more friends you have, the more friends you will have to be parted from when death suddenly descends and robs you of everything, even of this cherished body of yours. What is the point, in fact, of having so many friends? The best friends you could have might be a peaceful mind and self-control—strict teachers, perhaps, but friends kind enough to show you the way to liberation.

There is nothing definitive about obtaining whatever it is you long for. Observe how rich people get robbed, how generals get killed, and relatives separated. People crave the most lavish food and alcohol, and kill their fellow sentient beings to fulfill their desire for meat, even though, in the end, it all just turns to excrement. You could easily spend all your time trying to get rich enough to fulfill a taste for expensive clothes and the pleasure of owning more material goods. Craving, by its nature, brings only trouble and dissatisfaction.

The outer world and its living inhabitants are all impermanent. Your mind and body are together for the time being—but the mind is like a guest, and the body like a hotel in which that guest will only be making a short stay. Once you truly understand that, the seeming reality of your ordinary ambitions will fall away and you will realize that the really meaningful thing to do, for the present and the future, is to practice the Dharma.

ii. Abandoning any belief in the objects of aversion as truly existing

24

The various forms of suffering are like the death of
    one's child in a dream:
By clinging to deluded perceptions as real we
    exhaust ourselves.
Therefore, when encountering unfavorable
    circumstances,
To view them as illusions is the practice of a
    bodhisattva.

Faced with the prospect of something unpleasant happening to you, the usual reaction is to do everything possible to avert it. Whatever might be threatening you, whether sickness, poverty, or some emotionally unbearable situation, it would surely be unworthy of a person like you to be overcome by such a thing, you think—so you muster all your energy and resources, seek help from influential people, and do all you can to fight it off. In doing so, to give free rein to your attachment and hatred seems quite justifiable.

In reality, however, you have simply become the slave of your negative emotions. Try as you might to avoid or overcome unfavorable circumstances, there will always be more. They can never be completely eliminated.

The best way to deal with anything undesirable that happens to you is to reflect that this is the result of your own negative actions in the past. Whatever difficulties you are faced with now may seem disastrous, but remind yourself that compared with the overwhelming suffering you could face in the future in the realms of the tortured spirits or in the hells, your present problems are almost negligible. Pray from the depth of your heart that, through your experiencing these present difficulties, all your past negative actions and their results may be purified, leaving no karmic seeds for such rebirths in the future. Seen in this light, sickness and suffering are far from being undesirable.

Remember, too, how many sick people there are in this world, and pray that you may be able to take all their sickness and disease upon yourself, and that all their suffering and illness may be exhausted through your present experience of suffering and illness. Or, faced with material difficulties, even if you are utterly destitute, remember how many deprived and underprivileged people there are in the world, and pray that their impoverishment can be exhausted through your own.

It is the feeling that you will be unable to bear some impending suffering that drives you to take action outwardly in order to eliminate whatever it might be. Such attempts will never fully succeed—indeed, they will lead you into one pointless problem after another. But suffering does not have to be unbearable. Surely, it would be much more profitable to generate the inner serenity that would allow you to face such circumstances unperturbed.

If you are the target of some harsh criticism or insulting talk, for example, the harder you try to avoid being exposed to it, the more of it you seem to hear. It would be better to be like the great sages of the past, who felt neither upset when criticized nor pleased when praised, because they were able to perceive all sounds as empty echoes and to hear all criticism and praise about themselves just as though people were speaking about a person who had died long ago. They were aware that thoughts, perceptions, and feelings, if examined, have no intrinsic reality, so they could always remain simply present and not lose control of themselves.

A woman might have a dream in which she gives birth to a child, to her great joy. But should the child in her dream then die, she would feel devastated. In reality, nothing has happened at all. The same applies to your everyday perceptions. It is only because you give credence to their seeming reality that you feel sadness or joy. When you are watching a film, the people in it appear to be really fighting battles, loving each other, and so forth, but none of those things are actually happening. It is all just a fantasy. Try to see all your joys and sorrows as if you were watching a movie, letting go of the idea that you have to strive hard to avoid whatever is difficult or unpleasant. This will make your happiness indestructible. It is said:

> Whatever difficulty may arise, the way to bring it onto the path is not to dwell on it, which will only let your thoughts proliferate. People with narrow, crowded minds are besieged by a life full of suffering, attachment, and aggression. People with relaxed minds never lose their happiness.

The Kadampa teachers said:

> Happiness and suffering, that's all lies;
> It's just a matter of knowing or not knowing how to
>   deal with situations.
> Strong emotions, few emotions, that's all lies;
> It's just a matter of how strongly you counteract
>   them.

If you have contemplated the empty nature of all phenomena in your meditation sessions, it is easy to see the dreamlike nature of phenomena between sessions. At the same time, you will feel an effortless flow of compassion toward all those who suffer needlessly because they are unaware of the illusory nature of everything. Gyalse Thogme himself said:

> Between sessions see all phenomena as illusions;
> They appear, yet are devoid of any inherent
>   existence.
> To accomplish the benefit of others without clinging
> Is the postmeditation practice of absolute
>   bodhichitta.

3. The precepts for training in those practices

I. Training in the six transcendent perfections

II. Training in the four instructions taught in the Sutra

III. Training in how to be rid of the negative emotions

IV. Training in accomplishing others' good with mindfulness and vigilance

V. Dedicating the merit to perfect enlightenment

I. Training in the six transcendent perfections

The following six sections expound the practice of the six transcendent perfections, or paramitas: generosity, discipline, patience, diligence, concentration, and wisdom. Each of these virtues or qualities is considered to be qualified as truly transcendent (*paramita*) when it has the following four characteristics: (1) It destroys its negative counterpart—for example, generosity destroying miserliness. (2) It is reinforced with wisdom, that is, it is free from all concepts of subject, object, and action. (3) It can result in the fulfillment of all beings' aspirations. (4) It can bring others to the full maturity of their potential.

A. Transcendent generosity

25

If those who wish for enlightenment must give away
  even their own bodies,
How much more should it be true of material
  objects?
Therefore, without expectation of result or reward,
To give with generosity is the practice of a
  bodhisattva.

Generosity is the natural expression of a bodhisattva's altruistic mind, free from attachment. A bodhisattva is clearly aware of the suffering that can be caused by amassing wealth and by trying to protect and increase it. Should he ever have any wealth or possessions, his first thought is to give it all away, using it to make offerings to the Three Jewels and to support those who are hungry or without food and shelter. As it is said:

Generosity is the gem that fulfills all wishes
And the sublime sword that cuts through the knot
  of miserliness.

And the vinaya says:

> He who has never given anything away will not be
>   wealthy,
> Nor will he have any way even to gather people to
>   him—
> Let alone to attain enlightenment.

If you are truly generous, you will be free of all difficulties and will possess whatever wealth you need to carry out altruistic deeds until you attain enlightenment.

The Tibetan king Trisong Detsen is a good example of a bodhisattva who became a great ruler. He used his tremendous wealth to invite Guru Rinpoche, the great abbot Shantarakshita, the great pandita Vimalamitra, and 108 other Indian panditas to Tibet. It was because of his patronage that the teachings of both sutra and tantra were given in Tibet and that the first Tibetan translators were trained. His boundless generosity made the Dharma flourish, and there was immense happiness in the Land of Snows. Later, during the reign of other kings, the treasure rooms were locked and put under heavy guard, and both the Dharma and the prosperity of the Tibetan people declined.

People who are generous may not be trying to get rich, but the natural result of their merit will bring them ever-increasing wealth in their future lives. People tied up in their own miserliness, in contrast, will find themselves reborn in the realm of hungry ghosts, where not even the words *food* and *drink* are heard.

Never hope for anything in return for an act of generosity, and do not expect as a result that in your next life you will be treated well or be happy and prosperous. Generosity is complete in itself; there is no need for any other reward than having made others happy. If you give something motivated by self-interest, the joy you might have felt will be spoiled, and further unhappiness is certain to follow. But giving out of sheer devotion, love, or compassion will bring you a feeling of great joy, and your gift will create yet more happiness. The motivation behind the act of giving makes all the difference.

Recognizing all possessions to be like dreams or magical illusions, give them away as offerings or as charity without holding back. Through generosity, you will perfect your accumulation of merit, which leads in the end to the attainment of the major and minor marks of a buddha. Make sure that your generosity is always permeated with the enlightened attitude of bodhichitta, which is what makes it truly meaningful by turning it into an unerring cause for buddhahood.

There are three kinds of generosity. The first is material giving. A bodhisattva should give without reservation and without regret. If an offering is given with pure intention, its size is not important.

The second kind of generosity is to save life, and to provide beings with protection from fear. Follow the example of great bodhisattvas like Patrul Rinpoche and Shabkar Tsokdruk Rangdrol,[81] who would save thousands of domestic animals from slaughter by buying them and setting them free, convince people to give up hunting and fishing, obtain clemency for prisoners sentenced to death, and pacify bloody feuds.

The third kind of generosity is giving the Dharma. A bodhisattva should do everything he can to make the sound of the teaching of Dharma resound in places where it has never been heard before. He can bring the Dharma to people in a way that they can put it into practice and act in accordance with the Buddha's teachings. This is what enables the activity of all the buddhas to flourish and increase.

A very miserly man once came to see the Buddha for advice. He was totally incapable of giving anything away. The Buddha told him to begin training himself by giving small objects with his right hand to his left hand. As the man slowly got used to the idea of giving, the Buddha encouraged him to give small things to members of his family, then to friends, and then finally to strangers. Eventually, the man was able to give away whatever he had with great joy to anyone he came across. Through gradual familiarization, great aims can easily be achieved.

The essence of generosity is nonattachment. Transcendent generosity is generosity that is free of the three limiting concepts, that is, attachment to there being any substantial reality of a person giving, a recipient, and an act of giving. To be free from such concepts is precisely how a paramita, in this case generosity, works as a cause of enlightenment.

B. TRANSCENDENT DISCIPLINE

26

If, lacking discipline, one cannot accomplish one's
    own good,
It is laughable to think of accomplishing the good of
    others.
Therefore, to observe discipline
Without samsaric motives is the practice of a
    bodhisattva.

Discipline is the foundation of all Dharma practice. It provides the ground upon which all positive qualities can be cultivated. In the same way that all the oceans and mountains are supported by the underlying mass of the earth, all the practices of the Hinayana, Mahayana, and Vajrayana are supported by the backbone of discipline.

Discipline in each of these three vehicles is defined by one of the three corresponding levels of vows: the pratimoksha vows,[82] the bodhisattva precepts, and the Mantrayana samayas. These three sets of vows should be kept in harmony with one another.

As your practice progresses stage by stage through the three vehicles, the vows of the preceding vehicles are not discarded but rather are transmuted, like iron into gold. The discipline of the pratimoksha begins when you take the refuge vows and enter the path of Dharma. A person motivated by a strong determination to be free from samsara will then renounce worldly concerns and keep the vows of a lay disciple, the monastic vows of the novice, or the vows of a fully ordained monk or nun. To this basis, the discipline of the Mahayana adds the bodhichitta, the vow to bring all beings to perfect enlightenment. Mahayana practitioners therefore keep either lay or monastic vows themselves, adding the wish that all beings might keep perfect discipline in order to be free from samsara's bonds, and apply the various precepts of the bodhisattva. Thus infused with the bodhisattva's motivation, discipline grows greatly in its power. It culminates in the discipline of the Vajrayana, which is to maintain the samayas, the sacred links between the spiritual master and the disciple—the very life force of the Vajrayana.

Without discipline there is no way to achieve either the temporary happiness of liberation from suffering or the ultimate bliss of enlightenment. Whatever vows you take—whether the 253 vows of the pratimoksha, the 18 root and branch vows of the bodhisattvas, or the 100,000 samayas of the Vajrayana—they all need to be observed with great care, like that of a farmer doing everything possible to protect his crops against wild animals, thieves, hailstorms, and all other harmful eventualities.

Guard your own discipline, therefore, as carefully as you protect your own eyes. For discipline, if you can keep it, is the source of bliss; but if you transgress it, it becomes a source of suffering.

There are three kinds of discipline to be practiced. The first is to give up all actions that harm either others or yourself. The second is to undertake positive actions by practicing the six paramitas. The third is to do everything possible to benefit others in their present and future lives.

Without discipline, you will never even be able to accomplish any of your personal aims, let alone be able to help others. To keep pure discipline, it helps to spend your time with virtuous friends. Give up attachment and desire, remember the infallibility of the karmic law of cause and effect, reflect on the miseries of samsara, and follow the precepts of the three types of vows. It is said that those who keep perfect monastic discipline will not only be widely respected by humans, but celestial beings will take their robes when they die and place them in stupas in their heavenly realms. As the Buddha said:

> In this decadent age, to maintain even one monastic vow for a day brings greater merit than to offer a million buddhas quantities of food, drink, canopies, lamps, and garlands as vast as the number of grains of sand in the Ganges.

Perfect discipline is to keep the vows in a pure way with constant mindfulness, free from conceit or pride. In essence, discipline is to have a peaceful, self-controlled, and altruistic mind.

C. TRANSCENDENT PATIENCE

27

For a bodhisattva who desires the joys of virtue,
All who harm him are like a precious treasure.
Therefore, to cultivate patience toward all,
Without resentment, is the practice of a bodhisattva.

There are three kinds of patience. The first is to bear without anger whatever harm people may do you. The second kind is to endure without sadness whatever hardships you may experience for the sake of the Dharma. The third is to face without fear the profound meaning of the Dharma and the boundless qualities of the Three Jewels.

For the first, when you feel you are being harmed by someone, remember that the harm that person may be inflicting on you (or on someone dear to you) is the direct result of you yourself having harmed others in the past. Reflect that this person is so overpowered by delusion that he or she is as if possessed, and cannot resist harming you. As a result of this harm, he or she will have to suffer in samsara's lower realms in a future life. When you think how terrible that will be, you will feel only sadness and pity rather than anger.

Remember, too, that if you can patiently accept all this harm, many of your own past negative actions will be purified, and you will accumulate both merit and wisdom. Indeed, this person who appears to be harming you is therefore doing you a great kindness, and is a true spiritual friend. As an expression of your gratitude, dedicate whatever merit you have accumulated to him or her.

Seeing all such situations in this way, train yourself not to get upset when someone harms you, not to seek revenge, and never to bear the slightest grudge.

Moreover, when you look even more deeply into what is happening, you will see that the person being harmed, the person doing the harm, and the harm itself are all totally devoid of any inherent existence. Who is going to get angry at delusions? In these empty phenomena, what is there to be gained or lost, to want or to reject? Understand it all as being like the vast, empty sky.

Now for the second kind of patience, enduring hardships for the sake of Dharma. In order to be able to practice Dharma, it may happen that you have to endure illness, or suffer from heat, cold, hunger, or thirst. But since these short-term sufferings will help you purify your past negative actions and, in the long term, reach ultimate buddhahood, accept them with joy, like a swan gliding into a lotus pond. In *The Way of the Bodhisattva*, Shantideva says:

> Is a man not relieved when, though condemned to
>   death,
> He's freed, his hand cut off in ransom for his life?
> Enduring likewise merely human ills,
> Am I not happy to avoid the pains of hell?

The third kind of patience is to have the deep, inner courage that it takes to be ready, out of compassion, to work over many aeons for the sake of beings and to face without any fear the highest truths of the teachings—that ultimately all phenomena are totally empty by nature, that emptiness is expressed as radiant clarity, that there is a buddha nature, a self-existing primordial wisdom that is uncompounded, and an absolute truth beyond the reach of the intellect. If you are afraid to accept the reality of emptiness, and criticize practices such as the Great Perfection by which the true nature of all phenomena can be realized, you are rejecting the very essence of the Dharma and are preparing your own downfall into the lower realms. When Lord Buddha taught the profound teachings on emptiness, some of the monks who were present reacted to the deep truths of the teaching with panic so intense that they vomited blood and died forthwith. These truths are by no means easy to fathom, but it is of the utmost importance to try to grasp their true meaning, and not to have a negative view of them.

These three kinds of patience should be developed with the aid of wisdom and skillful means.

To practice the paramita of patience is essential, so that you can never be overcome by anger, hatred, and despair. Once you have entered the path of the bodhisattvas, you should in any case have kindness in your heart for all beings, seeing them as your former parents. So when people are against you and do you harm, you should have even more love, dedicating all your merit to them and taking all their suffering upon yourself.

Indeed, adversaries and people who try to harm you can be powerful sources of help on the bodhisattva path. By bringing about situations that would normally trigger your anger or hatred, they give you the precious opportunity to train in transforming those negative emotions with patience. On the path, such people will do you far more good than any well-disposed friend.

Now, Shantideva says:

> Good works gathered in a thousand ages,
> Such as deeds of generosity,

Or offerings to the blissful ones—
A single flash of anger shatters them.

And in the *Sutra of the Meeting of Father and Son* it is said:

Hatred is not the way to buddhahood.
But love, if constantly cultivated,
Will give rise to enlightenment.

So, if you react to an enemy with hatred and anger, he will certainly be leading you to the depths of the hell realms. But if you know how to see such a person with the deepest loving-kindness, he can only lead you toward liberation. No matter how much harm he tries to do you, it will only do you good. The difference is crucial. You may have studied various teachings and meditated for a while, and even feel rather proud of it. But if, as soon as someone says a few bad words to you, you burst with anger, that is a sign that you have not let the Dharma really permeate you—it has not changed your mind in the least.

Shantideva also says:

No evil is there similar to anger,
No austerity to be compared with patience.

If the land were full of sharp stones and thorns, you might try to protect your feet by covering over the whole countryside with tough leather. But that would be a difficult task. It is much easier to put the leather just on the soles of your feet. In the same way, even if the whole world is full of enemies, they can do you no harm as long as you keep loving-kindness and patience in your mind. Whatever apparent harm they do you would, in fact, help you on the path to enlightenment. As it is said:

When you encounter the emotions' formidable
    army,
Don the solid and excellent armor of patience;

Thus, unscathed by the weapons of harsh words and
    vindictive blows,
Pass through them to reach the land of nirvana.

There is no peace for a person whose mind is filled with anger and hatred. Anger and hatred need to be subdued by the great army of patience, for they are your only true enemies. It would be impossible for you to experience harm if your own anger and hatred had not, in the past, brought about the causes from which the present harm arises, like the returning echo of your own voice.

Look, too, at the true nature of harm itself. It is as ungraspable as writing on water. Let resentment vanish of its own accord, and as soon as the fiery waves of thoughts subside, let everything become like an empty sky, where there is nothing to gain and nothing to lose.

D. TRANSCENDENT DILIGENCE

28

Merely for their own sake, even shravakas and
    pratyekabuddhas
Make efforts like someone whose hair is on fire
    trying to put it out:
Seeing this, for the sake of all beings,
To practice diligence, the source of excellent
    qualities, is the practice of a bodhisattva.

To awaken and to develop all the paramitas, diligence is vital. Diligence is the joyous effort and active determination to carry out positive actions, without any expectations or self-satisfaction.

Diligence has three aspects. The first, called "armorlike diligence," is to develop a joyous courage and fortitude, which you wear like armor against discouragement. The second is "diligence in action," which is to set about accumulating merit through the practice of the six paramitas without delay or procrastination. The third is "diligence that cannot be stopped," an insatiable and unremitting energy to work for the sake of others. Diligence should permeate the practice of the other paramitas, and invigorate them all.

The first kind, armorlike diligence, is to put on the armor of a strong and courageous determination that you will never fall prey to obstacles created by the four demons (negative emotions, attachment to comfort, physical sickness, and death) but will persist, come what may, in your efforts to accomplish the extraordinary activities of a bodhisattva until you have established all beings in enlightenment.

The second kind, diligence in action, is determined perseverance in the actual application of that wish. Feeling a great joy to be able to practice, to travel the five paths and attain the ten levels,[83] you enthusiastically undertake endless meritorious activities, particularly study, reflection, and meditation. Engaging in all this, sustain an indomitable courage and never fall prey to discouragement, laziness, or procrastination.

The third kind, diligence that cannot be stopped, is the insatiable energy to work constantly for the sake of others. Day and night, engage in every possible way, directly or indirectly, in your thoughts, words, and deeds, to benefit beings. If you are not able to help them directly, you should keep nothing in your mind but the benefit of others, and dedicate everything you do toward their attainment of buddhahood. Never feel self-satisfied because of the few good qualities you may have been able to achieve, and never be diverted from your aims by people's abuse or other adverse circumstances. Just remain determined to continue constantly until you reach your goal.

Each of these three kinds of diligence has its opposite in a corresponding kind of laziness.

The first kind of laziness is the wish for nothing but your own comfort. It manifests as a tendency to sleep and idleness, to crave immediate satisfaction and comfort, and in so doing to ignore the Dharma. The antidote is to meditate on death and impermanence.

The second kind of laziness is faint-heartedness. You feel discouraged before you have even begun trying to do something, because you think a person like you will never reach enlightenment no matter how hard you try. The antidote is to strengthen your fortitude by reflecting on the benefits of liberation and enlightenment.

The third kind of laziness is a neglect of your true priorities. You become stuck in negative and unproductive habits. Forgetting or ignoring deeper aims, you stay preoccupied solely with matters limited to this life. The antidote is to realize that all such ordinary concerns are invariably causes of suffering alone, and to cast them far away.

People work with great endeavor, day and night, to accomplish things that are merely for their own comfort, fame, and power—in other words, for things that in the long term are utterly meaningless. Of the hardships you may undergo for the sake of the Dharma, however, not a single one will be without meaning. The difficult situations you experience will help you to purify the negativity accumulated in many past lives and to gather merit as a provision for lives to come. They are sure to be meaningful.

Without diligence, bodhichitta and the activities of a bodhisattva will have no means to take root and grow in your mind. As Padampa Sangye said:

> If your perseverance has no strength, you will not
>   reach buddhahood;
> People of Tingri, make sure you don that armor.

The Buddha Shakyamuni is renowned for having brought the paramita of diligence to its ultimate perfection. The power and merit generated by his endeavor over countless lifetimes could have brought him rebirth a thousand times over as a universal monarch, but instead he chose to direct all his efforts toward achieving enlightenment. As followers of the Buddha, we should use the story of his life and the stories of great saints of the past as inspiring models. Jetsun Milarepa, for example, displayed incredible endeavor, enduring many hardships to achieve his profound aims. Vairochana[84] left for India in search of the Dharma at a very young age, undergoing fifty-seven unbearable difficulties to obtain the teachings and often coming close to losing his life. He and the other great translators of Tibet encountered tremendous hardships on their travels—the burning heat and the fevers then endemic in the Indian plains, the harsh animosity of local rulers, and so forth. Nevertheless they persevered, and succeeded in bringing the authentic Dharma back to Tibet.

You are living today in countries where the Dharma has only just begun to take root, like a fragile new shoot in the ground. Only your sustained diligence will bring it to fruition. Depending on the effort you put into study, reflection, and meditation, and to integrating what you have understood into your spiritual practice, accomplishment may be days, months, or years away. It is essential to remember that all your endeavors on the path are for the sake of others. Remain humble and aware that your efforts are like child's play compared to the oceanlike activity of the great bodhisattvas. Be like a parent providing for much-loved children, never thinking that you have done too much for others—or even that you have done enough. If you finally managed, through your own efforts alone, to establish all beings in buddhahood, you would simply think that all your wishes had been fulfilled. Never have even a trace of hope for something in return.

A bodhisattva must have far greater diligence than a shravaka or pratyekabuddha, because the bodhisattva has taken the responsibility of accomplishing the ultimate happiness of buddhahood not only for himself but for countless beings. As it is said:

The hero who carries the burden of all beings on his
head has no leisure to walk slowly.

And:

Since I and all others are tied by a hundred bonds,
I must multiply my diligence a hundred times.

To increase your diligence, reflect on how impermanent
everything is. Death is inevitable and may come suddenly and
very soon. Think how shallow and superficial this life's ordinary
concerns really are in that light, and how free you could be if you
could turn your mind away from them. If you suddenly realized
that in your lap, in a fold of your clothes, a venomous snake was
hiding, would you wait to take action—even for a second?

E. TRANSCENDENT CONCENTRATION

29

Knowing that through profound insight thoroughly
grounded in sustained calm
The disturbing emotions are completely conquered,
To practice the concentration which utterly
transcends
The four formless states[85] is the practice of a
bodhisattva.

Examine body, speech, and mind, and you will find that mind
is the most important of the three. If your mind is thoroughly
trained in sustained calm and profound insight (shamatha and
vipashyana), your body and your speech will naturally follow
your mind along the path of liberation.

Hitherto your mind, like a restless monkey, has been running ceaselessly after forms, sounds, smells, tastes, and sensations
outside, and thoughts and feelings inside. But you can learn to

take control of it by maintaining mindfulness and vigilance. As you do so, study, reflect, and meditate on the teachings, integrating them into your mind. Finally you will become free of desire, hatred, and ignorance.

As Kharak Gomchung said:

> In the mind of a beginner
> There is clarity, but no stability;
> To stop it being consigned to the wind of thoughts,
> Fasten it with the rope of mindfulness.

To gain stability in concentration, it is helpful to stay in quiet, secluded retreat places free from distractions. Of sustained calm and profound insight, it is profound insight that is the most important; but profound insight cannot arise without a preliminary calming of the mind. What is crucial here is to calm all the wild thoughts that constantly agitate, unsettle, and condition your mind, for such thoughts give rise to negative emotions, which, in turn, you express as the words and actions that comprise the causes of suffering.

Calming the mind is like closing the glass of a lantern around the flame so that it can shine brightly and steadily, protected from the wind. There are many ways to practice sustained calm and profound insight, such as the "nine ways of settling the mind" and other methods explained in the Mahayana sutras.[86] All of these methods are directed toward supreme enlightenment. Techniques of concentration are also found in non-Buddhist paths, but they should not be confused with Buddhist methods, as they are not practiced with the same goal. Such contemplations, instead of being aimed at true enlightenment, are undertaken with the idea of bringing the elements to exhaustion, transcending form, and attaining a state of absorption in the formless realms as their ultimate goal.

Methods for attaining sustained calm, or shamatha, fall into two main groups: those in which an object of concentration is used, and those in which there is no object. Here, I will explain the first method, using as the object of concentration a visualization of Lord Buddha, which brings more blessings than some ordinary object.

Sit in the perfect seven-point posture of the Buddha Vairochana—your legs crossed in vajra posture, your two hands resting in the mudra of equanimity, your shoulders raised up, your vertebral column straight like a pile of gold coins, your chin slightly tucked in, your eyes steadily focused in the space in front of your nose, and the tip of your tongue touching your palate. If you find this posture difficult to maintain, at least sit upright and well balanced on a suitable cushion. Avoid leaning backward or to one side, or taking any other lax posture.

Allow your mind to settle naturally, and visualize Buddha Shakyamuni in the sky in front of you. He is seated upon a moon disk, on a lotus that rests on a throne supported by eight fearless lions. His body has all the radiance of gold. With his right hand he touches the ground near his right knee in the "gesture of taking the earth as witness,"[87] while with his left hand, in the "gesture of equanimity," he holds in his lap a begging bowl filled with nectar. He is sitting cross-legged,[88] wearing the three Dharma robes. His body is graced with all the thirty-two major and eighty minor marks of a buddha, notably the *ushnisha* on the top of his head,[89] wheel patterns or *dharmachakras* on the palms of his hands and soles of his feet, and a long hair between his eyebrows, curling counterclockwise like a white conch. From his body emanate infinite light rays of wisdom, which fill the whole universe. He is directly in front of you in the sky, gazing straight at you with compassion. Visualize the Buddha as alive, not inert like a statue made of clay or bronze or like a two-dimensional drawing. The colors and details of his form are perfectly clear and vivid, yet he is insubstantial and transparent like a rainbow. He is not made of flesh and bones, but appears as the empty but radiant unborn wisdom body of the buddhas, full of compassion and wisdom.

Try to concentrate one-pointedly on the visualization, seeing all the details as clearly as possible. Have total confidence that the

Buddha is actually there, remembering that for those with faith the Buddha is always present. As you visualize the Buddha, all your wandering thoughts will eventually subside. To keep your mind concentrated in this way on a clear and steady visualization is shamatha, or sustained calm.

To make your concentration more and more stable, you will need to counteract different disturbances of the meditation as they arise. If your mind grows wild and your thoughts begin to race, preventing you from achieving a clear visualization, look slightly downward in the space in front of your nose and concentrate on the lower parts of the visualization, the crossed legs of the Buddha, the lion throne, and the lotus seat. This helps to reduce wildness.

If your mind sinks into a state of drowsiness, slackness, or dull indifference, raise your gaze higher into the space in front of you and concentrate on the upper parts of the visualization, the perfect oval of the Buddha's face, his eyes, the hair between his brows. This clears away the sinking feeling of dullness and slackness.

As long as your mind stays balanced, neither wild nor dull, concentrate straight ahead on the Buddha's heart, the eternal knot of the secret treasure of pristine wisdom.[90] If the visualization is not yet clear, try again and again to make it better defined and more precise. If it is already clear, keep your mind concentrated on it in a natural, unforced way.

Concentrate on being aware of the presence of the Buddha in front of you, confident that he is actually there. As your visualization becomes more stable and your thoughts more infrequent, visualize more of the details of the Buddha's beautiful form, as though you were a skilled painter. Visualize the perfect mandala of his face, his two eyes gazing with compassionate wisdom upon all sentient beings, his perfectly proportioned nose and ears, his smile, the boundless rays of light emanating from him, and, gradually extend the visualization to all the details of both the upper and the lower parts of his body. This will make the whole visualization more vivid.

When your visualization is clear and your mind still and quiet, permeate the state of sustained calm with profound insight. First, consider who or what it is that is perceiving the visualization. You will become aware that it is the mind. You will also see that the image you are visualizing is not itself actually the Buddha who came into this world, but rather a projection created by your mind in order to develop concentration.

The mind has the ability to concentrate on an object, yet when you search for the mind, you cannot find it anywhere. As we saw earlier, if you look inward at the mind, and try to locate it or identify its shape, its color, its form, where it came from, where it is now, or where it goes to, you will never find anything. Ask those who know the teachings and have experience of meditation, and see if anyone has ever been able to point to anything as "the mind." And just as you will never find a particular entity that can be said to be the mind, the same is true for the body. What we call "the body" is simply a conglomeration of many elements put together. We give the name "heap" to a collection of grains, "sheaf" to a collection of dried straw, and "crowd" to a gathering of people, but none of them are entities in their own right. Likewise for this collection of things we call the body, if you take away the skin and the flesh, the marrow, the bones, and the different organs, once they have all been separated from one another there is no other entity present that you can identify as "the body."

All phenomena in their infinite variety throughout the universe, in fact, appear as a result of particular causes and conditions coming temporarily together. You take phenomena to be things that truly exist simply because you have not examined them properly. In truth, they have no solid, intrinsic existence at all.

When it becomes clear that your body, the image of the Buddha you are visualizing, and all phenomena are the display of the mind and that the mind's nature is empty, simply remain in the recognition of that nature without wandering, remaining attentive to whether or not thoughts interrupt this recognition. This is called profound insight, vipashyana. As Gyalse Thogme said:

> All appearances are one's own mind;
> Mind itself is primordially beyond conceptual
> extremes.
> Undistracted by dualistic subject-object notions,
> To remain one-pointed is called perfect
> concentration.

Uniting sustained calm and profound insight in this way is the key method for perfecting transcendent concentration.[91]

F. TRANSCENDENT WISDOM

30

In the absence of wisdom, perfect enlightenment
    cannot be attained
Through the other five perfections alone.
Therefore, to cultivate wisdom combined with
    skillful means
And free from the three concepts[92] is the practice
    of a bodhisattva.

The paramitas of generosity, discipline, patience, endeavor, and concentration can help you to accumulate merit, but they are still associated with concepts. Only wisdom can perfect the accumulation that leads you to realize primordial awareness free of all concepts. Generosity, discipline, patience, diligence, and concentration could be likened to five blind men who, without the eyes of wisdom, would never be able to find their way to the citadel of liberation. Indeed, only when accompanied by wisdom do they deserve the name *paramita*, "transcendent," or literally "gone to the other shore"—the shore across the ocean of suffering and ignorance, beyond the concepts of samsara and nirvana.

Transcendent wisdom has three aspects, which are stages in its progressive realization: first, the wisdom of the learning acquired through hearing the teachings; then, the wisdom that arises through reflecting on the meaning of these teachings; and finally, the wisdom that arises from meditating.[93]

You, the practitioner, should first of all be like a bee going from flower to flower collecting nectar. At the stage when you are listening to and studying the teachings, learn all of them carefully, in both words and meaning. Then, you should be like a wild animal. Not satisfied with a mere theoretical understanding, go and live in mountain solitudes where you can be free of all the busy involvement of ordinary life. Be self-sufficient and firm in one-pointed practice as you discover directly for yourself the profound meaning of the teachings. Finally, as you put the teachings into practice and integrate them with your being, you should be like a peg driven into hard ground. Unshaken by thoughts during meditation, remain unwavering. Cut away all limiting concepts of existence and nonexistence from within, and directly encounter the face of the ultimate nature of everything.

So here we have come to the very heart of the paramitas. Wisdom is not only the most important of the six—it is their very life force. To realize wisdom is the ultimate goal; it is the reason why all the branches of the teachings are explained.

For the first aspect of wisdom, to perfect the wisdom of the learning acquired through hearing the teachings, the scriptures to be studied include all the Mahayana teachings, which are referred to as "profound and vast." The profound teachings are those that expound emptiness, and the vast teachings those that explain the different stages on the bodhisattva path—the five paths, the ten bhumis, and so on. The profound teachings are found in sutras such as the *King of Concentrations Sutra* and the *Great Compendium Sutra*. The vast teachings are found in *The Ornament of the Mahayana Sutras, The Ornament of True*

Realization, and other texts. There are other treatises that explain the wisdom intention of the Buddha's words in a way that is easy for later followers of the Buddha to understand. You should hear all of these teachings from a qualified teacher.

However, hearing the teachings alone is not quite enough— even animals can hear the sound of the Dharma being taught. The second stage is to develop the wisdom that arises through reflecting on the meaning of these teachings. Think about what you have heard and extract the essential meaning from it so that the teachings do not just remain as intellectual knowledge. It is important to develop confidence in the meaning of the Dharma, and be sure you have understood it correctly. Whatever you are going to practice has to be considered very carefully. Clarify all your doubts and hesitations with your teacher. In particular, remember clearly what your teacher tells you about all the obstacles that can arise, and what deviations from the path you might find yourself making. Then, when you are ready to put your instructions into practice, it will be like setting out on a journey with full knowledge of all the different conditions you are likely to encounter, and all the money you will need to meet your expenses on the way.

Some teachings belong to the category in which the meaning expounded is provisional or expedient, or of relative truth; others to that in which the meaning is direct and definitive, or of absolute truth. Of the two, the absolute meaning is the more important, so you should put your effort into recognizing that absolute meaning and becoming familiar with it. The more you study and reflect on the teachings of the scriptures and of the rediscovered treasures,[94] the more your understanding, your confidence, and your certainty as to the meaning of the teachings will grow. When gold is being refined, the refining processes, such as melting and drawing off the pure metal, are repeatedly applied. In the same way, refine your understanding by reflecting, over and over again, on the meaning of the teachings so that you develop a clear confidence in their absolute meaning.

Study and reflection will cut through your more gross misconceptions. But the subtler ones can only be dispelled by meditation, and by integration of the absolute wisdom that arises from it into your very being. To engender it, go to a secluded place and stay as much as possible in meditation, practicing shamatha and vipashyana—sustained calm and profound insight—to realize emptiness, the ultimate nature of all phenomena. This is the wisdom that arises from meditation. To have recognized that all phenomena are empty by nature is to have recognized the ultimate point of all the teachings.

Through the understanding of emptiness, you will perceive no difference between yourself and others. You will be free of self-cherishing, compassion will arise spontaneously, and you will benefit beings without any effort. Even great bodhisattva acts such as giving your life for another's benefit will not be difficult for you, and you will be able to perform altruistic deeds effortlessly over many kalpas. Everything happens without effort because it all takes place within the continuum of the realization of emptiness. Here generosity, patience, and all the other perfections now truly merit the term *paramita,* as they are utterly beyond the realm of delusion. For a bodhisattva who has realized emptiness, the number of beings to be liberated and the time it might take to liberate them arouse feelings neither of discouragement nor of pride. Dawning freely in your enlightened mind is an all-inclusive compassion, devoid of all concepts of subject and object. Having realized the sameness of self and others, you remain as unchanging as primordial space.

A thorough, experiential understanding of emptiness is the only antidote to the belief in an "I," in a truly existing self. Once you recognize emptiness, all your attachment to such a self will vanish without a trace. Realization will blaze forth like a brilliant sun rising in the sky, transforming darkness into light.

At first, until you actually recognize emptiness, you have to gain an understanding of it through deep and careful reflection on the teacher's pith instructions. Then, when you first recognize it, your experience of emptiness will not be stable. To improve it, blend meditation and postmeditation periods. Try not to fall back into ordinary delusion, but to maintain the view of emptiness in all your daily activities. Meditation and the path of action will mutually enhance each other. Finally, you may reach a point where there is no difference between meditation and postmeditation, a point at which you no longer ever depart from emptiness. This is called the realization of great sameness. Within that great sameness, compassion for all beings will arise spontaneously—for the more you realize emptiness, the less there will be any impediment to the arising of compassion. With it will come a natural ability to benefit others without effort, in the same way that if, among a hundred blind people, one of them were to recover his sight, he would be able to guide all the others.

Without the realization of emptiness, both love and compassion are limited and narrow. As the *Bodhisattva-bhumi*[95] explains, there are three successive levels of boundless love, compassion, joy, and impartiality. Consider love to start with. At first, boundless love is focused on sentient beings. Remembering that all beings have been your parents, you wish that they may all have happiness. This is a form of love that everyone, from ordinary people to bodhisattvas, has in common.

At a second stage, boundless love has phenomena as its reference. The practitioner, while recognizing that in absolute truth nothing has any inherent existence, wishes nevertheless that within the illusory, dreamlike reality of relative truth all beings may find happiness. Love of this kind is unknown to ordinary people, but is common to practitioners of the Basic Vehicle (shravakas and pratyekabuddhas) and to those of the Mahayana (bodhisattvas).

The third and highest level of boundless love is nonreferential, beyond any concept of an object. From the outset of the meditation, the practitioner knows that the nature of both self and others is emptiness, free of all conceptual elaborations, like the sky. That intrinsic lack of substantial existence, omnipresent and vivid, unceasingly radiates a love that is lucid and spontaneous. This kind of love is, by nature, free of all concepts and without any goal. It is beyond the three ideas of there being a subject, an object, and an action. It is only found in the Mahayana.

These three successive approaches can be similarly applied to boundless compassion, joy, and impartiality.

The practice of the paramita of wisdom should be done in stages to begin with. First, divide your practice into meditation periods during which you meditate on emptiness, and postmeditation periods in which you try to improve your understanding of the view of emptiness by studying the philosophical system of the Madhyamika, until you attain certainty in it. The Madhyamika view leads to an understanding of the two truths. The recognition of the absolute truth is helped by understanding how all phenomena arise through a combination of causes and conditions.

As your practice becomes more stable, it will no longer be necessary to meditate intentionally on emptiness; it will be integrated into your understanding. You will reach a point when you see that emptiness and compassion, emptiness and phenomena, and absolute and relative truth, are intrinsically one, rather than being in each case two separate entities like the horns of a goat. The vaster your view of emptiness, the clearer your understanding will be of the infinite ways phenomena can manifest in accordance with the law of cause and effect. And it is from emptiness inseparable from compassion that a bodhisattva manifests.

This is the ultimate fruit of all the different teachings of the Mahayana and Mantrayana, of Madhyamika, Mahamudra, and Dzogchen. The most important point of these teachings is to realize them through your own experience, and no mere proliferation of words will be of much help to you in doing that. To put it simply and directly, developing perfect wisdom in your mindstream is the actual practice of the bodhisattvas.

II. Training in the four instructions taught in the Sutra[96]

A. To examine oneself for one's own defects and to give them up

31

> If I do not examine my own defects,
> Though outwardly a Dharma practitioner, I may act
>   contrary to the Dharma.
> Therefore, continuously to examine my own faults
> And give them up is the practice of a bodhisattva.

Ordinarily, whatever you do, say, or think is an expression of your belief in the true existence both of yourself as an individual and of phenomena as a whole. Your actions, as long as they are based on that false premise, can only be deluded, and permeated by negative emotions. As you follow a teacher, however, you can learn how to keep everything you do with body, speech, and mind in accordance with the Dharma.

Intellectually, you can probably recognize right from wrong, and truth from delusion. But unless you apply that knowledge in practice all the time, there can be no liberation. You have to bring your own wild mind under control by yourself—no one else can do it for you. No one else but you can know when you have fallen into delusion, and when you are free from it. The only way to do it is to keep looking into your own mind, as if you were using a mirror. Just as a mirror enables you to check if your face is dirty and see where the dirt is, so, too, being constantly present in every situation and looking within at your own mind allows you to see whether or not your thoughts, words, and deeds are in accordance with the Dharma.

Identify your own shortcomings, but never those of other people. As Gyalse Thogme himself said:

Despite not having the slightest learning or moral standing, you conceitedly pose as a good practitioner. Overlooking a mountain of your own faults, you discern the minutest of faults in others. Motivated entirely by your own ambition, you proclaim how you are taking care of others. You pretend to be practicing Dharma, but all you are achieving is ordinary self-aggrandizement. Anyone who, like you, fails to check his own behavior from the very start will deceive no one more than himself.

As a Tibetan expression puts it, "The promise went to Dharma, but the practice goes to sin."

Whenever you think or do something harmful or false, it is important to recognize it. As soon as a thief has been identified, he can be arrested. In the same way, negative thoughts and deeds, once you have seen them as such, will be powerless to continue as they were. As soon as negative emotions arise, swoop down on them with mindfulness. Whenever positive thoughts arise, reinforce them using the "three supreme points" described earlier.[97]

The only way to practice the Dharma authentically is to mix the teachings with your own mind. If you neglect to examine yourself for faults and mistakes, you might not be aware how lacking you are in any obvious learning, self-control, contentment, humility, or other positive qualities. Being blind to your obvious defects, you may begin to believe that you are a Dharma practitioner, and even get other people to believe it—while in fact it is no more than the outer facade, the mere pretense of a true practitioner. This is a major defect.

As Gampopa said:

> To be learned in the Dharma but not refrain from
>   wrong is a hidden fault of practitioners.
> To hold profound instructions but not transform
>   oneself is a hidden fault of practitioners.

> To skillfully praise oneself and skillfully disparage
> others is a hidden fault of practitioners.

Only by being mindful all the time, whatever the situation, can you keep yourself from falling prey to such dangers. Maintain a constant awareness of what should be done and what should be avoided, with the same care you might take on a perilous mountain path to keep constantly to the right track.

Among the precepts of the bodhichitta of application are four basic downfalls that you have to train yourself to avoid. The first is, out of desire for wealth or prestige, to praise yourself and disparage others. The second is, out of miserliness, not to give what you can to those who are destitute and suffering, or not to give the Dharma to those worthy of receiving it when you have the capacity to do so. The third is, out of animosity and hatred, to abuse others verbally, or worse, with physical violence, or to harbor resentment against wrongdoers who have sought forgiveness and changed their ways. The fourth is, out of ignorance, to criticize and reject the Mahayana teachings, or hypocritically to assume an outward appearance of Dharma. More generally, refrain from everything harmful or meaningless done merely to obtain wealth, fame, status, or gratification, for there is nothing to be gained from such actions but suffering. Cultivate actions that are in accordance with the Dharma, for they will take you closer to liberation and farther from delusion. To differentiate positive from negative actions, it is important to maintain constant awareness.

As well as distinguishing right from wrong, you will also need to keep your intelligence and faculties alert to make sure that you are indeed applying appropriate antidotes instead of just continuing to follow after your bad habits and tendencies. When you get angry, for instance, you need to counter it by practicing patience. When you have feelings of mindless bewilderment, the antidote is to cultivate a clear understanding of samsara and determination to be free from it. When you crave something, you should deal with your desire by reflecting how whatever it is you crave is, on deeper analysis, not really desirable at all.

The ability to transform your own mind will naturally bring you the ability to help others' minds. To be constantly alert, forever mindful and aware, observing the state of your mind so that you can correct and improve yourself, is the authentic practice of the bodhisattvas.

B. TO GIVE UP SPEAKING OF A BODHISATTVA'S FAULTS

32

If, impelled by negative emotions, I relate the faults
Of other bodhisattvas, I will myself degenerate.
Therefore, to not talk about the faults of anyone
Who has entered the Mahayana is the practice of a
     bodhisattva.

Not only can you consider all other Dharma practitioners as your close relatives, but in many ways all beings are, too. All of them have certainly been your parents in one life or another. What is more, all of them possess the same ultimate nature, the tathagatagarbha or buddha nature. As it is said,

Buddha nature is present in all beings:
Not a single one of them lacks it.

As Gampopa explains at the beginning of *The Precious Ornament of Liberation,* the fact that beings have the buddha nature is the basis that gives them the possibility, when fully actualized, of becoming buddhas. Disparaging any one of them is therefore inappropriate; we should rather all respect one another. As the Buddha said, "An ordinary person cannot assess another ordinary person, only a buddha can."

It is even more important not to criticize all those who are like sons and daughters of the same parents, in that they have taken refuge in the Three Jewels and started out on the path of the Buddha's teachings through confidence in the basic truth of what he taught—for example, that "All that is compounded is impermanent; all that is defiled is suffering; all phenomena are without inherent existence; that which is beyond suffering is peace."[98]

Even more closely related are those of us who have entered the Mahayana. Together, we should be like a thousand princes and princesses of one universal monarch who never feel animosity or contempt for one another, but instead always extol one another's virtues and qualities. Treat one another with great kindness and openness, and above all do not look for one another's mistakes. Once you start finding defects somewhere, you will see them everywhere and in everyone. By proclaiming someone's faults to all and sundry, you are burning yourself and hurting the other person—which can only be wrong. It is the sangha that upholds the teachings; its members must be in harmony, and their discipline perfect. Develop confidence and pure vision. To respect the sangha—all those who have taken monastic vows and all those who have entered the Dharma—is a commitment of the refuge vows. Consider all your brothers and sisters in the Dharma as being free from any faults.

Malicious criticism of other traditions of Dharma, in particular, is a major cause of the Dharma as a whole declining and being corrupted. View all traditions and views as noncontradictory, and as true expressions of the Buddha's teachings. As Panchen Lobsang Yeshe[99] said:

> The various different doctrinal views
> Are all the very teachings of the Victorious One.
> Instead of a blaze of enmity ignited by the demon of
> sectarianism, how much finer

To see everything lit up by the radiant jewel of pure
perception!

Your impure perception of the world can easily falsify the
way you see the actions of bodhisattvas. Indeed, any faults you
may perceive in them are due only to your own imperfections,
just as a white conch may look yellow to someone with jaundice.
Whenever you think you have seen some defect in a bodhisattva's
conduct or thinking, therefore, remind yourself that the problem
is your own distorted perception and that in reality that person
is free of all defects.

You should be aware that every action of enlightened beings,
spiritual masters, and bodhisattvas has a deep meaning that re-
flects their intention to benefit beings. As they manifest in infinite ways to help others, it is easy to mistake bodhisattvas for
ordinary beings. They might seem to be ordinary people engaged
in mundane activities; they may even take the form of wild animals, birds, or dogs. There have also been many bodhisattvas
who manifested as beggars or low-status, rough-looking people
with unsuitable occupations and no obvious good qualities.
Tilopa killed fish, Saraha was an arrow smith, and Shavaripa a
hunter. Anyone you meet, therefore, could actually be a fully ma-
tured bodhisattva who has assumed an ordinary appearance, or
even an offensive one; so you should respect all beings and regard them as teachers.

When you hear the stories of Buddha Shakyamuni's past
lives, you can understand how each time he manifested in a different way it was an expression of his intention to help beings, his
infinite bodhisattva activity. Bodhisattvas are free from all selfish
intentions, and everything they do is the application of skillful
means. In the same way that a drop of mercury that falls in the
dust remains spotlessly clean with nothing adhering to it, so too
bodhisattvas manifest in the world without being contaminated
by it.

To recognize bodhisattvas' perfect goodness, and with confidence and faith to see everything as pure, will ensure that your Dharma practice does not become rotten at the root. Faith is what opens the gate of the teachings wide. Of the seven noble qualities,[100] faith is the most noble of all. With complete confidence and devotion, see the teacher as a real buddha and whatever he does as a manifestation of his perfect wisdom.

The way you behave should be in harmony with the teacher and with all of your Dharma friends. Fitting all your actions smoothly with whatever the others are doing, make sure that your presence is never oppressive or constraining—like a comfortable belt that can be worn all the time without ever being felt. Enter into all situations without creating problems and difficulties—like salt that readily dissolves in any water. Receive teachings and guidance from your teacher without ever creating inconvenience for him, and act toward your spiritual friends in a way that does not trouble them at all—like a swan on a lotus lake, gliding serenely over the water without disturbing it, and navigating between the lotus flowers without any disruption of their delicate arrangement.

Keep your perception pure, considering all that appears to be infinite purity. Then everything will inspire you to practice the Dharma, and everything will be an illustration of the teachings. As Milarepa said:

> The world all around is the best of all books—
> I don't need to read a book in black and white.

For the Vajrayana, faith and pure vision are the two main roots of practice. If you do not have them yet, try to give rise to them. Once you have developed them, try constantly to increase them. As soon as you think or do something that goes against faith and pure vision, be aware of it, confess and counter it right away. Set your own defects right, instead of proclaiming those of others. This will help to preserve the purity of the samaya and maintain harmony within the sangha, performing a great service to the teachings.

After receiving empowerment from a Vajrayana master, you have to remain in harmony with your vajra brothers and sisters, those who entered the same mandala with you, until you all attain enlightenment, just as the wick and flame of a lamp stay alight together until both of them die. To spoil or weaken the samaya, the sacred links you have with other disciples, will obscure your spiritual experiences and realization, and hinder the attainment of all ordinary accomplishments and especially the supreme accomplishment of enlightenment. The antidote is to see the primordial purity of everything. This is the authentic practice of the bodhisattvas.

C. TO GIVE UP ATTACHMENT TO A SPONSOR'S PROPERTY

33

Offerings and respect may bring discord
And cause listening, reflection, and meditation to decline.
Therefore, to avoid attachment
To the homes of friends and benefactors is the practice of a bodhisattva.

By putting all your efforts into the affairs of this life, you could no doubt make yourself tremendously wealthy, amass gold in vast quantities, and reach the very pinnacle of fame and power. Yet even then you would probably be bitterly resentful of anyone even wealthier or more influential than yourself; you would regard with contempt the people you left behind, now your social inferiors, while toward your peers, you would feel competitive and jealous, waiting for any opportunity to get the better of them. Even beggars burn with jealousy when other beggars get the alms.

People get themselves into situations where they no longer even have the time to eat or sleep. You can be so preoccupied trying to achieve your ordinary ends that you become as busy as an ant, constantly out till late at night and up early in the morning—as the holy Physician of Dagpo, Gampopa, put it, "having stars for a hat and hoarfrost for boots."

Finally, however, the net result of all this unending activity is that you turn into someone ready to slide into obsequious hypocrisy, and become no more than a pathetic beggar prepared to face the bites of fierce guard dogs, all for the sake of a scrap of food. As Shantideva says:

> For I am one who strives for freedom;
> I must not be bound by wealth and honors.

And Jetsun Milarepa said:

> Thunder, mighty though its blast, is empty sound;
> Rainbows, superb though their hues, just melt away;
> This world, charming though it seems, is but a
>   dream;
> Pleasures of the senses, great though their joys, cause
>   evil.

Make a clean break from all ordinary activities. Be content with whatever you have and satisfied with whatever happens, day by day. Everything else will then fall naturally into place. As Gyalse Thogme said:

> To feel satisfied with whatever you have, that is the
>   ultimate wealth;
> Not to crave or be attached to anything at all, that is
>   the ultimate happiness.

When you practice Dharma, to begin with you may experience hardships. But later, those sufferings give way to great happiness and serenity. With worldly activities, however, it is just the opposite. To begin with, they seem to bring happiness. But later, they deteriorate into suffering—for such is their nature. To keep making the right choice in this matter is the practice of the bodhisattvas.

D. To give up harsh speech

34

Harsh words disturb the minds of others
And spoil our own bodhisattva practice.
Therefore, to give up rough speech,
Which others find unpleasant, is the practice of a
bodhisattva.

Now you have given rise to the idea of attaining enlightenment for the sake of others. From now on, therefore, you should never say things that hurt others—words that upset their feelings and are bound to lead to anger. Instead, you should only say kind and gentle words that will encourage them.

Most of the wars that devastate the world are started by harsh words. Quarrels, rancorous resentment, and endlessly perpetuated feuds all arise because tolerance and patience are lacking.

As Nagarjuna says in his *Letter to a Friend,* the words people speak are of three kinds, which the Buddha described as being like honey, like flowers, and like excrement. Words that help and please are like honey. Words that are honest and true are like flowers. But violent, harmful words and falsehoods are like excrement, and must be abandoned.

Kharak Gomchung says:

Stop shooting the poisoned arrows of harsh
speech,
And give up your ill-natured aggression.

If you allow unkind words to spew out of your mouth, you will upset not only other people's minds but your own mind, too. At such moments, the bodhisattva's way is lost. Those who divulge other people's failings, loudly proclaiming them everywhere, or disparage teachers and other spiritual lineages, are only building themselves a mountain of negativity.

The way a bodhisattva uses speech, in contrast, is to bring people onto the path of liberation. He or she would start by saying things and telling stories that open people's minds by making them happy, and then gradually and skillfully introduce to them the meaning of Dharma. The Buddha taught beings in ways that matched their differing capacities and degree of receptivity. Those with lesser capacity he instructed in the teachings of the Basic Vehicle, stressing the need to give up all ordinary activities focused on this life, to go forth from home to homelessness,[101] and to live in secluded places. Those with greater capacity he instructed in the vast and profound teachings of the Great Vehicle, explaining how to be generous, keep discipline, and be patient; how to start by renouncing all worldly affairs, entrust oneself to the guidance of a teacher, and practice his instructions one-pointedly in solitary retreat. He taught them how to sustain their determination by reflecting on the futility of the eight ordinary preoccupations,[102] and how to permeate their practice with bodhichitta by giving rise to a truly altruistic attitude and directing to the benefit of others everything they think and do.

III. Training in how to be rid of the negative emotions

35

When emotions become habitual, they are hard to
get rid of with antidotes.
Therefore, with mindfulness and vigilance, to seize
the weapon of the antidote

And crush attachment and other negative emotions
The moment they arise is the practice of a
    bodhisattva.

Whatever practice you are doing, it has to work as an effective antidote to your negative emotions and to your belief in substantial existence.

Now, any emotion can only begin as a tiny thought or feeling, which then grows stronger and stronger. If you can recognize that thought the very moment it first arises, it will be easy to let it subside again. An emotion recognized at that stage is like a small wisp of cloud in a clear and empty sky, which is not going to produce any rain.

If, on the other hand, you remain unaware of such thoughts and let them expand and multiply, there will soon be such a rapid succession of thoughts and feelings, each one adding to the one before, that you will find it increasingly hard not only to break the buildup of that emotion but also to hold back from the negative actions it is liable to induce. As *The Ornament of the Mahayana Sutras* warns, "The emotions destroy oneself, destroy others, and destroy discipline."

At the end of the chapter on carefulness in *The Way of the Bodhisattva*, Shantideva likens the negative emotions to enemies who must be repulsed and routed. But, he points out, unlike ordinary, human enemies, they do not have anywhere to retreat to. You get rid of them simply by recognizing them for what they are: "Miserable afflictions, scattered by the eye of wisdom!"

In the struggle against the emotions, if you lose your vigilance even for a moment, you have to revive it at once—in the same way that a swordsman in battle who lets slip his sword must pick it up again immediately. The very instant an emotion arises, the thought of using the antidote should occur to you. What else is the Dharma for, if it is not to stop you giving full vent to your negative emotions? As Drom Tönpa said,

Whatever works to counteract emotions, it is
    Dharma;
Whatever does not work is not Dharma.

Indeed, there is no time to waste. If you had been shot at with a poisoned arrow, would you just wait with it sticking in your flesh, or would you immediately set about extracting it and making the wound bleed?

As Shantideva also said:

Wandering where it will, the elephant of mind
Will bring us down to pains of deepest hell.
No worldly beast, however wild and crazed,
Could bring upon us such calamities.

But if, with mindfulness's rope,
The elephant of the mind is tied on every side,
All fears will come to nothing,
And every virtue drop into our hands.

When Yeshe Tsogyal asked Guru Rinpoche, "Who is the worst enemy?" he said, "Obscuring emotions."

Gyalse Thogme concludes:

Train yourself to control the three poisonous
    thoughts between sessions.
Until all thoughts and appearances arise as the
    dharmakaya,
There is no way to do without that training.
    Remember whenever you need it,
And never give deluded thoughts free rein, you
    Mani-reciters.

Always stay alert, therefore, and watch what your mind is doing. Think about it. Over countless lifetimes, have you not been deluded, fallen under the power of your negative emotions, and as a result had to undergo—time and time again—the sufferings of birth, sickness, old age, and death? Yet still you cling to samsara as if it were a happy place. You take things that are impermanent to be permanent. You work frantically to amass possessions you will never be able to keep, without ever being satisfied. Surely now it is high time to start observing your mind.

Be aware of everything that arises in your mind immediately, as though watching your face in a mirror. Identify your emotions as the enemies that have spoiled your past lives, and will spoil your future lives, too, if you fail to cut them at the root as soon as they appear. There is no emotion that you cannot be rid of, because emotions are simply thoughts, and thoughts are just like the wind moving through the empty sky. There is nothing to them.

However, in just the same way that someone who attains a high position may find that his worries and difficulties increase, so too, when you set yourself the ambitious goal of getting free from samsara, you may find that your thoughts and habitual tendencies seem even stronger and more numerous than before. If you fall immediately under their power, your practice will be interrupted. It may stagnate, to the point that you end up as an old hermit only interested in making money. Or you could stray into an intellectual approach, endlessly acquiring more and more knowledge. But if you can manage to overcome your wild emotions by concentrating on sustained calm and profound insight, you are sure to make steady progress on the path.

When your mind is distracted, you can be bitten by a mosquito without your even noticing it. But when your mind is quiet, you will feel a mosquito bite straight away. In the same way, the mind needs to be relaxed and quietened if it is to become aware of its empty nature. The practice of shamatha is done for this reason, and through such practice even a person with strong emotions will gradually acquire self-control and inner calm. When the mind comes to a stable state of relaxed concentration, your habitual tendencies fade away by themselves, while altruism and compassion naturally develop and expand. Eventually, you will come to a state of ease in the unceasing flow of the absolute nature.

Why are all of us beings wandering in samsara? As Chandrakirti said:

> Beings think "I" at first, and cling to self;
> They think of "mine" and are attached to things.
> They thus turn helplessly as buckets on a
>   waterwheel,
> And to compassion for such beings I bow down.[103]

The buddha nature, tathagatagarbha, is present in all of us, but we fail to recognize it, instead mistakenly taking what arises through its natural power of manifestation—the universe and its six realms (place), the various physical forms of the beings in those realms (body), and the eight consciousnesses (mind)—to be things outside and separate from ourselves. This dualistic perception is responsible for the split between self and others, from which arises the tendency we all have to cherish ourselves and to consider others much less important than we are. The root of all this is ignorance, the false belief in an "I." If your mistaken belief in a self disappeared, so too would the whole idea of "other." You would realize the essential sameness of self and other.

The separation of everything into yourself and others is how the entire play of attachment and aversion begins. "Others" can only be conceived in relation to yourself. Without the idea that there is an "I," how could the notion of "other" arise? When you recognize the empty nature of "I," you simultaneously recognize the empty nature of "other." When ignorance disappears, so too does the distinction between self and other. You stop treating people as adversaries to be overcome, and perceive friends and relatives as dreamlike magical illusions.

Be aware of whatever negative tendency may be contained in your thoughts as they arise, and apply the appropriate antidote.

For instance, if you are thinking of someone and the idea of this being an "enemy" arises, do not let any hatred develop. Instead, generate great love for that person as though he or she were your dearest friend. If attachment arises, view the person as an illusion, and remember that whatever comes together is bound to separate. When you let attachment subside, there will be no habitual tendencies or karmic seeds to accumulate for future lives. By trying to classify the infinitude of living beings into friends and enemies, you will only overload your mind. Instead, simplify everything and see everyone as your kind parents.

Only an omniscient buddha could know how long ago it was that you fell into the delusion of samsara, in which you have spent an incalculable number of lives. All beings must have been your parents in one life or another. Realizing this, feel a deep, impartial love for them all.

IV. Training in accomplishing others' good with mindfulness and vigilance

36

In short, wherever I am, whatever I do,
To be continually mindful and alert,
Asking, "What is the state of my mind?"
And accomplishing the good of others is the practice
     of a bodhisattva.

Every day, check to what extent you are applying the teachings, how often you are managing to control your mind, and how many times you are falling under the power of negative emotions. Examining your own progress in this way will help you to decrease your clinging to the ordinary concerns of this life, and to increase your confidence in the teachings.

Now, for once, you know exactly where the authentic path lies. It will take you without fail to enlightenment, as long as you make the right choices and do not mistake priceless jewels for ordinary stones. Right now is the time to practice Dharma, while you are free from physical illness and mental torments.

What do we mean by *Dharma*? The Tibetan word for Dharma, *chö*, means both "to repair all defects" and "to bring into being all positive qualities." The Sanskrit word *Dharma* means "to hold," implying that once you have made a connection with the Dharma, it will unfailingly take you from the depths of samsara to enlightenment—just as a fish once caught on the hook is sure not to be staying in the water for long. This is not an ordinary connection, but a very profound one.

Here, we come to the conclusion of the text, *The Thirty-seven Verses on the Practice of a Bodhisattva*. Its essence, in summary, is that whatever actions and whatever Dharma practice you do with body, speech, and mind, you should do them with the intention of benefiting the infinity of sentient beings. If your intentions are purely altruistic, without any self-clinging, perfection will naturally arise.

The way this pure, altruistic intention—the bodhichitta—is cultivated is analogous to cultivating a crop by plowing the soil and making it fertile. First you need the intention to attain enlightenment for the sake of all beings, which you can then bring to maturity by putting these thirty-seven precepts into practice. To be of real help to others may be beyond your capacities at present, but you should constantly keep in mind your aim to help them. As Langri Thangpa said, "In the Mahayana, there is nothing else to do but benefit beings. So don't let your armor of helping others be too small."

The essence of the practice of a bodhisattva is to transcend self-clinging and dedicate yourself completely to serving others. It is a practice based on your mind, rather than on how your actions might appear externally. True generosity, therefore, is to have no clinging; true discipline is to have no desire; and true patience is to be without hatred. That bodhisattvas can even give away their kingdom, their life, or their spouse and children is because they do not have the slightest inner feeling of poverty or need, and are ready to fulfill others' needs unconditionally. It does not matter how your actions might seem to anyone else—no particular "compassionate" appearance is necessary. What you do need is a pure mind. For instance, sweet and pleasing words spoken without any intention of helping others are meaningless. Even birds can sing beautiful songs. Wild animals such as tigers behave in a loving way to their cubs, but theirs is a partial love mixed with attachment. It does not extend to all beings. A bodhisattva possesses impartial love for all beings.

You might teach the Dharma to hundreds of thousands of students, and do thousands of spiritual practices and meritorious acts, but if self-clinging is still your mind's most firmly rooted theme, your activity will never be that of a bodhisattva. To be a bodhisattva and to carry out a bodhisattva's activity, you must uproot all trace of selfishness from within.

Outwardly, most of the great siddhas of India looked like unimpressive beggars. Their lives were not filled with conspicuous deeds of grandiose charity. But inwardly they had realized emptiness, and their minds were constantly overflowing with love and compassion for all beings. In Tibet, too, Jetsun Milarepa was the same. He never made grand offerings or performed a lot of meritorious deeds for everyone to see. Yet Milarepa is considered foremost among all the enlightened yogis of India and Tibet, and has been able to turn the minds of countless beings all over the world toward the Dharma because he completely cast off all self-clinging and realized emptiness.

If you remain unable to master your own mind, to have studied many scriptures and to have met many spiritual masters will be of no real help to you. You run the risk of becoming like the monk Good Star, who was exceedingly learned but ended up finding fault with the Buddha himself.[104]

What matters most is the strength of your compassion.

There was once an eminent lama of Lhasa who used to make a daily offering of water torma for the hungry ghosts, using beautiful vessels made of solid gold. One day, he was late making his offering, and some of the spirits appeared before him. They urged him to make haste. The lama asked them why they were in such a hurry, and the spirits replied that they wanted to go to receive Kharak Gomchung's water torma offering, as his was more satisfying than any other. Were they to miss it, they feared, they would have to starve.

The lama wanted to know more about this Kharak Gomchung, and made some inquiries. He discovered that he was a humble hermit living in a cave at Tsang Kharak.[105] Apparently, when Kharak Gomchung offered his water torma, he used half a walnut shell as the container, and put only a few grains in it. The water for the offering came from the tears of compassion that fell from his eyes. Because his compassion was limitless, all the spirits of Tibet came to receive his offering.

Everything depends on your intention. All the time, therefore, check your attitude and motivation. As Patrul Rinpoche said, everyone wants happiness, but the true way to reach perfect happiness yourself is to bring happiness to others.

V. Dedicating the merit to perfect enlightenment

37

Dedicating to enlightenment
Through wisdom purified of the three concepts
All merit achieved by such endeavor,
To remove the suffering of numberless beings, is the
    practice of a bodhisattva.

There are three sections to the teachings: a virtuous beginning, which is the arousing of relative and absolute bodhichitta; a virtuous middle, which concerns the illusory accumulation of merit and wisdom; and a virtuous end, which is the dedication of all merit to enlightenment. Dedication seals the practice, and enhances its benefits and results. As the *Ratnakuta Sutra* says:

> All phenomena are caused by circumstance,
> And so our destiny is determined by what we
> wish for.
> Depending on the aspirations that we make
> We shall obtain results that correspond.

Right dedication is to dedicate your meritorious actions of body, speech, and mind to the enlightenment of all beings, beginning with those who have harmed you and created obstacles for you.

If you share with all beings the merit of a practice or positive action, that merit will last until you reach enlightenment, just as a drop of water that you put into the ocean will never dry up for as long as the ocean remains. But if you neglect to share the merit, it is like pouring a drop of water on a hot stone—it evaporates right away. Or it is like a seed that bears fruit once and then dies. If you fail to seal your merit with authentic dedication, then however vast the offerings and positive actions you have performed may be, their results can only be ephemeral, and vulnerable to the destructive effects of your negative emotions, such as anger, pride, and jealousy.

It is also important to dedicate your merit to the right goal, and not just to the petty achievements of this life, such as wealth, good health, success, and influence. Your true goal should be total, unsurpassable enlightenment for the sake of others.

To dedicate merit in the best possible way—a way entirely free from the three concepts of a subject, an object, and an action—is possible only for someone who has fully realized emptiness. How, then, should we ordinary beings dedicate the merit, incapable as we are of such perfect dedication? We can do it by following in the footsteps of those who have that realization. The bodhisattva Samantabhadra mastered the ocean-like infinitude of a bodhisattva's aspirations, while Mañjushri and Avalokiteshvara mastered the oceanlike infinitude of a bodhisattva's activity to benefit beings. When you dedicate merit, do it with the idea of emulating the way these great bodhisattvas dedicated merit, and use the perfect verses spoken by the Buddha or his followers who realized the ultimate, empty nature of everything. It gives your prayers much more power and efficacy. Use *The King of Aspirations for Excellent Conduct*, or extracts from it, such as:

> Just as fearless Mañjushri did to attain omniscience,
> And in the same way that Samantabhadra, likewise,
>   did too,
> Just so, to follow all of them and train myself,
> I perfectly dedicate these meritorious actions.

Or this prayer, spoken by Lama Mipham:[106]

> By the power of omniscience, love, and prayers
>   arisen
> From the enlightened hearts of the sugatas,
> May we all realize
> The magical transformation of the guru's wisdom.

Or:

> By the blessings of the attainment of the Three
>   Bodies of the Buddha,
> By the blessings of the unchanging truth of the
>   dharmata,
> And by the blessings of the intentions of the
>   undivided Sangha,
> May all my aspirations, just as made while
>   dedicating now, in future come to be.

And:

> When, stricken by impermanence,
> They cross to the next existence,
> May I lead all beings in general
> And all those who have been connected to me
> In a positive or negative way.
>
> May I guide them efficiently,
> May I cut the stream of their suffering,
> May I ferry them across the four rivers.[107]
> May they soon obtain unsurpassable enlightenment!

And:

> Throughout all of our lives, may we never separate
>   from the perfect Teacher;
> May we avail ourselves of all the beneficial glory of
>   the Dharma.
> Fully perfecting the qualities of the paths and
>   bhumis,
> May we swiftly reach the very level of Vajradhara.

Actions done with neither pride nor regret, and then dedicated correctly, bear an unhindered energy that enables us to progress quickly toward enlightenment.

Concluding Verses

1. How and for whom this text was composed

> Following the teachings of the holy beings,
> I have arranged the points taught in the sutras,
>   tantras, and shastras
> As *The Thirty-seven Verses on the Practice of a
>   Bodhisattva*
> For the benefit of those who wish to train on the
>   bodhisattva path.

To write an authentic *shastra* or treatise, tradition requires the author to possess at least one of three qualifications. At best, he should have fully realized the absolute nature. If not, he should have been blessed by a vision of his yidam deity. At least, he must be thoroughly learned in all five branches of learning.[108]

Nagarjuna and Asanga, the two great panditas of India, are examples of the first type of author with a thorough understanding of absolute truth. The great bodhisattva Shantideva had a vision of Mañjushri in which he met him as if in person, and through the blessings he thus received, Shantideva attained a direct understanding of all the essential points of the teachings; he is an example of the second type of author. Most of the great panditas of India and Tibet were thoroughly versed in the five branches of learning and had a perfect knowledge of both the words and the meaning of the Buddha's teachings. They therefore belong to the third category of authors.

No text by a writer without any of these three prerequisites, composed according to his own inclinations, can be an authentic shastra. A true shastra should act as a remedy for the negative emotions and protect beings from falling into the lower realms of existence. Texts from outside the authentic tradition do not possess these qualities. The literal meaning of *shastra* is "that which explains the meaning of the Buddha's words and remedies ignorance." A shastra should enable those who study it and meditate on it to free themselves from confusion and to establish themselves firmly on the path to liberation and enlightenment. A shastra is, therefore, a manifestation of compassion.

Gyalse Ngulchu Thogme, author of *The Thirty-seven Verses on the Practice of a Bodhisattva*, possessed all these qualifications. He had immense knowledge and was blessed by numerous visions of wisdom deities. His very being was saturated with compassion, for indeed he was an emanation of Avalokiteshvara. The great Sakya master Jetsun Trakpa Gyaltsen,[109] who was his contemporary, used to say to his students, "You probably think of Avalokiteshvara as a deity residing far away in the buddhafield of the Potala Mountain. But anyone who receives teachings on the bodhichitta from Ngulchu Thogme is meeting Avalokiteshvara in person."

Countless commentaries and explanations of the bodhisattva path have been contributed by such masters as the "Six Ornaments of India" and the "Two Supreme Ones,"[110] as well as by all the learned and accomplished masters of Tibet, yet in our times no one has the capacity to assimilate all those teachings. People today have little true intelligence, and their endeavor is weak. Moreover, very few see the Dharma as the most important thing in life. Realizing this, Gyalse Ngulchu Thogme extracted the very essence of all the teachings on bodhichitta, as if churning butter from milk, and wrote it down in the form of this text. He organized it in a way that is easy to understand and yet still conveys the entire meaning with no risk of mistakes being made. It is a text that can be practiced by anyone.

The Thirty-seven Verses on the Practice of a Bodhisattva is the most direct and profound Mahayana teaching on attaining enlightenment. Gyalse Ngulchu Thogme wrote it not because he hoped for fame or recognition but out of sheer love and compassion. That is why these teachings have been able to help countless beings down through the centuries. They are the very words of Avalokiteshvara in human form. If you practice according to these precepts, all concern for yourself will be dispelled and you will find it easy to turn all your efforts toward benefiting others.

Aspirations bring their own results. A strong enough wish to accomplish some goal will probably be realized. If you direct all your efforts into becoming rich and famous, you may manage to achieve that goal—while if, instead, you strive hard through study and meditation to understand and accomplish the sublime goals of the spiritual path, you will eventually succeed. Like a boatman steering his boat, use your own mind to take your life in the direction you choose.

2. The unerring nature of these practices

The best teaching for you is whichever one works for you, and matches your level of realization. The teachings of Madhyamika, Mahamudra, and Ati Yoga are very profound indeed, and buddhahood can be attained in a single lifetime by meditating upon emptiness in the way they explain. But they are beyond the reach of ordinary beings like us. It is pointless to give rice and meat to a newborn baby instead of his mother's milk. For a start, he cannot chew such foods; and then, even if he does manage to swallow a little, he completely lacks the capacity to digest them.

The teachings you most need are teachings that will actually bring benefit and inspiration to your practice. You may receive teachings that are as high as the sky—but the sky is hard to reach and catch just with ordinary hands. On the other hand, by starting with practices you can truly assimilate, developing more and more love and compassion, and letting go of ordinary, worldly concerns, you will gradually gain stability until, in the end, you will be able to master the higher teachings, too.

Never think that training the mind is just a low-level practice. Mind training is a teaching tailored to our minds by the Buddha himself. Start by having a good heart, and reinforce it with compassion. Develop relative bodhichitta, the determination to achieve enlightenment in order to be able to benefit all beings, infinite as they are. That will lead you to absolute bodhichitta, the recognition and realization of ultimate primordial awareness.

Bodhichitta opens the door to whatever practice you do. It is the skillful means by which you can make progress on the path of liberation, and it is the indispensable catalyst that enables you to harvest the fruit. Bodhichitta should be the very heart, core, and life force of your practice.

When you practice, use Jamgön Kongtrul Rinpoche's commentary on the *Seven-Point Mind Training*, too. These commentaries describe a practice suitable for everyone, whatever their capacities. Unlike the practices of the development and completion stages of the Mantrayana, in which there are many ways that you could go wrong, the practice of mind training described in this text is without risk.

That is why Gyalse Thogme adds:

> Since my understanding is poor, and I have little
>   education,
> This is no composition to delight the learned;
> But as it is based on the sutras and teachings of holy
>   beings
> I think it is genuinely the practice of the
>   bodhisattvas.

3. A humble prayer for forgiveness

Great bodhisattvas always try to conceal their own infinite qualities, and will praise others' qualities, however insignificant. They never think proudly about what great learning or realization they possess, instead hiding their excellence like a treasure buried underground. Just as the branches of a tree laden with fruit bend low, so, too, the sage filled with good qualities and knowledge keeps to the very humblest position. An example of this attitude is found at the beginning of Shantideva's *The Way of the Bodhisattva:*

> What I have to say has all been said before,
> And I am destitute of learning and of skill with
>   words.
> I therefore have no thought that this might be of
>   benefit to others;
> I wrote it only to sustain my understanding.

Gyalse Thogme, too, therefore, expresses his humility and confesses any mistakes he may have made:

However, it is hard for someone unintelligent
like me
To fathom the great waves of the bodhisattvas'
activities,
So I beg the forgiveness of the holy ones
For my contradictions, irrelevances, and other
mistakes.

The Bhagavan, Buddha Shakyamuni, turned the wheel of Dharma in three stages. The first was in Varanasi, when he taught the Four Noble Truths; the second was in Rajgriha, when he taught the Dharma free from characteristics; and the third was at several different places and times when he taught the ultimate truth. He thus laid out the path to enlightenment in an inconceivably vast and profound way.

Here, Ngulchu Thogme has the intention to present the essence of all these teachings. But, feeling in his humility that he has not reached the ultimate point of all knowledge, reflection, and meditation, he requests all the learned and accomplished masters of the Eight Great Chariots of Transmission,[111] the Ten Great Pillars Who Supported the Explanatory Lineages,[112] and others to forgive any imperfections, irrelevances, or mistakes that could have occurred in his exposition of *The Thirty-seven Verses on the Practice of a Bodhisattva.*

4. Dedicating the merit of having composed this text

Through the merit arising from this
And through the power of the sublime bodhichitta,
relative and absolute,
May all beings become like the Lord
Avalokiteshvara,
Who is beyond the extremes of samsara and
nirvana.

So that both relative and absolute aspects of bodhichitta may flourish in the minds and actions of all beings, Gyalse Ngulchu Thogme now dedicates, with a pure mind permeated with compassion, whatever merit has been generated in composing this text.

He wishes that all beings may achieve enlightenment, both for their own sake and for the sake of others. The aspect of enlightenment he wishes for beings' own sake, through wisdom, will free them from falling into the extreme of samsara; while the aspect of enlightenment he wishes for the sake of others, through compassion, will free them from falling into the extreme of nirvana. He wishes that beings may be able to work tirelessly for the benefit of all living creatures, by manifesting in whatever form—ordinary beings, arhats, bodhisattvas, buddhas—would be beneficial to every single one of them.

The dedication is a sincere prayer that all beings may achieve Avalokiteshvara's level and that they may benefit all living beings just as he does. Avalokiteshvara is the source, or "father" of all the buddhas of this fortunate kalpa. From his thousand and two eyes emanated the thousand and two buddhas of our aeon; from his thousand and two arms emanated the thousand and two universal monarchs. In each pore of his body are countless buddhafields; and in each of those buddhafields, emanations of Avalokiteshvara teach the Mahayana to countless bodhisattvas and set beings on the path of liberation. On the absolute level, Avalokiteshvara is the nature of the vajra speech of all the Tathagatas, and possesses the five bodies and wisdoms of a fully enlightened buddha. On the relative level, he appears as a tenth-bhumi bodhisattva to beings within the realm of his compassionate activity.

5. The colophon

For his own benefit and that of others, Thogme, a teacher of scripture and logic, composed this text at Rinchen Phug, in Ngulchu.

The text was written by the great saint Gyalse Ngulchu Thogme in his hermitage, Rinchen Phug, "the Jewel Cave," which is in Ngulchu, central Tibet. The name Thogme means "unobstructed," and indeed his learning and insight regarding the most profound aspects of theory and practice knew no boundary or hindrance whatsoever.

FINAL ADVICE

Reflect deeply upon these precepts. Put them into practice in your everyday thoughts, words, and actions. You may not be able to integrate these precepts truly into your mind at the very beginning, but if you persevere, the stubborn clinging you have had, for countless lives, to the apparent solidity of the phenomenal world and to the permanence of things will gradually dissolve. Yangönpa said:

> Old bad habits keep recurring, as a roll of paper
> keeps on rolling up again,
> While new experiences are easily destroyed by
> circumstances.
> You won't cut through delusion in a short time—
> All you "great meditators," keep on meditating for a
> long time!

If you practice the Dharma you should never give up, from the beginning to the ultimate fruit. You should become determined to practice until you drop dead. As Milarepa said, "Do not hope for any result, but practice sincerely until your death."

Entrust yourself to the practice wholeheartedly and give up samsaric activities as much as is humanly possible. As you begin to see the positive quality of the Dharma germinate within you, your endeavor and determination to practice will blaze like fire.

You should realize how extremely rare it is for the Dharma to appear in this universe, and how precious it is to have the opportunity to hear it and reflect upon it. To hear even a single word of teachings—even the sound of a gong calling the sangha to assemble—can free you from falling into the lower realms. As the great sage Patrul Rinpoche said, "In this dark age, just to hear, understand, or explain four lines of the Dharma can be called the Dharma of transmission, and to meditate on sustained calm and profound insight for one day can be called the Dharma of realization."[113]

All these teachings are offered to you like a flower-covered meadow offered to the bees. Everything is now in your hands. You have everything you need to practice and to achieve enlightenment. Do not waste even a day. If you practice, relying upon a spiritual master and following his words exactly, your confidence in the truth of the teachings will grow daily, and within your lifetime you can achieve the supreme level of Vajradhara.

All the great enlightened beings were once ordinary individuals who became buddhas through their own endeavor. Endeavor is the quality you need most. As the Buddha said, "I have shown you the path. It is up to you to achieve liberation."

The Buddha is not going to project you to buddhahood, as if throwing a stone. He is not going to purify you, as if washing a dirty cloth. Nor is he going to cure you of ignorance, like a doctor administering medicine to a passive patient. Having attained full enlightenment himself, he is showing you the path, and it is up to you to follow it or not. It is up to you now to practice these teachings and experience their results.

May this text bring great benefit to all beings, and point out the essential unity of all the teachings of the Buddha!

Appendix 1

Supplementary Commentaries on the Spiritual Teacher (Verse 6)

A. The right and the wrong teacher
The following excerpts are from The Vase of Amrita
(2) by Dzatrul Ngawang Tendzin Norbu (folio 19 et
seq.)

The wrong teacher

The *Inner Tantra* (*nang rgyud*) says:

> Ignorant and proud,
> Lacking in intelligence, he teaches mere words;
> He cuts down others with disparaging statements;
> With little learning and a lot of arrogance
> He is a true evil for the disciple who fails to
>   recognize such a teacher.

Such a teacher does not have even a single one of the many good qualities that are born from listening and meditating. Nevertheless, because he belongs to a good family, he claims, "I am the son of so and so," and, like a Brahman, conceitedly wraps himself in his noble ancestry. Although he is no different from any ordinary person, he acts as if he were on the same footing as the great siddhas of the past. When he has done a little study and practice, he puffs up with self-infatuation as soon as others show him some marks of respect. He is so full of pride, so stupid and arrogant, that he cannot see the qualities of great beings. He is irascible and jealous, and the cord of love and compassion in him is broken.

If you, faithful one, meet and follow such a mistaken teacher, it is just as if you were shown the road by a mad guide. Your entire life of virtuous actions will be wasted. Seeking his protection is like wanting to take rest under the cool shadow of a tree that turns out to be a huge venomous snake.

The right teacher

With vast learning in the sutras, tantras, and commentaries, he is aware of the crucial points of the three vows. Having discarded all the veils of ignorance and realized all that is to be realized, he has the ability to cut through doubts and misconceptions with his sharp wisdom. His mind is imbued with love and compassion for others, like a mother for her only child. He can thus be followed and relied upon. He knows and can teach both the way samsara arises through confusing emotions and the way nirvana is attained through total purification.

He gathers fortunate disciples in four ways: through giving presents, speaking gently, teaching in accordance with the disciple's faculties, and behaving in accord with what he teaches.

Remaining near him, you will acquire his good qualities, just as logs of ordinary wood acquire a wonderful fragrance by remaining for years in a forest of sandalwood trees.

How to follow a qualified teacher

Although, in order to skillfully train ordinary people, he may appear to be and to act in tune with them, his mind is perpetually in the state of buddhahood, utterly beyond that of ordinary beings. Whatever he does is perfectly adapted to his disciples' natures and needs. He is able to bear all ill treatment that may be shown him in return for his kindness, as well as all saddening events, with a patience like that of a mother for her only child.

Therefore, have constant faith in him, see him as the Buddha in person, and perceive the perfection of all that he does and the truth of all that he says.

With fervor, prostrate to him and circumambulate the place where he lives. Speak to him with a mind filled with devotion, and gaze upon him insatiably—since such teachers are so rare, and so difficult to meet and to see.

How to behave in his presence

If he enters the room or gets up from his seat, you should get up also, unless you are sick and unable to do so. When meeting him, inquire about his well-being and present him with all that he needs. Do not be noisy, do not gesticulate, frown, look him fixedly in the eye, tell lies, slander, sit arrogantly in full lotus posture or laxly with your legs stretched out before you, crack your joints, wear hats, or hold weapons or sticks. Never step over his seat or his clothes, never use his personal objects, or ride his horse. If you accompany him, do not walk in front of him unless there is a danger or you need to show the way; do not walk on his right, the side of honor; do not walk immediately behind him, stepping upon his footsteps and his shadow, but walk slightly behind on his left side.

> B. A practice of Guru Yoga
> *This Guru Yoga, which is specifically connected to the practice of bodhichitta, can be found in volume 4 of the* Treasury of Spiritual Instructions (gdams ngag mdzod) *collected by Jamgön Kongtrul Lodrö Thaye.*

In general, for the Basic Vehicle as for the higher ones, the crucial necessity of following a teacher is always stressed. As it is said in the *Gandavyuha Sutra*:

Throughout countless lives,
We were unable to sail across the ocean of suffering.
Even though we possessed many qualities—
Without a spiritual master
We did not gain freedom from samsaric existence.

You may possess great worldly qualities, and as a Dharma practitioner you may have many spiritual qualities, such as consummate faith and endeavor, but unless you follow a master who blesses you, realization will not be born in your mindstream. If realization is not born, there is no way to attain liberation from samsara.

You therefore need to follow an authentic master, a master who holds the lineage and is himself realized. An authentic master is someone who has received the transmission of bodhichitta through an unbroken lineage from the Buddha to himself, like the lineage that came down through the Kadampa masters, the followers of Lord Atisha.

You should also know how to serve such a master. You must truly accomplish whatever he says, through your actions and in your words and thoughts. Pray to him constantly with great fervor, meditating on him at the center of your heart or above your head. For this there are three parts: the preparation, the main practice, and the conclusion.

As preparation, generate love, compassion, and the mind set on enlightenment. Then, visualize yourself, appearing yet empty, like an image in a mirror. Your heart is a brilliant mass of light.

For the main practice, visualize a lotus and moon disk above the crown of your head, on which sits the master to whom you have the strongest devotion. He is either his natural size or the size of a thumb—whichever you find the easiest to visualize.

Remember his face, his expressions, the way he sits and moves, the tone of his voice, and the wisdom of his mind. See him as indistinguishable and inseparable from all the masters of the lineage up to the Buddha himself, from all the teachers from whom you have received instructions, and from all the yidams, buddhas, and bodhisattvas. Offer whatever you can to him and, with folded hands, go for refuge as much as you are able, in his body, speech, and mind. Remember that the guru is free of all defects and has perfected all good qualities. Although in absolute truth he is as substanceless as the sky, he takes appearance in the realm of form for the sake of us all. Pray to him as follows:

"Bless me so that the bodhichitta in its two aspects may take birth in me right now, just as it took birth in the minds of the precious spiritual teachers of the lineage, just as it dwells in the wisdom mind of the buddhas and bodhisattvas, and just as it is described in the sutras of the ultimate direct meaning.

"Bless me so that whether I meet prosperity or ruin, renown or infamy, happiness or suffering, whether I am sick, dying, transmigrating, or being reborn, I may actualize the two kinds of bodhichitta. Bless me that I may know how to use all difficulties and obstacles as friends along this path!"

Having said this prayer three times, place your two hands one upon the other in the mudra of equanimity in your lap, and consider that the aperture at the crown of your head opens wide. The teacher shoots down through it like a shooting star and, descending, comes to dwell in the depth of your heart.

Then meditate one-pointedly without distraction, with utter faith and devotion, thinking that the teacher is the Buddha himself. After a while, the body, speech, and mind of the teacher merge totally with your body, speech, and mind, and you yourself melt into light. Remain for some time in that radiantly clear, skylike state.

To conclude, when you arise from that state, visualize the teacher as before, in the center of your heart or above your head, and dedicate all your merits, past, present, and future, to fulfilling the teacher's wisdom intention and to the blossoming of the two kinds of bodhichitta.

There are boundless ordinary and extraordinary benefits to this meditation. To mention a few of them, you will not be harmed by either human or nonhuman beings, you will attain all worldly and supramundane perfections, and you will actualize all instructions and teachings.

The two stages of this meditation will accomplish the transfer of consciousness into great luminosity and thus serve as the essential instruction needed at the time of death. If you persevere with this meditation, you will achieve whatever spiritual realization you aspire to.

There is no need to look for any other meditation than this. Za Rinpoche Chilbupa[114] said about this meditation, "If I take my living heart from my chest, I have only one to show; likewise this practice is the quintessential one."

This was written from the Teacher's own words. It was transmitted by the Buddha to the sublime Maitreya, and from him successively to Asanga, Vasubhandu, the Elder Kusulu, the Younger Kusulu, Serlingpa, Lord Atisha, Drom Tönpa, Potowa, Sharawa, Chekawa, Chilbupa, Lopon Lha, Lhading Pön, Dharma Siddha, Gyatön Changchup Gyaltsen, Khenpo Shonnu Changchup, Rinchen Jungne Pal Sangpo (1187–1254), Buddha Ratna (Sangye Rinchen), Kirti Shila (Trakpa Tsultrim), Jaya Bhadra (Gyalwa Sangpo), and Punye Ratna (Sönam Rinchen, 1214–86). May it be auspicious!

Appendix 2

Supplementary Commentary
on Desire (Verse 21)

The Dangers of Meat, Alcohol, and Sex
The following is an abridged translation from The
Vase of Amrita *(2) by Dzatrul Ngawang Tendzin*
Norbu, of a long description of the dangers of alcohol,
meat, and sex in the commentary to verse 21

The Buddha said that alcohol is the ax that cuts the life of spiritual practice. Some people say that drinking is forbidden in the sutras but allowed in the tantras. Yet the *Tantra of the Purification of the Lower Realms* (*ngan song sbyong ba'i rgyud*) states, "Do not drink intoxicating beverages, do not eat meat." And the *Adamantine Peak Tantra* (*rdo rje rtse mo*) says, "Alcohol is the root of all devastation, give it up!"

To those who think that the scriptures say that beer and meat must accompany a *ganachakra* feast offering, the answer is given in the *Kalachakra Tantra* (*dus kyi 'khor lo'i rgyud*): "Alcohol is to be offered as the sacramental substance of the Speech Family, but intoxicants are not to be taken by practitioners of the Mantrayana." And Drom Tönpa said, "Alcohol taken to the point of drunkenness is not a samaya substance."

Some of the great siddhas of the past who drank alcohol no longer had ordinary thoughts, and perceived all phenomena as deities. They had fully realized the two truths and could transform ordinary water into beer and poison into medicine. Trying to imitate them would be like a fox mimicking a tiger.

Jetsun Milarepa said, "Alcohol fuels craving and cuts the life of liberation." And Guru Padmasambhava, too, said, "Chang is one of the main roots of the suffering in the three worlds—forsake it."

Likewise, eating meat has heavy negative consequences. The sutras say:

> To make a profit
> You take the life of living beings.
> For the sake of eating meat
> You give away your wealth.
> These two are wrong acts,
> Main causes for rebirth
> In the Hell of Lamentations.

In the Mahayana tradition, practitioners commit themselves to protecting all infinite living beings. Rather than protecting them, if they mercilessly kill those supposedly protected beings and eat them, is that not a complete contradiction of their vows? It is totally unacceptable.

Similarly, a practitioner should be aware that compulsive sexual attraction between man and woman is the source of great difficulties. For the sake of a single smile from a beautiful girl, not only does a man forget what can happen to him in future lives, but he may even forget any sense of immediate decency and, disregarding the advice of his teachers and parents, run after her like a dog, jumping off the path of enlightenment and sinking like a stone in the ocean of the lower realms.

In brief, as Gampopa said,

Sinful meat,
Intoxicating beer,
And deceiving young companions:
These are deadly poisons for the Dharma
    practitioner.
If you want to do genuine practice, give these up.

The Lord of Siddhas, Kalden Gyatso[115] said,

Crave the taste of delicious food,
The smooth contact of soft clothes,
The enchanting form of beauties,
And the profound Dharma will be left far behind.

Appendix 3

Supplementary Commentaries on Transcendent Concentration (Verse 29)

A. Sustained Calm and Profound Insight
The following is excerpted from The Vase of Amrita
(2) by Dzatrul Ngawang Tendzin Norbu (folio 87 et
seq.)

How to meditate on sustained calm (shamatha):

1. Preliminary conditions for shamatha meditation

You need to be deeply weary of samsara and feel a strong sense of renunciation. You may be in a remote retreat place, physically isolated from all distractions, but unless your mind goes into retreat from all its thoughts and feelings, too, and stops being constantly agitated by ordinary concerns, you will be no different from an aging yak on a mountainside. You must apply the right antidote for whatever type of disturbing emotion predominates: when strong desire arises, reflect on the unpleasant aspects of the object of your desire; when anger is strong, try to feel more affection and kindness; when mental confusion prevails, reflect on the dependent origination of samsara; when jealousy arises, meditate on the essential equality of yourself and others; and when pride arises, mentally exchange places with others.

2. How to meditate

First, arouse bodhichitta with the aspiration to establish all beings in the very essence of enlightenment. Then make the seven-branch offering (prostration, offering, confession, and so on) and sit properly, adopting the seven-point posture of Vairochana:

i. Your legs should be crossed in the *vajrasana* posture, right on top of left.

ii. Your hands should be closed into fists, with your thumbs pressing into the bases of your ring fingers, and placed on your thighs where they join your pelvis; your elbows should then be locked straight. (Two variations of this are to place your hands, palm up, right over left, on your lap, with your bent elbows out on each side, or to place both your hands palms down, relaxed, on your knees.)

iii. Your shoulders should be raised and pulled slightly forward.

iv. Your spine should be kept straight, "like a pile of golden coins."

v. Your chin should be slightly tucked in toward your throat.

vi. The tip of your tongue should be curled up to touch your palate.

vii. Your eyes should be kept unwaveringly focused at a distance of twelve fingers' breadth ahead of the tip of your nose, without blinking.

You should then sit there, without falling into either slack dullness or wild agitation. If you can stabilize your mind and make it flexible enough to focus one-pointedly on any object, your ability to accomplish virtuous deeds will be much greater.

3. Three types of meditation

A. FOCUSING ON SPECIFIC OBJECTS

Meditate on the form of Buddha Shakyamuni, and concentrate on his qualities. At the end, observe that the mind that concentrates is impossible to locate or identify; its nature is empty.

B. FOCUSING ON ANTIDOTES

To remedy disturbances to your meditation caused by the arising of different states of mind, there are *five main disturbances* to be recognized: (1) laziness, (2) forgetting the instructions, (3) dullness and wildness, (4) lack of effort, and (5) excessive effort.

Remedy these with the following eight antidotes. Counteract *laziness* with (1) inspiration, (2) endeavor, (3) faith, and (4) the refined flexibility that comes through training body, speech, and mind. Counteract *forgetfulness* with (5) mindfulness, remembering both words and meaning. Counteract *dullness and wildness* with (6) alertness to these states of mind.

When any of these defects occur in meditation, counteract *lack of effort* by (7) making the effort to apply the appropriate antidote. When defects are absent, the antidotes are no longer necessary, and you should counteract *excessive effort* by (8) letting the mind rest in its natural state without antidotes.

C. FOCUSING ON THE NINE WAYS OF SETTLING THE MIND

There are nine ways to place the mind in evenness and acquire stability:

(1) *To place the mind* on objects of concentration, using the strength of having received the teachings.

(2) *To place it continuously,* through the strength of having reflected on and retained the meaning of the teachings.

(3) *To place it back again,* through the strength of mindfulness that swiftly recognizes whenever the mind has strayed from its object of focus to something outside.

(4) *To place it closely,* by repeatedly gathering in the mind when it expands due to excessively strong mindfulness.

(5) *To tame it* when it sinks into dullness, through the strength of alertness that comes from having reflected on the benefits of samadhi.

(6) *To calm it* when it is shaken by wildness and the pleasure of meditating is lost, alertness being too forced, by reflecting on the flaws of wildness and distraction.

(7) *To calm it completely,* through the strength of endeavor giving up all clinging to meditative states and pleasant experiences as well as sleepiness.

(8) *To place it one-pointedly,* again through the strength of endeavor eliminating dullness and wildness to the extent that it is possible to remain one-pointedly focused for a complete session of meditation.

(9) *To place it in total evenness,* through the strength of familiarity with one-pointed concentration, letting the mind remain therein of its own accord, spontaneously and without effort.

As you practice sustained calm, you will experience the gradual pacification of the mind in five steps, which are illustrated by five similes:

(1) Meditation like a waterfall pouring down over a cliff. The thoughts continuously follow one another, and at first seem even more numerous than usual, because you have become aware of the mind's movements.

(2) Meditation like a river rushing through mountain gorges. The mind alternates between periods of calm and turbulence.

(3) Meditation like a wide river flowing easily. The mind moves when disturbed by circumstances, but otherwise rests calmly.

(4) Meditation like a lake lightly ruffled by surface ripples. The mind is slightly agitated on the surface, but remains calm and present in its depth.

(5) Meditation like a still ocean. An unshakable, effortless concentration in which antidotes to discursive thoughts are redundant.

How to meditate on profound insight (vipashyana):

Sustained calm can momentarily limit negative emotions, but not eradicate them. Their full uprooting can only be achieved by the discriminating insight that recognizes the true nature of all phenomena during meditation and that is aware of everything as empty illusion during postmeditation. Sustained calm is thus the concentration aspect of meditation, while profound insight is its wisdom aspect. Shamatha prepares the mind for the insight of vipashyana to show the practitioner that all phenomena are inherently devoid of substantial existence. Both sustained calm and profound insight should be permeated by compassion. Uniting sustained calm and profound insight will eventually lead to a state of sameness in which all concepts of subject and object disappear.

As compassion is always united with wisdom, the union of sustained calm and profound insight is biased neither toward samsara nor toward nirvana. Wisdom is experientially understood during meditation; compassion is wisdom's natural expression and develops during postmeditation. Eventually, meditation and postmeditation merge into one, and the ultimate nature, devoid of conditions, concepts, or characteristics, is actualized. There is then no further need for discriminating insight, and both insight and its object disappear of their own accord—in the same way that two sticks rubbed together make a fire and are then consumed by the fire they started.

B. Concentration
The following is excerted from The Oral Transmission of the All-Knowing Ones *by Shechen Gyaltsap Pema Namgyal*

Three kinds of concentration:

1. The concentration practiced by ordinary beings

This consists of sitting properly in a secluded place, taking refuge, arousing bodhichitta, and dwelling imperturbably in a state free of thought and of any fixation. This leads to a samadhi in which phenomena continue to be perceived but no fixation or clinging attaches to them. Your mind rests in one-pointed concentration, free of dullness and wildness. This state of sustained calm (shamatha) cannot lead beyond the state of absorption in the formless realms, as it lacks profound insight (vipashyana), which ascertains and recognizes the ultimate nature of phenomena.

2. Clearly discerning concentration

In this concentration, all aspects of phenomena are examined down to their empty nature. Through profound insight, you establish beyond any doubt the lack of inherent existence of any kind of self, and meditation culminates in insight free of any conceptual affirmation. Meditating in this state, you accomplish the path that unites sustained calm and profound insight. This corresponds to the levels of the paths of accumulation and of joining. This type of concentration confers the higher perceptions and the ability to benefit beings.

3. The excellent concentration of the Tathagatas

If you persevere in the practice of clearly discerning concentration for a long time, all dualistic perceptions of subject and object vanish in the absolute expanse, and you enter the path of vision, reaching the first bhumi. Concentration has then metamorphosed into "the excellent concentration of the Tathagatas," the third type of concentration.

From this moment until reaching the seventh bhumi, there will remain a distinction between the state of meditation (in which you remain without discursive thoughts) and the state following meditation (in which notions of subject and object still exist). From the eighth bhumi onward, although the terms *meditation* and *postmeditation* are still used, these are no longer distinct, discrete states.

Finally, on reaching the level of a buddha, you remain constantly in the evenness of primordial wisdom, a state from which you do not waver for even an instant.

Appendix 4

Supplementary Commentaries on Transcendent Wisdom (Verse 30)

The following excerpts are from The Vase of Amrita *(2) by Dzatrul Ngawang Tendzin Norbu (folio 97 et seq.)*

Without wisdom, the means of compassion cannot bring you to nirvana; you will remain in the extreme of samsara. Without the means of compassion, wisdom will lead you to remain in the extreme of nirvana. Wisdom and compassion must be united.

There are three levels of wisdom:

1. *Conventional, worldly wisdom.* In essence, this consists of four of the five traditional sciences: healing, logic, languages, and crafts.

2. *Absolute wisdom beyond the worldly.* This is the fifth "inner science," or philosophy, based on the teachings of the shravakas and the pratyekabuddhas, and leads to the understanding that the physical aggregates are unclean, necessarily involve suffering, and are impermanent and devoid of inherent existence.

3. *The wisdom of realization.* This is based on the Mahayana teachings and leads to the recognition that the ultimate nature of all phenomena is intrinsically empty, unborn, groundless, and without a source.

Each of these wisdoms must be practiced gradually through hearing, reflecting, and assimilating them through meditation.

In brief, transcendent wisdom is knowing that phenomena are devoid of any intrinsic existence. In nirvana, clinging to the apparent solidity and existence of phenomena, as well as clinging to the notion of their nonexistence, both vanish. The realization of nirvana is within the scope of wisdom-awareness, not within that of the ordinary intellectual and discursive mind.

To actually realize this lack of substantial existence, which is intrinsic and beyond any conceptual idea, you need to meditate. Although gold is present in ore, it needs to be worked and refined and released from the ore; likewise although phenomena are primordially empty and free of all limiting conditions, if you do not realize this through sustained meditation and familiarization, you will never be free from samsara's suffering.

As Shantideva said:

> All who fail to know and penetrate
> This secret of the mind, the Dharma's peak,
> Though they may wish for joy, all sorrows spent,
> They'll wander uselessly in misery.

And the *Sutra of the Increase Toward Great Liberation* says:

> The darkness of thousands of years
> Is instantly dispelled by one lamp;
> The negativities of a thousand kalpas
> Are instantly purified by realizing the nature of
>   mind.

Furthermore, Tilopa said, "The nature of mind is the space beyond the contents of thoughts."

Thus, all other Dharma practices are condensed in the practice of realizing the nature of the mind. As a result of meditating on wisdom and realizing the nature of the mind, you will naturally be inclined toward performing positive and beneficial actions, your emotions will decrease, your compassion will increase, and ultimately you will attain supreme enlightenment.

The other commentary, The Vase of Amrita *(1) by Minyak Kunzang Sönam, adds:*

Wisdom, as the shastras make clear, is in essence an accurate distinguishing or investigating knowledge of the phenomenon in question. This includes:

1. *Wisdom that understands relative truth,* which is the wisdom of expertise in the traditional five sciences

2. *Wisdom that understands absolute truth,* which is wisdom regarding the absence of true existence, whether understood as an abstract notion or by direct experience

3. *Wisdom that understands how to accomplish beings' benefit,* which is knowledge of how the temporal and ultimate benefit of beings may flawlessly be achieved.

There are several other ways in which wisdom may be classified.

Appendix 5
Mind Training Prayer

The Gateway to the Ocean of Bodhichitta[116]
*A Mind-Training Prayer by Jamgön Kongtrul Lodrö
Thaye*

By the truth of the ultimate mind of enlightenment,
Generated by mighty and sublime Avalokiteshvara
And all the buddhas and bodhisattvas,
May supreme bodhichitta be born
In myself and in all beings under the sky.

May the cause of suffering, the anger of all beings,
And its result, the heat and cold of the hells,
Come to me! Dissolve into me!
I give to all beings under the sky
All the merit of my loving-kindness
And my freedom from anger.

Thus may anger's realms, the hells, be emptied.
May all hell-beings become Avalokiteshvara of the
    Vajra family,
And realize sublime mirrorlike wisdom.

May the cause of suffering, the greed and
    attachment of beings,
And its result, the thirst and starvation of the spirit
    realm,

Come to me! Dissolve into me!
I give to all beings under the sky
All the merit of my open-handed generosity
And my freedom from attachment.

Thus may the realms of the starving spirits be emptied.
May all such beings become Avalokiteshvara of the
    Padma family,
And realize sublime discriminating wisdom.

May the cause of suffering, the stupidity of beings,
And its result, the dumb dullness of beasts,
Come to me! Dissolve into me!
I give to all beings under the sky
All the merit of my generation and refinement of
    insight
And my freedom from ignorance.

Thus may the animal realm be emptied.
May all animals become Avalokiteshvara of the
    Buddha family,
And realize the sublime wisdom of the absolute
    expanse.

May the cause of suffering, jealousy, which corrodes
    the hearts of beings,
And its result, the warring of the asuras,
Come to me! Dissolve into me!
I give to all beings under the sky
All the merit of my patience, expressed in body,
    speech, and mind,
And my freedom from jealousy.

Thus may the asura realm be emptied.
May all such beings become Avalokiteshvara of the
    Karma family,
And realize sublime all-accomplishing wisdom.

May the cause of suffering, the overwhelming pride
    of beings,
And its result, the eventual fall of the gods,
Come to me! Dissolve into me!
I give to all beings under the sky
All the merit of my endeavor,
And my freedom from pride.

Thus may the realms of the gods be emptied.
May all celestial beings become Avalokiteshvara of
    the Ratna family,
And realize the sublime wisdom of equality.

May the cause of suffering of beings,
Negative acts and obscurations since beginningless
    time,
And its result, the suffering of birth, illness, old age,
    and death,
Come to me! Dissolve into me!
I give to all beings under the sky
All the merit I have accumulated since beginningless
    time
With my body, speech, and mind.

May the realms of destitution be emptied.
May all beings become stainless dharmakaya
    Avalokiteshvara,
And realize sublime self-existing wisdom.

Downfalls, degenerations, breaches, and
    transgressions
Of the pratimoksha, bodhisattva, and secret
    Mantrayana vows
Committed by all beings,
Come to me! Dissolve into me!
I give to all beings under the sky
The merit of upholding the three kinds of vows.

May their vows become utterly pure,
Unstained by the slightest degeneration.
May they all achieve the level of Vajrasattva,
Embodiment of all families.

May the negative karma, obscurations, and short life
Caused by killing, destruction of sacred objects, and
    the like,
Come to me! Dissolve into me!
I give to all beings under the sky
My generation of bodhichitta and the ten
    transformations.

May premature death become a term unheard of.
May all beings achieve the level of Vajra Amitayus.

May the illnesses of beings,
Caused by imbalances of wind, bile, phlegm, and
    other elements,
Come to me! Dissolve into me!
I give to all beings under the sky
All the merit of my abandonment of any kind of
    violence,
And provision of medicine, and other beneficial
    things.
I offer them my own health and well-being.

May all beings achieve the level of the Medicine
    Buddha,
The Body of Lapis-Lazuli Light,
Which dispels the ills of the three poisons.

May the thirst, hunger, and poverty
Caused by stealing and taking by force the goods of
    others,
Come to me! Dissolve into me!

I give to all beings under the sky
Dharma, wealth, and the fruits of generosity.

May they enjoy this sky-treasure:
The effortless and spontaneous fulfillment of all needs.

May the negative karma and obscurations
Caused by constant harmful activities that lead
To rebirth in impure fields,
Come to me! Dissolve into me!
I dedicate to all beings under the sky
My generation of bodhichitta and the ten
     transformations.

May they be reborn in pure buddhafields,
Such as True Joy and Realm of Bliss.

May the negative karma and obscurations
Caused by the constant harboring of false views,
Which displease the Three Jewels,
Come to me! Dissolve into me!
I give to all beings under the sky
The merit of developing the three kinds of faith.

May they develop complete conviction
In the infallibility of the law of cause and effect,
And replace their negative acts with positive ones.

May attachment and aggression,
Which arise from constant focus on the self,
And lead to perceiving everything as a threat,
Come to me! Dissolve into me!
I give to all beings under the sky
All my merit born of the four boundless thoughts.

May their minds be filled with kindness,
     compassion,
Sympathetic joy, and equanimity.

Source of all suffering,
The deluded mind which takes illusory perceptions
    as real,
Come to me! Dissolve into me!
I offer to all beings under the sky
The realization of egoless emptiness.

May profound emptiness dawn in their minds,
And may they attain perfect buddhahood.

In short, I take all suffering brought about by change:
By encountering what one does not wish—
The sixteen sources of fears and so forth;
By being parted from what one likes—
Relatives and friends, places, food, and riches;
By being unable to keep what one has—
When protecting kinsmen, vanquishing opponents,
And toiling in agriculture and trade;
By being unable to get what one wants—
Power, possessions, and fame;
By being struck by sudden adversities and evil
    influences.

I take all these upon me, on top of my own
    ego-clinging,
While, without keeping anything, I give to all beings
All my merit of past, present, and future;
I give to all beings my influence and power,
My body, my very life.

May all beings enjoy happiness and well-being
And perform the deeds of the bodhisattvas.

May all beings who have made a connection with
    me in good or in bad ways,
Through my teaching them the Dharma and urging
    them to virtue;

Or through my eating their flesh, drinking their
    curds, or riding upon them;
Or through having faith and respect in me, and
    giving me food and wealth;
Or through criticizing me, doubting me, thinking ill
    of me,
Robbing me, beating me, harming me—
In short, whoever has seen me in person,
Heard my name, thought of my good or bad
    qualities,
Or has even been touched by the wind coming from
    my direction:

May their harmful actions and obscurations,
Built up since time without beginning,
Come to an end.
May they be led to the Realm of Bliss
By the Great Compassionate One, the sublime
    Mahakarunika.

May I be able to benefit beings
Through my body, speech, and mind.
Even through my shadow.

May all beings of ill will, human and nonhuman,
Who strive to harm my body and my life,
Be the very first to reach enlightenment.

And may not even the least harm
Ever come about because of me.

When we investigate phenomena,
We find nothing has any true existence.
Everything is as a dream, a mirage,
A reflection, like the moon in water.
Nonetheless, everyone is fooled by taking things
    as real.

In absolute truth,
I and all other beings under the sky,
Even nonhuman entities, evil spirits, and
    obstacle-makers,
Are equal in the sphere of emptiness.
Yet, in taking what is empty as real,
We are all deluded.

In relative truth,
There is not a single being
Who has not been the parent of everyone else.
And who in the whole world has more kindness
Than a father or a mother?
What a delusion it would be
For a mother to wish to harm her child!

This is why, remembering without preference
The kindness of all those parent beings,
I shall offer them gain and victory,
And take loss and defeat for myself.

By the power of this, my pure intention,
May all beings purify their misdeeds and perfect the
    accumulations,
Effortlessly arouse sublime bodhichitta,
Which is emptiness suffused with compassion,
The unerring path of the Victorious Ones,
And swiftly attain the omniscience of buddhahood.

To give form to his aspiration for mind training, Jamgön Kongtrul Lodrö Thaye made this heartfelt prayer in a lonely mountain hermitage. May it be beneficial and auspicious.

Notes

1. Including, for instance, Lopön Kunga Gyaltsen (*slob dpon kun dga' rgyal mtshan*), Khenchen Changchup Sempa Sönam Trakpa (*mkhan chen byang chub sems dpa' bsod nams grags pa, 1273–1345*), Pang Lodrö Tenpa (*spang blo gros brtan pa*), Jonang Kunkhyen Dolpopa Sherap Gyaltsen (*dol bu pa shes rab rgyal mtshan, 1292–1361*), Butön Rinpoche (*bu ston rin po che, 1290–1364*), Rinchen Lingpa (*rin chen gling pa, 1295–1374*), and about thirty other renowned masters. He received transmissions of major teachings from the four main schools— Nyingma, Kadam, Sakya, and Kagyu—as well as from the Kalachakra and other lineages.

2. One of the "Two Supreme Ones" among the "Six Ornaments of India." See note 111.

3. The *Bodhicharyavatara* of Shantideva: see bibliography.

4. The *Prajñaparamita*.

5. His writings include commentaries on *The Way of the Bodhisattva* (*Bodhicharyavatara*), *The Supreme Continuity* (*theg pa chen po rgyud bla ma'i bstan bcos* T.4024), and *The Ornament of the Mahayana Sutras* (*theg chen po'i mdo sde'i rgyan*)—three fundamental Mahayana teachings that explain the practice, paths, and levels of the bodhisattvas in terms of relative and absolute truth. He also considered composing commentaries on the *Prajñaparamita* and the *abhidharma*, but

out of concern that they might cast a shadow upon the commentaries of the Dharma Lord Chöje Wanglo, he decided against doing so. He also wrote explanations of Serlingpa's *Seven-Point Mind Training* (*blo byong don bdun ma*), which were later included by Jamgön Kongtrul Lodrö Thaye in vol. 4 of his compilation, the *Treasury of Spiritual Instructions* (*gdams ngag mdzod*); a text for the transmission of the bodhisattva vows; prayers and praises to various deities; pieces of advice encouraging spiritual practice; and many other spiritual instructions centered on the exercise of compassion and the realization of wisdom, which were gathered in a collection of miscellaneous writings (see note 26 and bibliography).

6. The Kashmiri Pandita Shakya Shri (1127–1225): initiated the "upper" transmission of the monastic lineage in Tibet, so called in comparison to the "lower" transmission initiated by the great abbot Shantarakshita, who, in 827, gave the first monastic ordination in Tibet to seven young men. *Upper* and *Lower* are geographical references, as these two lineages first spread from what are called Upper (western) and Lower (central and southern) Tibet.

7. The Lord of Dharma Gyalwa Götsangpa Gonpo Dorje (*chos rje rgyal ba rgod tshang pa mgon po rdo rje*, 1189–1258): one of the most remarkable saints of the Drukpa Kagyu lineage, who spent years in retreat in solitary caves meditating on compassion, fervent devotion, and pure perception. He performed many miracles and left numerous inspiring writings on many aspects of contemplative life.

8. Jamyang Dönyö Gyaltsen (*'jam dbyangs don yod rgyal mtshan*, 1310–44): the second son of Danyi Chenpo Sangpo Pal's sixth wife. "His brother" probably refers to Lama Dampa Sönam Gyaltsen (*bla ma dam pa bsod nams rgyal mtshan*, 1312–75), the third son.

9. Changchup Sempa Sönam Trakpa, also known as Khenchen Changchup Sempa (see note 1): a great practitioner of the mind-training teachings, he was born in Nyemo (*snye mo*) and became abbot of Chölung (*chos lung*).

10. At the beginning of an empowerment, the master visualizes

himself as a wrathful deity, expelling all hindrances and obstacle makers from the mandala.

11. *spyan-ras gzigs,* Skt. Avalokiteshvara.

12. For this story, see the commentary to verse 18.

13. Khenchen Changtse, alias Lochen Changchup Tsemo (*lo chen byang chub rtse mo,* 1303–80): an abbot of Bodong Monastery and a great scholar and meditator, especially in the Kalachakra tradition. He was the disciple of Pang Lotsa Lodrö Tenpa (*dpang lo tsa ba blo gros brtan pa,* 1276–1342) and of the Jonang abbot Cholé Namgyal (*phyogs las rnam rgyal*), from whom he received the Kalachakra teachings. He received the Path and Fruit (*lam 'bras*) transmission from the great Sakya master Lama Dampa Sönam Gyaltsen (*bla ma dam pa bsod nams rgyal mtshan,* 1312–75).

14. Khasarpani is a form of Avalokiteshvara.

15. *Tsa tsa:* A small molded stupa, symbol of the Buddha's enlightened mind, that can be made of clay or other substances. Some are filled with relics, while others, as in this case, are made with a mixture of clay and bones or remnants of deceased people or animals with the prayer that they may be freed from the lower states of existence and realize the buddha nature.

16. Lama Dampa Sönam Gyaltsen: see note 13.

17. The most famous and revered statue of Tibet, which was blessed by Lord Buddha himself, and brought from China by Queen Gyasa Konjo when she came to Tibet to wed King Songtsen Gampo (617–98).

18. Where he was invited and honored by Situ Changchup Gyaltsen (*t'ai si tu byang chub rgyal mtshan,* 1302–71), the first of the seven Phagdru kings who ruled Tibet after ending the Sakya rule.

19. Jowo Je Atisha (*jo bo rje dpal ldan a ti sha*) Dipamkara Shri Jñana (982–1054): Born in Bengal of royal descent, he first studied in India with great Vajrayana masters such as Maitripa; Rahulagupta; Virupa; Guru Dharmarakshita, a great master of compassion who gave his own flesh in generosity; and Maitriyogin (*'byams pa'i rnal 'byor*), who could take in reality others' suffering upon himself. He then crossed the sea to

Sumatra, where he studied for twelve years with Dharmakirti, often known as Serlingpa (*gser gling pa chos kyi 'grags pa*). On his return to India he became the abbot of the famous Buddhist University of Vikramashila. He was invited to Tibet by Yeshe Ö (*ye shes 'od*) and Changchup Ö (*byang chub 'od*), reached Tibet in 1040, and lived there until his death at the age of seventy-three at Nyethang Drolma Lhakhang, south of Lhasa. He was the father of the Kadampa school. He had countless disciples, among whom the main ones in India were Kshitigarbha (*sa'i snying po*), Pitopa, Dharmakaramati, Mitraguhya, and Jñanamati, and in Tibet the three known as Khu, Ngok, and Drom—that is, Khutön Tsöndru Yudrung (*khu ston brtson 'grus g.yung grung*), Ngok Chöku Dorje (*rngog chos sku rdo rje*), and Drom Tönpa ('*brom ston*)—as well as Gönpapa (*dgon pa ba*) and the "four yogis" (*rnal 'byor pa bzhi*).

20. Butön Rinpoche (*bu ston*, 1290–1364): an encyclopedic scholar who wrote thirty volumes of commentaries and revised the arrangement of the Tangyur (*bstan 'gyur*), the 213 volumes of the commentaries upon Lord Buddha's words by Indian siddhas and panditas.

21. Yogic practices focused upon the spiritual channels (Skt. *nadi*), energies (Skt. *prana*), and essence (Skt. *bindu*).

22. Two veils: the veil, or obscuration, created by the *kleshas* (confusing emotions), and the veil that masks ultimate knowledge.

23. See also the story of another great bodhichitta master, Langri Thangpa, in the commentary to verse 11, p. 112.

24. Mild earthquakes are considered to be marvelous signs that indicate when a great bodhisattva is born or departs from this world.

25. This biography of Gyalse Thogme, entitled *Drops of Ambrosia, the Life of the Precious Bodhisattva Thogme* (*rgyal sras rin po che thogs med pa'i rnam thar bdud rtsi'i thigs pa*), was written by Drögön Palden Yeshe ('*gro mgon dpal ldan ye shes*), a close disciple of his who also collected some of Gyalse Thogme's writings in a collection known as *The Great Oral Transmission of the Mind Training* (*blo sbyong snyan brgyud chen mo*). See bibliography for a list of Gyalse Thogme's writings.

26. The four formless states, or absorptions (*gzugs med pa'i snyoms par 'jug pa bzhi*): (1) the sphere of infinite space (*nam mkha' mtha' yas skye mched*), (2) the sphere of infinite consciousness (*rnam shes mtha' yas skye mched*), (3) the sphere of nothing at all (*ci med pa'i skye mched*), and (4) the sphere of neither perception nor non-perception (*'du shes med 'du shes med min skye mched*). They correspond to the states experienced by the gods of the four formless realms, which are the result of sustained absorption in samadhi without profound insight.

27. The three concepts: subject, object, and action.

28. The Eight Great Chariots of Transmission (*sgrub mtha' shin rta chen po brgyad*): (1) Ngagyur Nyingma (*snga 'gyur snying ma*), (2) Kadam (*bka' gdams*), (3) Kagyu (*bka' brgyud*), (4) Shangpa Kagyu (*zhangs pa bka' brgyud*), (5) Sakya (*sa skya*), (6) Chöd and Shiché (*gcod* and *zhi byed*), (7) Kalachakra (*dus 'khor* or *sbyor drug*), and (8) Orgyen Nyendrub (*o rgyan bsnyen sgrub*). See also note 112.

29. Shantideva (*shi ba lha*): one of the eighty-four *mahasiddha*s of India. He composed his famous *The Way of the Bodhisattva* (*Bodhicharyavatara, byang chub sems dpa'i spyod pa la 'jug pa*), and the *Collected Precepts* (*Shikshasamucchaya, bslab pa kun las btus pa*), two major texts describing the ideal and practice of a bodhisattva.

30. King Songtsen Gampo (*srong btsan sgam po*, 617–98): the first of the three great Buddhist kings of Tibet, an emanation of Buddha Avalokiteshvara.

31. Guru Padmasambhava, the Lotus-Born Guru, was an emanation of the dharmakaya Buddha Amitabha, of the sambhogakaya Buddha Avalokiteshvara, and of the nirmanakaya Buddha Shakyamuni. Born immaculately from a lotus, he brought the teachings of sutra and tantra to Tibet, and concealed countless spiritual treasures, or termas, to be rediscovered in due time for the benefit of successive generations.

32. See bibliography.

33. These names correspond to various aspects of Avalokiteshvara. King of the Sky (*nam mkha'i rgyal po*), Bountiful Lasso (*don yod zhags pa*), He Who Dredges the Depths of Samsara (*'khor*

ba dong sprugs), Greatly Compassionate Transformer of Beings (*'gro 'dul thugs rje chen po*), and Ocean of Victorious Ones (*rgyal ba rgya mtsho*), as explained in Dilgo Khyentse's *The Heart Treasure of the Enlightened Ones* (Boston: Shambhala, 1992, pp. 133–40), can be seen as the pure nature of, respectively, the skandhas of form, feeling, appraisal, impulse, and consciousness, while Khasarpani (*kha sarpa Ni*), Lion's Roar (*senge sgra*), Unwinding in Ultimate Mind (*sems nyid ngal gso*), and Sovereign of the Universe (*'jig rten dbang phyug*) represent the pure nature of body, speech, mind, and the continuum of dharmakaya (ibid., pp. 140–44).

34. Bodhisattvas are beings who have realized the empty nature of phenomena and the nonexistence of individual self. They are free from the kleshas, or ordinary emotions. There are ten bodhisattva levels, or *bhumi*s. The eleventh bhumi is that of consummate buddhahood, which is realized when both obscurations—that of the kleshas and that which veils total wisdom—have been cleared in an irreversible way. In a broader sense, a bodhisattva is described as a being engaged in practicing the Mahayana teachings.

35. Shariputra was said to be particularly gifted with deep insight, and Maudgalyayana particularly gifted with miraculous powers.

36. The Tibetan term *gyalsé* (*rgyal sras*, in Sanskrit *Jinaputra*), literally "child of the Victorious Ones," has, however, for readability, been translated throughout this text by its synonym, *bodhisattva* (*byang chub sems dpa'*).

37. *Arhat*, in Tibetan *drachompa* (*dgra bcom pa*), means "one who has defeated the enemy," that is, the negative emotions.

38. Gyalwa Longchen Rabjam, Trimé Öser (*rgyal ba klong chen rab 'byams dri med 'od gzer*, 1308–69): also known as Longchenpa, the foremost teacher of the Nyingma tradition who, in his *Seven Treasuries* (*mdzod bdun*), wrote an explanation of the nine vehicles in general and of the Great Perfection (*rdzogs pa chen po*) in particular.

39. These two sets of eight conditions necessary for the practice of Dharma (*'phral byung rkyen gyi mi khom rnam pa brgyad* and *ris chad blo yi mi khom rnam pa brgyad*) are described in

Longchenpa's *Wish-Granting Treasury* (*yid bzhin mdzod*). See also *The Words of My Perfect Teacher*, pp. 30–31.

40. Tibetan beer made from fermented millet.

41. Ignorance includes (a) basic ignorance (*ma rig pa*), the non-recognition of primordial awareness and of the empty nature of phenomena; (b) a dense mental state (*ti mug*), chiefly a lack of discernment regarding what should be accomplished and what should be discarded in order to gain freedom from samsara; (c) doubt (*the tsom*) regarding the truth of karma (the law of cause and effect), the existence of past and future lives, and so on; and (d) obscured view (*lta ba nyon mong can*), the belief that the aggregates (Skt. *skandhas*) form an individual self, and that phenomena have a real, inherent, and autonomous existence, and so on.

42. The five traditional sciences: medicine, logic, languages, crafts, and metaphysics. See note 109.

43. Mani-reciter (*mani pa*): someone who recites the *mani*, the mantra of Avalokiteshvara, the Buddha of Compassion. Here "Mani-reciters" is used as an affectionate term for Dharma practitioners.

44. *The Way of the Bodhisattva*, p. 121.

45. Drom Tönpa Gyalwai Jungne (*'brom ston pa rgyal ba'i 'byung gnas*, 1004–64): the closest Tibetan disciple of Lord Atisha, with whom he remained for eighteen years. He founded the monastery of Reting (*rwa sgreng*) where he remained and taught for seven years before passing away at the age of sixty.

46. See *The Words of My Perfect Teacher*, p. 237.

47. The *Saddharmanu-smrtyu-pasthana-sutra* (Tib. *dam pa'i chos dran pa gnyer bzhag pa'i mdo*): a sutra that explains how we should identify which actions, words, and deeds are suitable and which unsuitable, and how we should then keep our sustained attention focused upon them.

48. Gampopa, Sönam Rinchen (*sgam po pa bsod nams rin chen*, 1079–1153): born in Nyal, eastern Tibet, he first trained as a physician, hence his name Dagpo Lharje (*dwags po lha rje*), the Physician of Dagpo (the name of the province in which he was to spend many years). He was ordained at the age of twenty-

six after his two children and wife died in an epidemic. After studying and practicing the Kadampa teachings, at the age of thirty-two he met Jetsun Milarepa, whose foremost disciple he was to become. His main disciples were the first Karmapa, Dusum Khyenpa (*dus gsum mkhyen pa,* 1110–70), Phagmo Drupa (*phag mo gru pa rdo rje rgyal po,* 1110–70), and Dharma Wangchuk (*dhar ma dbang phyug*).

49. Meditation on impermanence has three roots, nine considerations, and leads to three definite conclusions.

The three roots to consider: (1) death is certain, (2) there is no certainty what will cause it, and (3) anything other than Dharma is totally useless at the moment of death.

The nine considerations: For the first root, (1) no one in the past has ever escaped death, (2) the body is compounded and bound to disintegrate, and (3) life runs out second by second. For the second root, (1) life is incredibly fragile, (2) the body is without any enduring essence, and (3) numerous circumstances can cause death, while few circumstances prolong or support life. For the third root, (1) relatives and friends will be of no use at the moment of death, (2) wealth and food will be of no use, and (3) my own body will be of no use.

The three definite conclusions: (1) we should practice the Dharma, since it will definitely help us at death; (2) we must practice it *right now,* since we do not know when we will die; and (3) we should devote our time exclusively to practicing the Dharma, since nothing else is of any use.

50. For details of the qualities of true and false teachers, as set out in Dzatrul Tendzin Norbu's commentary to this verse, see appendix 1 (pp. 205–7). See also *The Words of My Perfect Teacher,* chap. 6.

51. Pratyekabuddhas (*rang sangs rgyas*): "those who attain buddhahood by themselves." With the shravakas they constitute the sangha of the Basic Vehicle.

52. Marpa Lotsawa Chökyi Lodrö (*mar pa lo tsa ba chos kyi blo gros,* 1012–97): father of the Kagyu lineage, born in Lhodrak, in southern Tibet. He first studied with Drogmi Lotsawa, then traveled to India three times to meet his root teacher, the maha-siddha pandit Naropa, as well as his other gurus, Maitripa,

Kukuripa, and Jñanagarbha. Jetsun Milarepa, Shepai Dorje (*rje btsun mi la ras pa bzhad pa'i rdo rje*, 1040–1123), his foremost disciple, is perhaps the most famous example of a perfect spiritual disciple, practitioner, and teacher.

53. A practice of Guru Yoga related to these teachings is set out in part B of Appendix 1 (pp. 207–10).

54. There are four things to remember regarding the karmic law of cause and result: (1) a karmic result is certain, (2) the result of an action tends to increase, (3) you will never experience anything that is not the result of an action of your own in the past, and (4) karmic seeds sown by your actions are never wasted and never disappear on their own.

55. There are six basic miseries in samsara: (1) friends and enemies are changeable, (2) we never seem to have enough, (3) we die again and again, (4) we are reborn again and again, (5) we go up and down in samsara again and again, and (6) we are essentially alone.

56. Drogön Tsangpa Gyare (*'gro mgon tsang pa rgya ras, ye shes rdo rje*, 1161–1211): the archetype of the enlightened renunciate. Following a prediction given to him by Gyalwa Lorepa (1187–1250) in a vision, he opened the door to the secret land of Tsari, and there had a vision of Chakrasamvara, who predicted that his teachings and lineage would spread the distance of eighteen days' flight of an eagle. He and his immediate spiritual successors, Gyalwa Götsangpa (1189–1258) and his disciple Gyalwa Yangönpa, were highly accomplished masters of the Drukpa Kagyu tradition.

57. Jigme Gyalwai Nyugu (*'jigs med rgyal ba'i myu gu*): an emanation of Avalokiteshvara, and one of the two chief disciples of Kunkhyen Jigme Lingpa. He was the teacher of Jamyang Khyentse Wangpo and Patrul Rinpoche.

58. Patrul Rinpoche, Orgyen Jigme Chökyi Wangpo (*dpal sprul O rgyan 'jigs med chos kyi dbang po*, 1808–87): a re-embodiment of Shantideva and the speech emanation of Jigme Lingpa. He displayed the most perfect life of spiritual realization and renunciation. Except for some years in Shri Singha, the monastic college of Dzogchen Monastery in Kham, he spent most of his life in

caves, forests, and the most secluded hermitages, moving at random from one place to the other. Dressed as a simple lay nomad, he traveled unrecognized most of the time. In his youth he committed most of the important treatises (the *Seven Treasuries* of Longchenpa, for instance) to memory, and thus he could teach the most complex subjects for months at a time without using any books, as he did in Shri Singha College. When he passed away, his only possessions were a copy of Shantideva's *The Way of the Bodhisattva* and a begging bowl. He was a disciple of Jigme Gyalwai Nyugu, Gyalse Shenphen Thaye, Dzogchen Mingyur Namkhai Dorje, and other great teachers; and among his disciples were Lama Mipham, Nyoshul Lhungthok, Onpo Tenga, and many others. Minyak Kunzang Sönam's commentary of the *Thirty-seven Verses on the Practice of a Bodhisattva* is said to have been written according to Patrul Rinpoche's oral instructions.

59. Skt. *Candamaharosana* or *Bhrikuti*, Tib. *khro gnyer can ma.*

60. The practice of Chöd considers the body as an offering to the Three Jewels, a present to the Dharma-protectors, a gift to sentient beings, and repayment of outstanding karmic debts to harmful spirits. There are also the methods of water torma (*chu gtor*), and burned offerings, sur (*gsur*), two offerings dedicated to spirits who suffer endlessly from thirst and hunger.

61. Langri Thangpa (*glang ri thang pa rdo rje seng ge,* 1054–1123): an emanation of Buddha Amitabha, and the sun-like disciple of Geshe Potowa (*po to wa*).

62. See note 45.

63. Kunkhyen Jigme Lingpa (*kun mkhyen 'jigs med gling pa,* 1729–91): an emanation of Vimalamitra, King Trisong Detsen, Gyalse Lharje, and Ngari Panchen Pema Wangyal. He had numerous visions of Guru Padmasambhava, Yeshe Tsogyal, and Kunkhyen Longchen Rabjam. The collection of his mind treasures, the *Longchen Nyingthig* (see note 65), and of his other writings fills nine volumes. Foremost among his disciples were the four "fearless ones"—Jigme Trinle Öser, Jigme Gyalwai Nyugu, Jigme Kundrol, and Jigme Gocha.

64. Dodrup Jigme Trinle Öser (*rdo grub 'jigs med phrin las od zer,*

1745–1821), the first Dodrup Chen Rinpoche: foremost disciple
of Jigme Lingpa and heir of the Longchen Nyingthig lineage.

65. The *Longchen Nyingthig* (*klong chen snying thig*): the cycle of
spiritual instructions revealed by Guru Rinpoche to Kunkhyen
Jigme Lingpa in visions in the eighteenth century. It has become one of the most practiced of the various spiritual treasures (terma) of the Nyingma tradition. See bibliography.

66. The "four things that you do not want to happen": loss (*ma
rnyed*), suffering (*sdug bsngal ba*), disgrace (*mi snyan pa*), and
disparagement (*smad pa*). Their opposites are gain (*rnyed pa*),
pleasure (*bde ba*), fame (*snyan grags*), and praise (*bstod pa*),
and all together these eight are called the "eight ordinary concerns" (*'jig rten chos brgyad*).

67. See note 60 on the practice of Chöd.

68. The four principles of positive training (*dge sbyong gi chos
bzhi*) in Tibetan: (1) *gshe yang slar mi gshe bar bya*, (2) *khros
kyang slar mi khro bar bya*, (3) *'tshang brus kyang slar mtshang
'bru bar bya*, and (4) *brdeg kyang slar mi brdeg par bya*.

69. Shawopa, or Shawo Gangpa (*sha bo sgang pa*, 1067–1131): a disciple of Langri Thangpa (see note 61) and of the Three
Brothers—Potowa (*pu to ba*), Chengawa (*spyan snga ba*), and
Puchungwa (*phu chung ba*)—who were the three main disciples of Drom Tönpa.

70. Kharak Gomchung (*kha rag sgom chung*): an eleventh-century
Kadampa master. He was one of the most perfect examples of
a renunciate who gives up all activities other than spiritual
practice. Mindful of the inevitability of his impending death,
he would not even cut steps to his cave, nor remove the thorny
bushes at its entrance, thinking that it would be a terrible waste
of his time if he were to die that day. He was famous for his unlimited compassion. His *Seventy Pieces of Advice* (*ang yig bdun
bcu pa*) are said to condense the very essence of the Kadampa
teachings. He was the foremost disciple of Geshe Gonpa (*dge
bshes dgon pa*) and among his own students were Ngul Tön
(*rngul ston*) and Dharma Kyap (*dhar ma skyabs*).

71. *The Ornament of the Mahayana Sutras* (see bibliography)

mentions the eight supreme qualities that arise from meditation on love: (1) gods and men will rejoice, and (2) they will protect you; (3) you will not be able to be harmed by poison, nor (4) by weapons; (5) you will have a happy mind; (6) you will experience all sorts of happiness; (7) you will effortlessly accomplish your aspirations, and (8) even if you do not achieve liberation immediately, you will be reborn in the highest realm.

72. The three great religious kings of Tibet: Songtsen Gampo (609–98), Trisong Detsen (790–844), and Tri Ralpachen (reigned 815–38). It was thanks to their faith, their efforts, and their generosity that in each of their reigns the Buddhist scriptures, commentaries, and teachers were brought to Tibet.

73. The ten negative actions: three of the body—taking life, taking what is not given, and sexual misconduct; four of speech—lying, sowing discord, worthless chatter, and harsh words; and three of the mind—wishing harm, covetousness, and wrong views. The ten positive actions are to avoid the ten negative ones and to practice their opposites.

74. Geshe Potowa, also known as Rinchen Sal (1031–1105): one of the Three Brothers, the three main disciples of Drom Tönpa. (See note 45 and 69.)

75. Dzatrul Rinpoche's commentary here includes a long description of the dangers of alcohol, meat, and sex, of which an abridged translation is set out in appendix 2, pp. 211–13.

76. The story is recounted in the *Jataka* tales of the Buddha's previous lives. King Mandhatri—in Tibetan, Ngalenu (*nga las nu*)—had been a small boy in a previous life at the time of the Buddha Vipashyin (*rnam gzigs*), whom he met when the Buddha was going to beg for alms. He instantly felt great faith in the Buddha and wanted to make an offering to him, but could only find a handful of peas in his pocket. He threw them toward the Buddha in a gesture of offering. Four peas fell in the Buddha's begging bowl, two peas fell at the level of the Buddha's heart, and one remained stuck to the Buddha's robe. As a result of this the boy was reborn as King Mandhatri, who had power over the four continents. He then gained power

over the Four Great Kings and, finally, reached the Heaven of the Thirty-three, where he shared the celestial throne with thirty-seven successive Indras. According to one version of the *Jataka* tales, the boy had also thrown four peas on the ground with a negative attitude at the end of his offering, and his fall was the result of these final four peas.

77. Vasubandhu (*dbyig gnyen*): the younger brother and disciple of Asanga. He is said to have mastered the entirety of the Buddha's teachings and was one of the greatest panditas of India. (See note 111).

78. Tilopa (988–1069), and his disciple Naropa (1016–1100): the two famed mahasiddhas of India.

79. Dzatrul Rinpoche quotes the fifth Dalai Lama (1617–82), who says:

> All phenomena are primordially pure; they cannot
> be located, and are empty;
> Empty though they are, like a magic show they
> clearly appear to our perception;
> What appears to our perception, when we look into
> its nature for something identifiable, is
> nonexistent.
> Nonexistent though it is, it can give rise to the
> experience of all happiness and suffering.

80. This particular quote is from Ben Gung Gyal ('*ban gung rgyal*), a bandit who later became a perfect Dharma practitioner because of his profound understanding of the total renunciation of worldly affairs. He was a close disciple of Potowa (1031–1105).

81. Shabkar Tsogdruk Rangdrol (*zhabs dkar tshogs drug rang grol*, 1771–1851): a lama of Amdo Rekong famed for his great compassion. Wherever he traveled throughout Tibet and Nepal, he ransomed the lives of domestic animals and set them free; he convinced many local people to give up hunting and reduce slaughtering. He himself had vowed to give up eating meat (unusual for Tibetans) in front of the Jowo Rinpoche statue in Lhasa. When he was in retreat in the wilderness, he protected

small water birds from large birds of prey, prevented insects from eating each other, and performed other such compassionate actions. On many occasions, he pacified bloody feuds between rival tribes in Amdo. See *Life of Shabkar,* 2nd ed. (Ithaca, N.Y.: Snow Lion, 2001). Patrul Rinpoche did the same in eastern Golok, where he saved countless human and animal lives.

82. Pratimoksha (*so sor thar pa*), "self-liberation": the goal of this discipline is to free oneself from cyclic existence or samsara.

83. See note 35.

84. Lochen Vairochana (*lo chen bai ro tsa na*): the foremost of the great Tibetan translators, or *lotsawas,* of the Early Translation period (*snga 'sgyur*) and one the eight closest disciples of Guru Padmasambhava.

85. See note 27.

86. At this point in Dzatrul Rinpoche's commentary, *The Vase of Amrita,* a more detailed teaching on the practice of sustained calm and profound insight is included, of which excerpts are set out in appendix 3: "Supplementary Commentaries on Transcendent Concentration (Verse 29)," "A. Sustained Calm and Profound Insight" (pp. 215–20).

87. The symbolic gesture the Buddha made, in response to the skepticism expressed by Mara, to take the earth as witness of the merit he had accumulated over countless lifetimes in preparation of his enlightenment. As he made the gesture, the earth shook and opened, and the Earth Goddess appeared and proclaimed the Buddha's perfection.

88. Having his two legs crossed is a symbol of the oneness of samsara and nirvana within all-pervading emptiness.

89. The ushnisha (*gtsug tor*), or crown prominence, one of the major marks of a fully enlightened Buddha, is usually represented in paintings and statues as a protuberance resembling a topknot in size, but is said in fact to rise up from the top of a buddha's head to the infinity of space. Its full extent, however, can only be seen only by a bodhisattva who has attained the first bhumi. In the *Kalachakra Tantra,* the ushnisha corresponds to the Sky Chakra (*nam mkha'i 'khor lo*), the sixth chakra, which extends upward without limit and represents

the unlimited wisdom of enlightenment. In the *thögal* practice of the Great Perfection, the ushnisha corresponds to the visions of five-colored lights and buddhafields that manifest above one's head as the infinite display of sambhogakaya realization.

90. The "eternal knot" mentioned here refers to the unchanging pristine wisdom of the buddhas, rather than to any particular form (such as the drawing of an eternal knot) that is supposed to be visualized.

91. In parallel to the other transcendent perfections, there are also three kinds of concentration described in the texts: "the concentration practiced by ordinary beings," "clearly discerning concentration," and "the excellent concentration of the Tathagatas." In the present teaching, Dilgo Khyentse Rinpoche chose not to mention them, but a brief summary may be found in the excerpt from Shechen Gyaltsap's *The Oral Transmission of the All-Knowing Ones* set out in appendix 3: "Supplementary Commentaries on Transcendent Concentration (Verse 29)," "B. Concentration" (pp. 220–21).

92. The concepts of subject, object, and action.

93. For a detailed explanation of these three aspects of transcendent wisdom from the commentaries by Dzatrul Rinpoche and Minyak Kunzang Sönam, see appendix 4: "Supplementary Commentaries on Transcendent Wisdom (verse 30)" (pp. 223–25).

94. In the Nyingma tradition, the teachings are divided into the scriptures (*bka' ma*), transmitted from the time of the Buddha and other great masters from master to disciple over the generations, and the rediscovered teachings, or terma (*gter ma*), the profound teachings hidden by Guru Padmasambhava for the sake of future generations, to be rediscovered according to his prophecies at the appropriate time by accomplished siddhas known as spiritual treasure rediscoverers, or tertöns (*gter ston*).

95. The *Bodhisattva-bhūmi*, or *The Levels of the Bodhisattvas* (*byang sa*), is a text by the great fourth-century Indian master Asanga; see bibliography.

96. These four instructions are taken from the *Sutra That*

Encourages Noble Superior Intention (*Arya-adhyasayasañco-dana-sūtra, 'phags pa lhag pa'i bsam pa bskul ba'i mdo,* T.69), a teaching given by the Buddha to Maitreya and others on the conduct of bodhisattvas, which is part of the *Ratnakuta* (*dkon mchog brtsegs pa*).

97. See the commentary to verse 10, pp. 98–106.

98. These statements are the "four seals of the Buddha's teachings" (*bka' rtags kyi phyag rgya bzhi*). See *What Makes You Not a Buddhist,* Dzongsar Jamyang Khyentse (Boston: Shambhala, 2007).

99. Lobsang Yeshe (*blo bzang ye shes,* 1663–1737), the fifth Panchen Lama (the second to hold the title).

100. The seven noble qualities, or riches (*'phags pa'i nor bdun*): faith (*dad pa*), discipline (*tshul khrims*), conscientiousness (*ngo tsha shes pa*), modesty (*khrel yod pa*), learning (*thos pa*), generosity (*gtong ba*), and wisdom (*shes rab*).

101. "To go forth from home to homelessness" (*khyim nas khyim med par rab tu byung ba*): an expression used in the sutras to denote renouncing the life of an worldly householder and taking ordination as a monk or nun.

102. The eight ordinary preoccupations (*chos brgyad*): pleasure and pain, gain and loss, praise and defamation, fame and obscurity.

103. This famous quote comes from the opening stanzas of Chandrakirti's *Madhyamaka-avatara,* a detailed presentation of Nagarjuna's Middle Way (madhyamika) philosophy according to the Prasangika viewpoint.

104. The monk Good Star (*legs pa'i skar ma*) remained very close to the Buddha for a long time, and learned the twelve branches of the teachings by heart. But his pride and jealousy led him to tell people that besides the aura of light around the Buddha's head, there was no difference between himself and the Buddha. He decided he did not want to listen to the Buddha's teachings any longer. As a result, he took rebirth as a tortured spirit who always approached the Buddha when he was teaching and turned his back toward him.

105. Tsang Kharak (*gtsang kha rag*): a place in central Tibet on the way from Lhasa to Nyemo.

106. Kunkhyen Lama Mipham (*mi pham phyogs las rnam rgyal*): also known as Mipham Jamyang Gyatso (*mi pham 'jam dbyangs rgya mtsho*) and Jampel Gyepai Dorje (*'jam dpal gyes pa'i rdo rje*) (1846–1912), an emanation of Mañjushri, an accomplished siddha and the greatest Nyingmapa scholar in modern times.

107. The four rivers of suffering, in which living beings, especially humans, are helplessly carried along: birth, sickness, aging, and death.

108. The five branches of learning, or five sciences (*rig pa'i gnas lnga*): (1) the science of language (*sgra'i rig pa*), (2) the science of logic (*gtan tshigs kyi rig pa*), (3) the science of philosophy (*nang gi rig pa*), (4) the science of medicine (*gso ba'i rig pa*), and (5) the science of material arts and crafts (*bzo gnas kyi rig pa*).

109. Jetsun Trakpa Gyaltsen (*rje btsun grags pa rgyal mtshan*, 1147–1216): one of the foremost masters of the Sakya tradition, who had a vision of Mañjushri.

110. The "Six Ornaments of India" (*rgyan drug*): the two ornaments of the abhidharma, Asanga (*'phags pa thogs med*) and Vasubandhu (*slob dbyig gnyen*); the two ornaments of the science of logic, Dignaga (*phyogs kyi glang po*) and Dharmakirti (*chos kyi grags pa*); and the two ornaments of the madhyamika, Nagarjuna (*mgon po klu sgrub*) and Aryadeva (*'phags pa lha*). Among these six, Nagarjuna and Asanga are considered the "Two Supreme Ones" (*mchog gnyis*) in some texts, while in others the term refers to the two masters of the vinaya, Sakyaprabha (*sa kya 'od*) and Gunaprabha (*yon tan 'od*).

111. See note 29. The principal masters of the Eight Great Chariots are known as the Eight Great Pillars Who Supported the Accomplishment Lineages (*sgrub brgyud 'degs pa'i ka chen brgyad*): (1) Pagor Vairochana (*pa gor bai ro tsa na*, Ngagyur Nyingma); (2) Drom Tönpa (*'brom ston pa*, Kadam); (3) Marpa Lotsawa (*mar pa lo tsa ba*, Kagyu); (4) Khyungpo Naljorpa (*khyung po rnal 'byor pa*, Shangpa Kagyu); (5) Drogmi Lotsawa (*'brog mi lo tsa ba*, Path and Fruit, or Sakya); (6) Padampa Sangye (*pha dam pa sangs rgyas*, Chöd and Shiché); (7) Kyijo Lotsawa (*skyi jo lo tsa wa*, Kalachakra); and (8) Orgyenpa (*o rgyan pa*, Orgyen Nyendrup).

112. The Ten Great Pillars Who Supported the Explanatory Lineages (*bshad brgyud 'degs pa'i ka chen bcu*): Thönmi Sambhota, Vairochana, Kawa Paltsek, Chokro Lu'i Gyaltsen, Zhang Yeshe De, Rinchen Sangpo, Drom Tönpa Gyalwai Jungne, Ngok Lotsawa Loden Sherab, Sakya Pandita, and Gö Khukpa Lhetse.

113. Of the two aspects of the Dharma, the Dharma of transmission (*lung gi chos*) corresponds to the words of the Buddha, and to the scriptures themselves, and the Dharma of realization (*rtogs pa'i chos*) corresponds to the actual realization of these teachings through one's inner experience, culminating in enlightenment.

114. Za Rinpoche Chilbupa, also known as Chökyi Gyaltsen (*sbyil bu pa chos kyi rgyal mtshan*, 1121–89).

115. Jetsun Kalden Gyatso (*rje btsun skal ldan rgya mtsho*, 1607–77), a much venerated teacher, emanation of Shariputra, whose life and teachings had a wide influence in the area of Rekong in Amdo). He wrote many beautiful songs and poems on contemplative practice.

116. *bLo sbyong smon lam byang sems rgya mtsho'i 'jug ngogs*. Tibetan text in *gDams ngag mdzod* (see bibliography), vol. 4, pp. 279–82.

Bibliography

I. TEXTS QUOTED IN THE INSTRUCTIONS

The following sections list the translated names of the sutras, tantras, and shastras, as they appear in the text, along with their Sanskrit and Tibetan titles. All the sutras, tantras, and Indian shastras are found in their Tibetan originals in the Kangyur and Tangyur. T numbers refer to the Tohoku University catalog of the sDe dge edition. For the shastras, references are provided to selected English translations.

Sutras

Great Compendium Sutra—*Avatamsaka-sutra, phal po che'i mdo* (T. 44).

King of Aspirations for Excellent Conduct—*Bhadracharya pranidhana raja, bzang po spyod pa'i smon lam gyi rgyal po.* A section of the *Sutra Arranged as a Tree,* which is itself part of the *Great Compendium Sutra* (T. 44).

King of Concentrations Sutra—*Samadhiraja-sutra, ting 'dzin rgyal po'i mdo* (T. 127).

Sutra Arranged as a Tree—*Gandavyuha sutra, sdong po bkod pa'i mdo,* part of the *Great Compendium Sutra* (T. 44).

Sutra Designed as a Jewel Chest—*Ratnakaranda-sutra, za ma tog bkod pa'i mdo* (T. 116).

Sutra of the Increase Toward Great Liberation—*Ghanajamaha-*

bhrichaphulakarma-sutra, thar pa chen po phyogs su rgyas pa'i mdo (T. 264).

Sutra of the Jewel Mound—Ratnakuta-sutra, dkon mchog brtsegs pa'i mdo.

Sutra of the Meeting of Father and Son—Pitaputra-samagamana-sutra, yab sras mjal ba'i mdo (T. 60).

Sutra of the Supreme Dharma of Clear Recollection—Saddharmanusmrtyupastana-sutra, dam pa'i chos dran pa nye bar gzhag pa' mdo (T. 287).

Sutra That Encourages Noble Superior Intention—Arya-adhyashayasañchodana-sutra, 'phags pa lhag pa'i bsam pa bskul ba'i mdo (T.69). A teaching given by the Buddha to Maitreya and others on the conduct of bodhisattvas, which is part of the *Sutra of the Jewel Mound.*

Sutra of the White Lotus of Compassion—Karunapundarika-sutra, snying rje pad ma dkar po'i mdo (T. 111–12).

Tantra

Vajra Peak Tantra—Vajrashekhara mahaguhya yoga tantra, rdo rje tse mo'i rgyud (T. 480).

Indian Shastras

Hundred Verses, Shatagatha, tshig bcad brgya pa, by Acharya Vararuchi (T. 4332).

Introduction to the Middle Way, Madhyamaka-avatara, dbu ma la 'jug pa, by Chandrakirti (T. 3861). Published in English, with Jamgön Mipham's commentary, as *Introduction to the Middle Way,* translated by the Padmakara Translation Group (Boston: Shambhala, 2002).

Letter to a Friend, Suhrlleka, bshes springs, by Nagarjuna (T. 4182). Published in English, with Rendawa's commentary, as *Nagarjuna's Letter: the Suhrlleka,* translated by Geshe Tharchin Lobsang and A. Engle (Dharamsala, India: LTWA, 1979). Also published with Kangyur Rinpoche's commentary as *Letter to a Friend,* translated by the Padmakara Translation Group (Ithaca: Snow Lion, 2005).

Levels of the Bodhisattvas (*Yogacharya-bhumau*) *Bodhisattva-bhumi,*
rnal 'byor spyod pa'i sa las byang chub sems dpa'i sa, or *byang sa,*
by Asanga (T.4037). In English, see J. D. Willis, *On Knowing
Reality: The Tattvartha Chapter of Asanga's Bodhisattvabhumi*
(Delhi: Motilal Banarsidass, 1982).

*Ornament of the Mahayana Sutras, Mahayana-sutralamkara, theg pa
chen po'i mdo sde'i rgyan,* by Maitreya-Asanga (T. 4020).

*Ornament of True Realization, Abhisamayalamkara, mngon rtogs
rgyan,* by Maitreya-Asanga (T. 3786).

*Supreme Continuity, Mahayanottaratantra-shastra, theg pa chen po
rgyud bla ma'i bstan bcos,* by Maitreya-Asanga (T.4024).
Published in English, with commentary by Thrangu Rinpoche
and Khenpo Tsultrim Gyatso, as *Maitreya on Buddha Nature,*
translated by Ken and Katia Holmes (Forres: Altea, 1999). Also
published with Jamgön Kongtrul's commentary as *Buddha
Nature,* translated by R. Fuchs (Ithaca: Snow Lion, 2000).
Forthcoming translation with Jamgön Mipham's commentary,
translated by the Padmakara Translation Group.

*Way of the Bodhisattva, Bodhicharyavatara, byang chub sems dpa'i
spyod pa la 'jug pa,* by Shantideva (T. 3871). Multiple English
editions exist. *A Guide to the Bodhisattva's Way of Life,* translated by S. Batchelor (Dharamsala: LTWA, 1979). *The Bodhicharyavatara,* translated by K. Crosby and A. Skilton (Oxford:
Oxford University, 1996). *The Way of the Bodhisattva,* translated
by the Padmakara Translation Group (Boston: Shambhala,
2006).

Tibetan Shastras

*Direct Path to Enlightenment, theg pa chen po blo sbyong don bdun ma'i
khrid yig blo dman 'jug bder bkod pa byang chub gzhung lam,* by
Jamgön Kongtrul Lodrö Thaye (*'jam mgon kong sprul blo gros
mtha' yas*). In *gDams ngag mdzod* (*Treasury of Spiritual Instructions*), vol. 4, pp. 243–75 (*see* Other Reference Works). Published
in English as *The Great Path of Awakening: A Commentary on the
Mahayana Teachings of the Seven Points of Mind Training,* translated by K. McLeod (Boston: Shambhala, 1987).

Precious Ornament of Liberation, dam chos yid bzhin nor bu thar pa rin po che'i rgyan, usually known as *dwags po thar rgyan,* by Gampopa (*sgam po pa*). Published in English as *Gems of Dharma, Jewels of Freedom,* translated by Ken and Katia Holmes (Forres: Altea, 1994).

Seventy Pieces of Advice, ang yig bdun bcu pa, by Kharak Gomchung (*kha rag sgom chung*).

Terma

Longchen Nyingthig (Heart Essence of the Vast Expanse), klong chen snying gi thi gle, by Jigme Lingpa (*'jigs med gling pa*).

II. REFERENCES

Works by Gyalse Thogme

rGyal sras lag len (The Thirty-seven Verses on the Practice of a Bodhisattva). Zhang kang: zhang kang then mA dpe skrun khang, 2004.

rGyal sras lag len so bdun ma dang de yi mchan 'grel yid kyi mun sel (Dispelling the Darkness, a Commentary on *Thirty-seven Verses on the Practice of a Bodhisattva).* Karnataka: Namdroling Monastic Jr. High School, 2000.

Byang chub sems dpa'i spyod pa la 'jug pa'i 'grel pa legs par bshad pa'i rgya mtsho (The Ocean of Noble Speech, Commentary on the *Bodhicharyavatara).* Thimphu: Kunsang Topgye.

rGyal sras thogs med kyi gsung thor bu (Miscellaneous Writings of Gyalse Thogme). Thimphu: National Library of Bhutan, 1985.

rGyal ba'i sras po thogs med bzang po dpal gyi mdzad pa'i blo sbyong don bdun ma'i khrid yig (Commentary on the *Seven-Point Mind Training* by Gyalse Thogme). In *gDams ngag mdzod,* vol 4, pp. 189–214 (*see* Other Reference Works).

bLo sbyong bla ma brgyud pa'i gsol 'debs (A Prayer to the Lineage Masters of the Mind Training).

bLo sbyong don bdun ma'i sngon 'gro'i zur 'debs (A Supplement for the Preliminary Practice of the Seven-Point Mind Training). Chengdu: Dmangs khrod dpe dkon sdud sgrig khang, 2001.

bLo sbyong gi bla ma'i rnal 'byor (*Guru Yoga Practice for the Mind Training*).

Theg pa chen po mdo sde'i rgyan gyi 'grel pa rin po che'i phreng ba (*The Precious Garland, a Detailed Commentary on Asanga's Ornament of the Mahayana Sutras*). Gangtok: Gonpo Tzetan, 1979.

rGyud bla ma'i ti ka (*A Commentary on Asanga's Supreme Continuity*).

rTen 'brel gyi khrid yig (*A Detailed Explanation of Interdependence*).

sMyung gnas kyi cho ga (*The Ritual of the Fasting Observance*).

Thugs chen la phyag 'tshal ba'i tshigs su bcad pa (*Verses of Obeisance to the Great Compassionate Avalokiteshvara*). Dehradun: G.T.K. Lodoy, N. Gyaltsen & N. Lungtok, 1970.

Commentaries on This Text

rGyal sras lag len gyi 'grel pa gzhung dang gdams ngag zung 'jug bdud rtsi'i bum bzang (*The Vase of Amrita* [1], Commentary on the *Thirty-seven Verses on the Practice of a Bodhisattva*), by Minyak Kunzang Sönam, Chökyi Trakpa (*kun bzang bsod nams, chos kyi grags pa*). Recently incorporated in the woodblock edition of the *rGyud sde kun btus*. Derge: Derge Parkhang. Also published in booklet form, Chengdu: Si khrun mi rigs dpe skrun khang (Sichuan Minorities), 1995.

rGyal sras lag len so bdun ma'i 'grel pa gzhung dang gdams ngag zung 'jug bdud rtsi'i bum bzang (*The Vase of Amrita* [2], Commentary on the *Thirty-seven Verses on the Practice of a Bodhisattva*), by Dzatrul Rinpoche, Ngawang Tendzin Norbu (*dza sprul ngag dbang bstan 'dzin nor bu*). Woodblocks at Thubten Chöling Monastery, Solokhumbu, Nepal.

Biography of Gyalse Thogme

rGyal sras rin po che thogs med pa'i rnam thar bdud rtsi'i thigs pa (*The Drops of Ambrosia, the Life of the Precious Bodhisattva Thogme*), by Palden Yeshe (*dpal ldan ye shes*). Tibetan text, 23 folios. Thimphu, Bhutan: Kunsang Topgye.

Other Reference Works

gDams ngag mdzod (*Treasury of Spiritual Instructions*). Collected by Jamgön Kongtrul Lodrö Thaye (*'jam mgon kong sprul blo gros mtha' yas*). Tibetan text in 18 vols. Delhi: Shechen, 1998.

Byang chub lam gyi rim pa la blo sbyong ba thog mar blo sbyong chos kyi sgo byed (*The Initial Opening of the Door to the Dharma of Mind Training, Training the Mind on the Stages of the Path to Enlightenment*), by Lodrö Gyaltsen (*blo gros rgyal mtshan*). In *gDams ngag mdzod*, vol. 3, pp. 429–544.

Theg pa chen po'i blo sbyong don bdun gyi khrid yig (*Explanations on the Seven-Point Mind Training of the Great Vehicle*), by Jetsun Taranatha (*rje btsun taranatha*). In Taranatha's *Collected Writings*, Leh, Ladakh: C. Namgyal and Tsering Taru, sMansa sris shes rig dpe mdzod, 1987, vol. 13, pp. 85–105.

rGyal ba'i bstan pa la 'jug pa'i rim pa skyes bu gsum gyi man ngag gi khrid yig bdud rtsi'i nying khu (*The Quintessense of Amrita, Explanations of the Instructions for the Three Kinds of Beings on the Stages for Entering the Buddha's Teaching*), by Jetsun Taranatha (*rje btsun taranatha*). In Taranatha's *Collected Writings*, Leh, Ladakh: C. Namgyal and Tsering Taru, sMansa sris shes rig dpe mdzod, 1987, vol. 13, pp. 107–223.

Theg pa chen po'i blo sbyong gi man ngag zab don sbrang rtsi'i bum bzang (*The Honey Vase, Pith Instructions on the Mind Training of the Great Vehicle*), by Shechen Gyaltsap, Pema Namgyal (*zhe chen rgyal tshab 'gyur med pad ma rnam rgyal*), 270 folios. In vol. 4 of *The Collected Works of Shechen Gyaltsap*, Paro: H. H. Dilgo Khyentse Rinpoche, 1975–94.

rDo rje theg pa'i thun mong gi sngon 'gro spyi la sbyor chog pa'i khrid yig kun mkhyen zhal lung rnam grol shing rta (*The Chariot of Complete Liberation, the Oral Transmission of the All-Knowing Ones, Instructions Applicable to All Preliminary Practices of the Adamantine Vehicle*), by Shechen Gyaltsap, Gyurme Pema Namgyal (*zhe chen rgyal tshab 'gyur med pad ma rnam rgyal*), 364 folios. In vol. 7 of *The Collected Works of Shechen Gyaltsap*, Paro: H. H. Dilgo Khyentse Rinpoche, 1975–94.

Byams khrid and *Byams snying rje'i khrid yig zhal gdams* (*Advice and*

Instructions on Love and Compassion), by Gyalwa Götsangpa (*rgod tshang pa mgon po rdo rje*). In his *Collected Works,* vol. 4, pp. 501–48 and 549–601. Darjeeling: Kargyud Syngrab Nyamso Khang, 1972.

III. SELECTED BIBLIOGRAPHY IN ENGLISH

Atisha and Buddhism in Tibet, compiled and translated by Doboom Tulku and Glenn H. Mullin. New Delhi: Tibet House, 1983.

Commentary on the Thirty-Seven Practices of a Bodhisattva, by H. H. the fourteenth Dalai Lama. Dharamsala: LTWA, 1996.

Mind Training: The Great Collection, various authors. Translated by Thupten Jinpa, Library of Tibetan Classics. Somerville, Mass.: Wisdom Publications, 2005.

Songs of Spiritual Change, by the seventh Dalai Lama. Translated by Glenn H. Mullin. Ithaca, N.Y.: Snow Lion, 1983.

Sutra of the Wise and the Foolish, Mdo mdzangs blun, or *The Ocean of Narratives.* Translated from the Mongolian by Stanley Frye. Dharamsala: LTWA, 1981.

Thirty-seven Practices of All Buddhas' Sons. Bilingual Tibetan and English pocket book. Dharamsala: LTWA, 2001.

The Thirty-Seven Practices of Bodhisattvas: An Oral Teaching by Geshe Sönam Rinchen. Translated by Ruth Sönam. Ithaca, N.Y.: Snow Lion, 1997.

Transforming Adversity into Joy and Courage: An Explanation of the Thirty-Seven Practices of Bodhisattvas, by Geshe Jampa Tegchok. Edited by Thubten Chodron. Ithaca, N.Y.: Snow Lion, 2005.

Uniting Wisdom and Compassion: Illuminating the Thirty-Seven Practices of a Bodhisattva, by Chokyi Dragpa. Somerville, Mass.: Wisdom, 2004.

The Wheel of Sharp Weapons, by Dharmarakshita. Translated by G. Ngawang Dargye et al. Dharamsala: LTWA, 1976. Revised edition, 1981. (Tibetan text: *Theg pa chen po'i blo sbyong mtshon cha'i khor lo,* in *gDams ngag mdzod,* vol. 4, pp. 47–60; *see* Other Reference Works.)

The Words of My Perfect Teacher, by Patrul Rinpoche. Translated by the Padmakara Translation Group. Boston: Shambhala, 1998.

Index

abhidharma (cosmology and meta-
    physics), 81
absolute bodhichitta, 137. *See also*
    meditation practice; postmedita-
    tion practice
absolute body. *See* dharmakaya
actions, negative. *See* negative
    actions
alcohol, 211–13
Amitabha, Buddha, 114–15
Amitayus, 15
anger, 124, 133, 134, 159, 160. *See also*
    hatred; negative emotions
arhat, 53
Asanga, 197
aspiration. *See* intention
Atisha, Lord, 73, 105
    confessions, 88
    on criticism and fault finding, 125
    on desire, 136
    Drom Tönpa and, 112–13
    on faith, 78
    illness, 113
    on solitude, 67
attachment, 44–45, 63–65. *See also* loss;
    meditation practice; negative
    emotions
    freedom from, 101, 102
    to possessions, 95–97
    to sponsor's property, giving up,
    182–84

authors of treatises, qualifications of,
    197
aversion and attachment, 44–45
Avalokiteshvara, Lord, 49, 50, 195,
    197–98, 202. *See also* mind-train-
    ing prayer
    mantra of, 50
    nature of, 48, 50, 197, 202
    Padmasambhava and, 113
    purpose of, 49

bardo, 71
Basic Vehicle, 145–46, 185
beggars, 13–14, 17–18, 180
bhumis, 221
Bhutan, 6, 8
bodhichitta, 47, 99, 100
    of application, 106, 177 (*see also* ab-
    solute bodhichitta; meditation
    practice; relative bodhichitta)
    Drom Tönpa and, 112–13
    enlightenment and, 47, 52, 98–105
    as essence of Mahayana, 100
    of intention, 98–106
    nature of, 43
    teachings on, 47
bodhisattvas, 180–81
    attitude of, 102, 127
    examples and manifestations of, 48,
    53–54, 180
    learning about the practice of, 54

bodhisattvas (*continued*)
  nature of, 53
  precepts of, 51, 154
  purpose, 48
  and the self, 47
body, 142–43, 168
boundless love, levels of, 173
Buddha, 6, 52–53, 76, 82, 145, 158. *See also* Amitabha, Buddha; Shakyamuni, Buddha
  Dharma and, 53
  on judgment, 178
  Mara and, 113
  on monastic discipline, 156
  most supreme offering to, 115
  omnipresence, 84
  on past lives, 72
  past lives of, 86, 117–18, 133
  relying on the wisdom of, 89
  taking refuge in, 85
  teachings, 29, 43, 47, 52, 62, 82, 87, 115, 153, 185, 204
  visualizing, 166–68
buddha nature, 62, 81, 158, 178, 189, 221
  aspects of, 80–81
Buddhafield of Bliss, 51
Buddhist path, aim of, 145
Bulwa, 19
Butön Rinpoche, 20

calm, sustained, 165
  how to meditate on, 215–19
  methods for attaining, 165–66
celestial beings, 57, 130
Chandamaharoshana, 105–6
change. *See also* impermanence
  suffering of, 59
Chenrezi. *See* Avalokiteshvara
Chökyi Lodrö, Dzongsar Khyentse, 5
compassion, 50, 98, 108–9, 118. *See also* generosity; kindness; meditation practice, of exchanging oneself and others; self-sacrifice
  Avalokiteshvara and, 48, 50, 113
  boundless, 118–19, 173, 174
  Padmasambhava and, 113
  wisdom and, 219, 223
concentration, 94
  clearly discerning, 220

practiced by ordinary beings, 220
  of Tathagatas, 221
  transcendent, 164–69
confession, 88

Dakinis, 82
Dalai Lama, 7, 49
death, 58, 70–73
dedication, 102–4
deprivation, 128–30
desire, 112. *See also* meditation practice
  objects of, 135–37
Devadatta, 117
"devil," 95–96
Dharma (practice), 53, 54, 57–58, 81–82, 203–4. *See also specific topics*
  advantages conducive to, 55, 57
  attachment, hatred, and, 64–66
  enduring hardships for the sake of, 157
  essence, 99–100
  factors causing people to drift away from, 55–56
  foundation, 60
  Gyalse Thogme on, 58
  importance, 58–59
  Padmasambhava on, 92–93
  solitary places and, 64–67
  states in which there is no freedom to practice, 55
  texts of, 62
dharmakaya (absolute body), 80, 81
dharmas, black and white, 88
diligence
  in action, 160–61
  armorlike, 160, 161
  aspects, 160–62
  opposite(s) of, 161–62
  that cannot be stopped, 161
  transcendent, 160–64
discipline, 94
  transcendent, 154–56
  types of, 155
disgrace, 121–23
disparagement, 123–25
distraction, 68
downfalls. *See* four basic downfalls
Drom Tönpa Gyalwai Jungne, 119–20, 128

on alcohol consumption, 211
Atisha and, 112–13
bodhichitta and, 112–13
on emotions and Dharma, 186–87
on solitary places, 67
Drubthop Chöyung, 72

emotions. *See also* negative emotions;
  specific emotions
  detachment from, 149–50
empathy. *See* meditation practice,
  of exchanging oneself and
  others
emptiness, 90, 104, 142–45, 158
  realization of, 172–74
enemies, 45, 46, 119–20, 159
enlightenment, 47, 56. *See also*
  liberation
  attaining, 60, 61, 82, 202
  bodhichitta and, 47, 52, 98–105
  spiritual teachers and, 76–78

faith, 78–79, 84, 181
  levels of, 84–85
fame, 123
faults
  examining and giving up one's,
    175–78
  facing one's, 124–25
  giving up speaking of a bod-
    hisattva's, 178–82
forgetfulness, 217
forgiveness, humble prayer for,
  200–201
four basic downfalls, 177
four boundless attitudes, 118–19
Four Noble Truths, 61, 201
freedom. *See also* liberation
  from attachment, 101, 102
  propensities limiting potential to
    attain, 55, 56
friends, 45, 46, 75, 146–47, 181
  unsuitable, 74–75

Gampopa, 4, 176–78, 183, 212
generation phase, 100
generosity. *See also* compassion; kindness; self-sacrifice
  transcendent, 151–54
  types of, 153
gods, 59

Great Perfection, 83, 113
great sameness, realization of, 173
Great Seal, 113
Great Vehicle, 145–46, 185
Guru Yoga, practice of, 207–10
Gyalse Ngulchu Thogme, 169, 187, 197,
  201–3
  beggars and, 13–14, 17–18
  compassion, kindness, and
    generosity, 12–19
  on Dharma practice, 58, 94
  humility, 200–201
  illness and death, 21–23
  on illusion, 150
  on judging and criticizing others,
    175–76
  on Mahayana, 99
  overview and life history, 9–26
  on satisfaction and happiness, 183
  on solitary places, 65–66
  on suffering, 99
Gyalwa Götsangpa, 72
Gyalwa Karmapa, 49
Gyalwai Nyugu, Jigme, 105

happiness, 46, 106–7, 149–50, 183
harsh speech, giving up, 184–85
hatred, 63–65, 159, 160, 177. *See also*
  anger; negative emotions
  objects of, 132–35
hell realm, 108, 133, 159
Hinayana, 47, 83
human vs. celestial beings, 57, 130
humiliation, 124–25, 127–28
humility, 200–201

"I," 120–21, 142
ignorance, 63, 177. *See also* negative
  emotions
illness, 22, 23
  taking on others', 148
illusions, 101–2, 150
illusory goals and ambitions, 92. *See
  also* liberation, striving toward
impartiality, boundless, 119, 173, 174
impermanence, 68–73, 164
intention, bodhichitta of, 98–106

Jamgön Kongtrul Lodrö Thaye
  Rinpoche, 227–34

Jamgön Kongtrul Lodrö Thaye
    Rinpoche (*continued*)
  commentary on *Seven-Point Mind
    Training*, 199–200
  Treasury of Spiritual Instructions,
    207
Jigme Lingpa, Kunkhyen, 4, 71, 113, 114,
    124
joy, boundless, 119, 173, 174
judgment. *See* faults

Kalden Gyatso, Jetsun, 213
karma, 89
kayas (bodies), 80
Kharak Gomchung, 129, 165, 184, 193
Khenpo Shenga, Dzogchen, 4–5
khyen-tse, 4
Khyentse Rinpoche, Dilgo, 1–2
  overview and life history, 3–8
Khyentse Wangpo, Jamyang, 4
kindness, 45, 83. *See also* generosity;
    meditation practice, of exchang-
    ing oneself and others; self-sacri-
    fice
  being wronged in return for, 124–27
  returning humiliation with, 127–28
*King of Aspirations for Excellent
    Conduct, The*, 195
kleshas, 61

Langri Thangpa, 112, 122–23, 191
laziness, 217
  types of, 161–62
liberation. *See also* enlightenment;
    freedom
  meaning, 94
  striving toward, 91–97
Lobsang Yeshe, Panchen, 179–80
Longchen Rabjam, Gyalwa, 55, 60,
    64–65, 70, 113
loss, 116–19
love
  boundless, 118, 173–74
  strength and power of, 129–30

Madhyamika, 174
Mahayana, 83, 100
  attitude of, 103
  discipline of, 155
Mahayana teachings, 23, 47, 100
  criticizing and rejecting, 177

practicing, 53
"profound and vast," 170
Mandhatri, King, 135–36
Mani mantra, 89
Mañjushri, 53, 54, 113, 137, 195
Mara, 113
master. *See* teacher(s)
material possessions. *See* possessions
meat, dangers of eating, 211–13
meditation, 62, 67–68, 173, 208–10.
    See also calm; shamatha medi-
    tation
  concentration and, 220–21 (*see also*
    concentration)
  types of, 217–19
meditation practice. *See also* postmed-
    itation practice
  of exchanging oneself and others,
    106–16
  of remaining in state free of con-
    ceptual elaborations with cling-
    ing, 137–46
merit, dedication of, 102–4
Mipham Rinpoche, 3, 195
Milarepa, Jetsun, 95, 181, 192, 203
  on alcohol, 212
  on the "devil," 95–96
  on generosity and Dharma, 131
  hardships endured by, 163
  Marpa and, 77
  on treating humans like celestial
    beings, 130
mind, 138–43, 168
  calming the, 165–66, 215–19
  empty nature of, 142–45
mind training, 199
mind-training prayer, 227–34
mindfulness, 74
monastic discipline. *See* discipline
monastic vows. *See* vows
motivation, 217

Nagarjuna, 52, 90, 184, 197
negative actions, 87–91, 148
negative emotions, 133, 148. *See also
    specific emotions*
  exchange of self and other as way of
    dealing with, 111
  meditating on, 112
  solitude and, 63–65
  sustained calm and, 219

training in how to be rid of, 185–90
"unsuitable friends" who increase, 74–75
negative spirits, 129. *See also* "devil"
Nepal, 6, 7
Ngulchu Thogme. *See* Gyalse Ngulchu Thogme
nirmanakaya (manifestation body), 80, 81
nonattachment. *See* attachment; emotions
nothingness, 142. *See also* emptiness

Oddiyana, Great Master of, 143–44
Ornament of True Realization, 99

Padampa Sangye, 162
Padmasambhava, Guru, 49–50, 74, 90, 92–93, 113, 212
paramitas. See perfections
parinirvana, 84
past lives. *See under* Buddha
patience, 124
    types of, 156–58
Patrul Rinpoche, 116, 129, 130, 193, 204
perception, 138–40
perfection phase, 100
perfections, transcendent (*paramitas*), 151, 169. *See also* concentration; diligence; discipline; generosity; patience; wisdom
positive training, principles of, 123–24
possessions, 95–97, 100. *See also* loss
postmeditation practice, 219, 221
    of abandoning belief in objects of aversion, 147–50
    of abandoning belief in objects of desire, 146–47
    of using unfavorable circumstances on the path, 116–37
Potowa, Geshe, 134
prajña, 94
pratimoksha vows, 154, 155
pratyekabuddhas, 77
present thought, 140–41
pride, 101. *See also* self-aggrandizment
profound insight (vipashyana), 145, 164, 165, 168–69, 172
    how to meditate on, 219–20

sustained calm and, 34, 145, 164, 165, 168, 169, 172, 188, 204, 208, 219
profound teachings, 170
prosperity, 130–32

Rahula, Prince, 53
realization, wisdom of, 223
reflection, 62, 67–68. *See also* faults
refuge, taking, 79–87
    faith and, 84–85
    motives for, 82–83
    things to be avoided after, 85
    things to be done after, 85–86
reincarnation. *See under* Buddha
relationships, 74. *See also* friends
relative bodhichitta, 106. *See also* meditation practice; postmeditation practice
    stages, 106
relaxation. *See* calm
renunciation, 96–97
Rinyewa, Lama, 14

Samantabhadra, 195
sambhogakaya (body of perfect endowment), 80
samsara, 45, 46, 59–61, 93–94
    liberation from, 51, 58–61, 76
    steps to being free from, 61–62
Sangha, 82. *See also* Three Jewels
self, 47. *See also* "I"
self-aggrandizement, 176. *See also* pride
self-reflection. *See* faults, facing one's; reflection
self-sacrifice, 107, 148. *See also* generosity; kindness; meditation practice, of exchanging oneself and others
selfishness, 45, 161–62. *See also under* Shantideva
sense perception, 138, 140
sexual attraction, 212
Shakyamuni, Buddha, 53, 81, 117, 162, 180, 217
shamatha, 145, 165–66
shamatha meditation
    how to meditate, 216
    preliminary conditions for, 215
    types of meditation, 217–19

Shantideva, 124, 125, 158–59, 183, 187, 197, 224
  on emotions and existence, 57
  on negative emotions, 186
  on selfishness vs. concern for others, 46, 110–11, 114
  on solitude, 66
  The Way of the Bodhisattva (Bodhicharyavatara), 1, 11, 57, 110–11, 114, 116, 157, 186, 200
shastra, 197
Shechen Gyaltsap Pema Namgyal Rinpoche, 2, 4, 5, 220–21
solitude and solitary places, 64–67
Sönam Trakpa, 14
Songtsen Gampo, King, 49
speech, giving up harsh, 184–85
spirits, negative, 129. *See also* "devil"
spiritual teachers. *See* teacher(s), spiritual
suffering, 71–72. *See also* compassion; deprivation; samsara
  causes of, 45, 106
  efforts to eliminate, 148–49
  exchanging one's happiness for others' (*see* meditation practice, of exchanging oneself and others)
  Gyalse Thogme on, 99
  negative actions and, 87–91
  of six realms, 108
  types of, 59
  using it on the path, 119–21
Sutra of the Wise and the Foolish, 68
sutras (condensed instructions), 81

Tara, Arya, 105–6
tathagatagarbha, 62, 178, 189. *See also* buddha nature
Tathagatas, excellent concentration of, 221
Teacher, 82
teacher(s), spiritual, 76–79, 124, 181, 205–6. *See also* authors of treatises
  false, 74
  how to behave in presence of, 207
  how to find qualified, 206–7
  necessity of following a, 207–8
  the right, 206
  serving, 208–9

Three Baskets (*Tripitaka*), 81–82
Three Jewels
  boundless qualities of, 156
  taking refuge in, 79–87
Three Roots, 82
three supreme points, 101–2, 176
Tibet, 15
Tilopa, 139, 224
tolerance. *See* patience
Trakpa Gyaltsen, Jetsun, 197–98
transcendent perfections. *See* perfections, transcendent
Trinle Öser, Dodrup Jigme, 113
Tripitaka (Three Baskets), 81–82
Trisong Detsen, King, 3, 4, 152
Tsangpa Gyare, Drogön, 96–97

Upagupta, Brahman, 73–74

Vairochana, Lochen, 163
Vajrayana, 181–82
vast teachings, 170–71
vegetarianism. *See* meat
Vimalamitra, 4, 152
vinaya (discipline), 81
vipashyana. *See* profound insight
virtues, 87
vision, pure, 181
visual perception, 138, 140
visualizations, 166–68, 208–9. *See also* meditation practice
vows, types/levels of, 154–56

Way of the Bodhisattva, The (Bodhicharyavatara). See under Shantideva
wisdom, 98, 100, 223–24
  aspects of, 170
  compassion and, 219, 223
  transcendent, 169–74, 223–25
  types and levels of, 223–25

Yangönpa, 203
Yeshe, Palden, 2
Yeshe Tsogyal, 187
Yidam, 82

Za Rinpoche Chilbupa, 210